**W9-BRJ-616**

# THE
# DOG LOVER UNIT

Also by Rachel Rose

*Marry & Burn*
Poetry, Harbour Publishing

*Thirteen Ways of Looking at Can Lit*
Poetry, BookThug

*Song and Spectacle*
Poetry, Harbour Publishing

*Notes on Arrival and Departure*
Poetry, McClelland & Stewart

*Giving My Body to Science*
Poetry, McGill/Queen's University Press

# THE
# DOG LOVER UNIT

## Lessons in Courage from the World's K9 Cops

## RACHEL ROSE

THOMAS DUNNE BOOKS
St. Martin's Press
New York

THOMAS DUNNE BOOKS.
An imprint of St. Martin's Press.

THE DOG LOVER UNIT. Copyright © 2017 by Rachel Rose.
All rights reserved. Printed in the United States of America.
For information, address St. Martin's Press,
175 Fifth Avenue, New York, N.Y. 10010.

www.thomasdunnebooks.com
www.stmartins.com

Title page photograph courtesy of
Freeimages.com

Designed by Kathryn Parise

The Library of Congress Cataloging-in-Publication Data
is available upon request.

ISBN 978-1-250-11074-9 (hardcover)
ISBN 978-1-250-11075-6 (ebook)

Our books may be purchased in bulk for promotional, educational,
or business use. Please contact your local bookseller or the Macmillan
Corporate and Premium Sales Department at 1-800-221-7945,
extension 5442, or by email at
MacmillanSpecialMarkets@macmillan.com.

First Edition: October 2017

10  9  8  7  6  5  4  3  2  1

*For the dogs*

# Contents

# THE
# DOG LOVER UNIT

# Prologue

I crouch, shivering, behind the shed. I'm about to be attacked by a huge black monster of a police dog named Cade, and I'm not sure I can control my panic. Twenty feet away from me, Cade is lunging, barking furiously, throwing his full eighty pounds against the taut line of his handler, Constable Darrell Moores. Cade wants to get me so badly, he's frothing at the mouth, snapping the air with his teeth. Inside the padded arm I'm wearing is a steel bar. I grip it hard, digging my boots into the mud.

I asked to be here. I wanted to experience what it felt like for suspects to be attacked by these turbocharged police dogs. I knew I could write it better if I lived it. This was all part of my plan, but in the moment my plan seemed *insane*. Why had I opened my big mouth a few minutes ago and said to Darrell, "What do I have to do around here to get permission to take a bite?"

"Nothing on my watch," Darrell replied. "You want to take a bite right now?"

He's an imposing man. With his strong nose, dark hair, and piercing, hooded eyes, there's something of the hawk in his appearance. As a member of the Royal Canadian Mounted Police (RCMP), Darrell was part of ERT, the federal Emergency Response Team, before he joined the Police Dog Services (PDS). Before that he was in the military. Darrell got his start in the armed forces at eighteen years old, with a tour of duty in Yugoslavia, and he hasn't stopped since. He's a big man, six foot two, rugged and restless, as eager as his dog Cade for the next adventure. Darrell's the kind of man who talks like he's done anger management courses, like he's keeping a lid on it, but it simmers underneath. He says *friggin'* a lot, probably because his wife's told him to knock it off with *fuck*. He says that a lot, too.

"Take a bite *now*?" I'd been thinking months of preparation and paperwork. Just like that, Darrell Moores calls my bluff.

"Sure. Let me get you the bite sleeve."

The sleeve is made of coarse jute. It's what you wear to prevent puncture wounds. I've already learned that some dogs don't like the sleeve because it doesn't have enough give to it. Some dogs just bite their way up the sleeve like a cob of corn, to get to the tender human meat underneath. Is Cade one of those dogs?

"Ready to go?" Darrell asks.

"Ready," I manage.

"Okay. Head over there, by that shed. When I call you to come out, just resist a little bit. Whatever you do, stay on your feet and protect your face."

We are up in the mountains north of Squamish, BC, halfway to Whistler, me and Cade and Darrell and about eight or nine other police dog handlers, all men. A couple of the cops mill around, watching. I can't back down. I have to give this my best attempt if I want to keep hanging out with the cops and their dogs. I want that more than anything, and no, I don't know why. My heart jackhammers in my chest.

Whatever happens, it will soon be over. I told myself this as I went into labor for the first time. I say it again now, gripping the steel bar, gritting my teeth. "Police! Hey, bad guy, come out!" shouts Darrell. I know it's just practice, but it feels terribly real.

"I'm not coming out!" I shout back, hoping my voice isn't shaking.

"Come out, bad guy, or I'm sending my dog!"

I take a deep breath, square up my stance. "NO! I'm not coming out!"

"*Hag* 'em up!" Darrell shouts. "*Hag!*" And then Cade hurtles through the air like a black demon and grabs my arm, shaking me in his jaws like a giant chew toy.

What I haven't anticipated is the force of his strike. I make the mistake of bracing, fighting Cade as he shakes me, rather than moving along with him as the experienced quarries do. Quarries are what they call the suckers like me who *volunteer* to get chewed on. Most of them are cops who want to be police dog handlers. They apprentice on their own time and their own dime, week after week, year after year, in hopes that they can someday have a dog of their own in the force. But quarry is also a word for prey, for those who are hunted, and I am learning all the definitions of the word at this precise moment. *Hag* is a word with Nordic roots, found in both Scottish and German, meaning to bite, to cut, or to harass. The Germanic harshness of it tears the air, evoking Nazis and police batons bashed over the backs of cowering prisoners, fierce shepherd dogs rushing in to inflict damage. Cade is waltzing me in some kind of convulsive box step as he drags me around. The adrenaline rush narrows everything around me: the other cops disappear; the whole world is nothing but Cade gripping my arm. Life is simple: I'm fighting to escape and Cade is making sure I can't.

Moores watches me carefully. After what seems like an eternity but is probably only a minute, he calls Cade off. Cade lets me go reluctantly, leaping to bite the reward of a Kong chew on a rope that Moores offers as a substitute for my arm.

"Good *dawg*!" Moores praises Cade, swinging him around in the air by the rope chew. "What a good *dawg*!" Moores says again, as he leashes Cade up. Cade regards me with his bright black eyes.

"You okay?" Darrell asks, and I nod, not trusting myself to speak. In general, Darrell is not a patient guy. He's energy trapped by ordinary life, like mercury in a thermometer. But at this moment, he checks me over carefully.

"I saw your face when he was coming at you and you looked so scared I friggin' almost called off my dog. You sure you're okay?"

"I'm fine," I say. "I'm great! That was better than three espressos!" He laughs. "You should have seen your face!"

"I was afraid I'd wet my pants," I confess.

"You wouldn't be the first," Darrell rumbles down at me. "People have been known to urinate, scream, defecate, pass out, whatever." I laugh out loud. Darrell decides I'm fine.

"So," says Darrell. "You ready for another go?"

Oh God, no. "Sure am," I say.

Darrell tells me the new scenario. I'm supposed to walk away and Cade will come at me from the side. Once again, I get behind the shed, digging my boots into the mud to brace myself. Darrell shouts at me to surrender. I refuse. He sends Cade, who flies through the air and strikes, using my leg as a springboard as he leaps to savage my arm. That's when I feel a knife blade of pain enter my bad knee, the knee I snapped in a judo match in Japan more than twenty years ago. Cade shakes me like a rag doll. I gasp but don't scream. I am dimly aware that all is not well with my left ankle, which is on fire. My right shoulder is humming a new refrain of pain.

The first time maybe Cade was just warming up. I struggle in silence as he throws his weight, and me, around. When Darrell finally calls Cade off, I do my best to stand up straight and walk normally. It's not easy. Those jaws that just bit my arm can exert three hundred pounds of crushing pressure per square inch. Both the dog and I are panting, and I hurt all over.

I'm also grinning like a fool. At this precise moment, I am more awake than I've been in my entire life.

I say nothing about my knee. I'm good at silence in the face of pain. I want to come on as many training expeditions as I can, just me and the guys. I know I have to suck it up and not be seen as someone who needs to be babysat, though of course that is exactly how they see me, despite my best efforts. So I limp behind one of the cabins and lean against the rotting wall to collect myself. I try a few stretches, but give up with the jolt of pain running down my leg. The rain has soaked through my boots and the bottoms of my jeans. I am shaking with adrenaline. I can practically feel the steam coming off me.

"Hey, Rose, ready to try some tracking?" calls Moores. Cade trots along beside me, his thick black tail wagging as we leave the trail and plunge into the brush. Cade's no longer in attack mode; he's been told to search, but not for me. I'm not afraid of him at this moment. I'm just vigilant. The men are talking about hunting bad guys. I'm learning the difference between the kind of hiking I've done, which always involves groomed trails, and tracking, which involves directions and possibilities and bushwhacking. Tracking requires addressing the terrain in front of you to make decisions about where you think someone might have gone. Hikers hike. Hunters track.

I'm wondering how long I can keep up, and what the hell I'll do if I fall behind. My knee has swelled up so that my jean leg looks like a sausage casing. But the smile on my rain-soaked face, as I struggle over wet logs and across icy creeks, branches smacking me, is 100 percent genuine.

It cost me a lot to get here. I was once a victim of a man who left a trail of other child victims in his wake. I never found justice. The experience left me distrustful of all who were supposed to serve and protect. No one protected me. So here I am, having made a commitment to spend long days and nights with those who are the first to arrive at crime scenes, the first to deal with victims. I figure I'll spend a few sessions riding along with police dog teams around my city. I have no idea what is in store for me. I have no idea that I am beginning a project that will obsess me for the next four years, a project that will lead me through four different countries as I follow the dogs.

All I know when I start is that I'm stuck, and can't see my way out. My relationship with my partner, Isabelle, is on the rocks. Isabelle's a police doctor, a very stressful job that leaves her unavailable and away from home much of the time. On top of that, one of our three children is struggling, but Isabelle doesn't see a problem. I know something is wrong, but I can't imagine the diagnosis that is yet to come. What I see is that my child and my partner have both detached from me, and I can't find any way to reconnect. All I can think to do is to redouble my efforts on all fronts, even though they don't seem to make any difference. I'm trapped in domestic quicksand, my own ambitions on hold. There is nothing lonelier than being in a broken marriage while trying to reach a child adrift. There are nights I just don't want to go on. In desperation, I buy this child a puppy, a fluffy white Maltese-poodle cross, called Dandelion. We call her Dandy for short. She looks like a baby seal and can meow like a cat, and it's hard to believe this sweet white dog could even be the same species as the police dogs I ride along with. She is as different from the German shepherds like Cade as I am from the men like Darrell, but even so, Dandy is a working dog with a purpose and a job. She brings my child love and tranquility and the warm, accepting touch of another living being. It is one of the few things I do that is unequivocally right during this dark time. My child will allow no physical contact, and hasn't for years, but somehow Dandy the dog is acceptable as a snuggling partner. As a bonus, Dandy and I quickly grow inseparable. When the kids are at school, she pushes herself against me, sighing companionably, watching me with those bright black eyes, asking only that I scratch her ears from time to time.

At home, I feel numb and lost myself, stunned at how we all ended up here, and desperate to find the plan to get us back on track. It is precisely this feeling that pushes me out of the house and into the company of these rough men and their dogs. On the road with the dogs, I am free. There is nothing as bracing as fear to release me from the trap my life has become. The last thing in the world I can imagine doing is exactly what I'm doing at this very moment: tracking in the woods with Darrell and Cade and a bunch of other police dog teams. Just to escape the house, leaving behind all the problems I don't know how to solve, is an incredible relief. Every time I get in the car to go to the dogs, I feel my heart unclench just a bit. I'm trapped, yes, but at least I can get lost for a while, out of my head and into the backwoods of Canada, into a world that is as foreign to me as any country I've visited. It is a pure, fierce curiosity about this world, and a hunger to be in the company of these dogs and their masters, that propels me forward.

As Cade trots beside me, I allow my fingers to graze his black ruff. I am not supposed to do this. Nobody but the dog's handler is supposed to touch him. I know, as only a criminal who has taken a bite can know, that police dogs are not pets. But I brush Cade, so lightly it could almost be an accident, as he trots beside me. He swings his big head to look at me, black eyes utterly fearless, pure Alpha, and I swear he grins back at me, light glinting off his canines.

# 1

---

## From Puppy to Police Dog—
## Drive and Determination

I fly to Calgary in May, and then ride the bus for an hour and a half to Red Deer, the murder capital of Canada. I'm not used to such a flat landscape. It feels too open, too exposed upon the earth. There are no looming mountains, no canyons—just the spring green of the grass, the magpies in their tuxedos scolding from budding trees, strip malls jammed with jacked-up trucks. I pass what I take to be a small mountain of topsoil, but as I roll by I see it is actually snow, dirtied by rocks and grime, still unmelted. Spring will soften Red Deer as best spring can, but this is a hard, open landscape, unfamiliar and unforgiving. The land is so flat that my eyes grow tired of looking for the horizon line.

The next morning, I meet Senior Police Dog Trainer Tom Smith in the lobby of the Sandman Hotel at six thirty a.m. so he can drive us to the kennels. I'm right on time, dressed in hiking boots and jeans, with layers that I can strip off if it gets too hot. Tom Smith is a man of medium build with salt-and-pepper hair. Most of the time, he's soft-spoken and easygoing. It's only when he is telling me some of his past experiences as a K9 cop that a hardness enters his eyes. Tom is not someone to be messed with. Beneath that mellow exterior is a tough and opinionated survivor.

A few months earlier, I spent my first week working with Tom as he validated police dog teams in the Lower Mainland, near Vancouver. Each team that graduates from the RCMP kennels program is required to be validated annually to ensure that they continue to meet or exceed standards. Tom tells me that if he can't pass a team, they have a maximum of fifteen remedial training days. If they still are unsuccessful, trainers have to make a decision as to which part of the team is at fault. If the dog is the problem, he will be retired, and the handler will go back to the kennels to be rematched with a new dog. If the handler is the problem, he will be removed from the program and his dog will be reteamed with a new handler. Validation is taken extremely seriously, and it means that dog and handler must stay at the top of their game.

That time with Tom and the teams was a great introduction in learning to read police dogs' body language. I got to see the precise moment when the dogs hit the scent and set off on a scent track, and when they were closing in on their quarry. To me it never got old.

After one of those long days out with Tom, I sat in the kitchen, talking with Isabelle after dinner. Maybe it was just the change of routine, but some of the tension between us had lessened.

"So today Tom was talking about how anxious the new dog handlers get when it's testing time. He said, 'They're always saying, "My dog never did this before, he must be sick, he might have hurt himself over that last fence," one excuse after another. The last one was complaining about his dog's tracking and I said to him, "This is what you should do. You go to your dog, lift up his tail, and kiss his ass, because he's been working great for you all week." ' "

Our daughter popped her head into the room, where she'd been quietly eavesdropping. "And did he do it? Did he actually lift up his dog's tail and kiss his ass, Mom?"

How long had it been since we'd laughed together until we had to lean on each other? I couldn't remember the last time.

■

I know Tom well enough to call him Tom and to ask him any question that pops into my mind, but being in Alberta now, on his home turf, feels different than the time we spent together in British Columbia. For the rest of the week, I will be in the company of Tom, the dogs, and the other police dog handlers of the RCMP.

In Celtic, Innisfail means Isle of Destiny, and this is where every RCMP police dog in Canada (and many that end up as K9s in the United States) is bred, born, and raised. Police dogs for the RCMP used to come from anywhere and everywhere. Some of those dogs worked out wonderfully, but in other cases the results were uneven. Because of the unreliability, dog trainers and veterinarians took over the responsibility of breeding all the dogs, ensuring complete control over the bloodlines and every aspect of puppy and young dog training. The science behind the breeding program at the RCMP is carefully monitored at all levels.

Innisfail is where a pup will meet his or her destiny. Few will succeed. Out of all the litters born, many of these purebred German shepherd dogs don't have what it takes. The tests to become a police dog are challenging, and begin when the pups are just seven weeks old. Every new level presents another opportunity to fail.

Innisfail is also where cops who want to become police dog handlers come to meet *their* destiny. By the time these police officers make it to Innisfail, they have already proven both their dedication and their skill. Most of the time, dog handlers are cops who have already put in up to five or six years of voluntary, daily, unpaid training and dog care on top of their regular duties as police officers. They sign up to volunteer as quarries. They raise and imprint young police pups in their homes, passing them on to experienced handlers when the dogs are old enough to work. They do all this in hopes of one day being chosen to go to Innisfail themselves. Most of them never will. Many drop out along the way, as the demands of a police dog on top of life, family, and career become too much, or as they realize that there is no end to this work. There are no guarantees and no rewards but the work itself.

I will be meeting those who have made the cut. This remote training ground in Alberta is the place where the chosen few come to make their dreams a reality. By the end of it, with a little luck and months of hard work, they will earn the right to call themselves police dog handlers.

This is where it all happens. Tom and his wife Roxanne are based in Innisfail, Alberta, but live in Red Deer. As a police dog trainer, Tom spends months away from home, living out of a suitcase in a hotel. Over the years, he has worked with most every dog and handler in the country to make sure they remain capable, competent, and prepared to face whatever comes their way. Roxanne has worked for many years as a 911 dispatcher, so she'd understood better than most what Tom was signing up for when he went to work as a canine cop.

"That must have been nice for you, having your wife really get what your work was like," I said.

"I tell you what, it could be a real pain in the ass," says Tom, grinning. "If she was on call while I was out after a suspect, she'd be checking in on my radio every thirty seconds, requesting my location and coordinates, making sure I was safe."

I laugh. That's one way to keep track of your husband while he's out facing unknown dangers: be his dispatcher. But in fact, the 911 dispatchers can easily be traumatized by what they hear when they are miles away and can't do anything to help. I don't envy Roxanne what she's had to listen to over the years.

Tom continues: "Once you are on a track you don't want to be talking on the radio. It's like, 'Leave us alone, let us get to work.' You don't want to be calling to update them. It's just different when it's your wife and she's worried."

"Do you think she called you more than others?"

"No, probably not, they worried about everybody, but it's just you don't need them to call all the time. You're just trying to focus on the track."

We head to Innisfail with a full truck—four new police dog recruits and their dogs. I try to prepare mentally for the long day ahead of me, but short of training for the Ironman, there's no way to be ready. Luckily, I don't know this at the time.

Once we arrive at the kennels, Tom puts me in the very capable hands of another police dog trainer, Eric Stebenne, for the week. Stebenne knows dogs like only a trainer can. He's just the kind of guy you want leading your team, because he wants all his recruits to succeed, and he wants all his dogs to make it, too. He is friendly and patient with any cop who is going through challenges with his dog. Stebenne must be a good decade older than I am, but over the two weeks I spend in Innisfail, I get to know his back and shoulders better than his face, because it's his back end I'm constantly following as I run after him.

These are the things I learn while out with the dog teams: no matter what kind of shape you are in, nothing prepares you for tracking. Running in hiking boots through uneven, boggy pasture, jumping from one clump of grass to another, is tough work. You may think toxic mosquito repellant should be banned until you've run through the clouds of mosquitoes in Alberta. After that, you will happily spray yourself until you gleam all over and green poison drips from your earlobes like shiny earrings.

I know the handlers work much harder than I do. They have to circle around for the scent, not taking any shortcuts, keeping up with their dogs the whole time (but, on the other hand, the dogs pull them along). They have to make the decision to crawl after their dogs under barbed wire fences, or to heave their dogs over the fences and then follow, but whatever their dog does, they must do too, or risk having their long lines become hopelessly, hazardously tangled. When they lose a scent, the team has to loop back, running concentrically growing circles until they find their trail again. At all times, handlers have to be reading their dogs' behavior, trusting them, but also thinking ahead.

All I have to do is follow Stebenne's backside, but this is almost more than I can do. My knee twinges in pain, the screws holding the bone together protesting long and loud, but I know one of the handlers, Kent MacInnis, is running with all kinds of hardware in his body. Kent MacInnis's dog was killed, and he nearly died in a terrible car accident; he's here to be matched with a new dog. I grit my teeth and push on.

After three tracks, though, I can barely stumble back to the truck, and I'm so far behind that I hear, rather than see, that moment where the dog finds the quarry and attacks, growling and barking. A fug of sweat and mosquito repellant drips down my face as I struggle to speak.

"I don't know how you guys do it," I gasp, leaning against the truck. One of the guys laughs and takes off his belt, containing gun, flashlight, radio, and a whole bunch of other gear. He straps it around my hips, and steps back. I can barely stand erect with the extra twenty-four pounds pulling me down. But I like the feeling of the harness cutting into my hips above my jeans.

What would I do with a Taser, a gun, and a heavy flashlight? I have no business wearing these things, but I like knowing what it feels like to carry this weight. It feels heavy, but good.

"Do you really run with all this? I guess I have to shut up now," I say, and the guys laugh again.

We are out in stunning countryside, with an endless sky and fields and plains so open it feels like you could run forever. The long days pass in a blur. As I run along, I learn how to read police dogs' body language, how to tell when a dog is aimlessly searching, and that sweet moment when he hits the scent and becomes totally focused. I learn how it feels to pee in a ditch in a landscape so flat there is no shelter, while six male cops pretend not to look in my direction. I learn how to keep going and keep going. I fall into bed at the end of every day dog tired.

At one point, I've stayed behind with a couple of guys while Stebenne and two other handlers lay a track. This involves planning a route that the quarry will take to really challenge the dogs, a route that crisscrosses roads and fences and ditches of still water. I'm happy to be sitting this one out. From far off I hear a sound like thunder. Dozens of horses gallop over a ridge, coming to see what we're doing here. They run to the fence and I can't help myself. I grew up with horses, love horses—I crawl under the barbed wire and try to meet them, holding new grass in my hands. But this herd of beauties is shy, or uninterested; they watch me but don't let me get close enough to touch. The guys wait for me, good-natured, but I know I'm holding them up, following the horses. Reluctantly I crawl back under the fence again.

I spend some afternoons hanging out at the kennels. I am in the capable hands of the two Louises who are core staff, Louise Paquet and Louise Falk. The breeding program at Innisfail couldn't operate without them. Physically, they couldn't look more different. Louise Falk is a trim, even-featured young woman with a blond bob. Louise Paquet is a solid, comfortable older woman, well weathered and talkative. But both the Louises know dogs like nobody's business. Both of them have dedicated their lives to raising and training police dogs.

It goes without saying that Louise Paquet loves dogs, but she lets me know it anyway. "My oldest boy found this mutt. We named him Jesus Murphy. I have Thea and Deenna at home, too. Deena belongs to the RCMP."

Deena is one of the RCMP's breeding mothers. Like the other mothers, she lives with families when she is not in the kennels with a new litter.

While I was in Alberta, I visited the rural home of John and Sue Charles, who have been providing a foster home for RCMP mother dogs since 2000. John and Sue are salt of the earth people, friendly and welcoming. They call themselves brood keepers. While the RCMP pays them to care for the mother dogs, they clearly consider it an honor. The dog I meet who lives with them, Dea, is a big, restless female. Dea remains in nearly constant motion for the duration of our visit. Sue tells me that she had Dea's grandmother and Dea's mother as well. As we talk, Dea runs laps around the property, patrolling but also running for the pure joy of it, bounding up to meet us and to greet her foster parents, then bounding away. I'm glad that Dea spends most of her life here with John and Sue, who obviously adore her, glad that she lives in a place where she has room to run.

The mothers like Dea are not pets, but neither are they police service dogs. They perform an essential service, though. Five days before a brood dog is due to whelp, she leaves her foster family and comes back into the kennels, where she stays under the watchful eye of the Louises and the other staff until the pups are weaned. It's a tough job, especially if she has a big litter of twelve or thirteen pups. By the time a mother dog like Dea's been on full-time puppy duty for six or eight weeks, she is more than ready to wean and go back to her foster family.

Louise tells me that she makes sure the mothers get their rest and recreation, even at the kennels, even with a new litter of puppies. Every day, she lets the mothers at the kennels out to run, under supervision. "Rain or shine, those dogs get to run," she says.

As I follow Louise Paquet through the kennels, some of the brood mothers stand outside, leaving their pups in the brood boxes in which they were whelped. I watch the mothers sniff the spring air, basking in the thin May sunshine for a few moments, before they return with a sigh to their whimpering puppies. I feel for these long-suffering bitches; who *wouldn't* be ready to wean, to get out of the kennel and back to the farms and their foster families, especially when part of your duty as den mother includes licking bottoms so the little ones defecate in your mouth, not in the den?

It's a big job the Louises have. Along with the other kennel staff, they do the early socializing of every litter of puppies and take care of all the adult dogs as well. The puppies start their training on their first day of life, when the kennel staff begin getting them used to human touch. They are each marked with a dab of nail polish on their rumps or their necks to identify their gender.

At fifteen days, the pups are started on a socialization regimen that involves removing them from the nest and getting the pads of their little paws used to feeling a variety of surfaces underfoot. Every dog's features are distinct, if you look closely enough and get to know them well enough. Still, with the limited contact I have, it is almost impossible for me to keep track of them or tell the dogs apart.

When I walk the rows of kennels where the dogs are caged, they run to the fence, barking furiously, jumping on the wire that separates us. They scratch and whine, begging to be released, to go out and do something, anything. Their kennels are two little rooms with bare cement floors, open to the outside, easy to hose down and clean, but neither cozy nor stimulating. It is here, when the dogs are housed between assignments, that I pity them the most. No animal wants to live like that. I wish they didn't have to. But these animals are not pets; they are soldiers. They live in barracks as devoid of color or comfort as any army post.

By some whim of fate, we each are born into our stations in life, and dogs are no exception. Helpless puppies may be born in a trash heap in Guatemala, or a breeder's pen in Palo Alto. They may roam the streets of Taipei, dying an early death of rabies, or follow a homeless man through Brooklyn as he pushes his shopping cart to the doorway they'll share for the night, an outlaw pack of two. They may be kept in the purse of a movie star in Beverly Hills, or become the playmate for an autistic boy. The odds are likely that most dogs in this beautiful, broken world will have a rough go of it. Even in developed countries, one trip to a shelter, where rows of dogs await possible adoption or probable death, is enough to break your heart.

In comparison, police dogs have enviable lives. Dogs as intelligent as these thrive with a job to do. They follow tracks and search for suspects with skill and zest. They take their responsibilities seriously. These dogs have the good luck to be out on the road with their handlers most of the time, unlike the average dog, who spends hours alone in an empty house while his owners are working.

But none of this reconciles me to the rows of mournful canines at the kennels in Innisfail. These dogs bide their time, waiting to be released. It's hard for me to walk down these smelly aisles of dogs, each of them barking deafeningly, scrabbling with desperate paws at the wire mesh separating us, begging with whimpers and cocked ears to be set free. A few of the dogs lunge aggressively, growling and barking, but most of them approach pleadingly, looking at me with their dark, soulful eyes, hoping that I might be the one with the key who will let them out.

Luckily, dogs don't spend long at the kennels. They are a holding station, not a place where dogs live long-term. Police dogs might go to the kennels while their handlers are recovering from an injury, or while they are waiting to be rematched with a new handler. But the work these dogs do is valuable, and they are in demand. Most of the police dog handlers go to great lengths to avoid leaving their dogs at the kennels. They like to keep their animals close. They are so connected, so used to each other's company, that it feels strange for a handler to be without his trusty sidekick. And, even though the dogs are turned out daily and have access to runs, there is nobody training them. It doesn't take long for a police dog to become rusty. Handlers work so hard to make their dogs successful police dogs. Any setback to this routine is something they avoid. Vacations with a police dog handler tend to be camping trips out in the bush where the dogs can come along. Anyone who marries into a police dog family knows, or quickly learns, that it's a package deal: the bonus is the big German shepherd who will be part of the family until the day he dies.

The kennels are built so that they can be cleaned and each dog fed without having to make contact, but staff still have to move dogs around and exercise them. I wonder what you are supposed to do if a dog goes after you. I know how unlikely this would be, but once I imagine it, I can't get the scenario out of my head.

"Louise, what should I do if a dog is trying to attack me?"

"Turn and walk away," she says, without missing a beat. "Cross your arms over your chest, or put your hands in your pockets and do a one-eighty. And you have to look at your dog. Nine times out of ten, if it's regarding the dogs I know and work with, it's just bad manners. If he's right in your face, barking, that's fear. If it's aggression, he'll go right after you, just run for you—you won't see it coming."

I shiver, thinking of ride-alongs I've done with Cade at night, his black form disappearing into the blackness around me. I can never see him, except for a gleam from the moon or streetlights that illuminates his eyes. I can hear him, though—or rather, I feel him as he rushes me. If I didn't trust Moores to handle Cade, I would be down on the ground, begging for mercy every time. I know Cade is not a vicious dog by nature. Edgy, yes, but not vicious. I also know with every step of my still-aching knee and shoulder the kind of damage he can do, that any of these dogs could do. It's taken me months of physio just to get back to where I was before Cade's attacks.

"More dangerous are the fear biters," Louise continues, "because it's unpredictable how they'll react."

I can't imagine walking away, hands in my pockets, with a dog savaging my body, ripping into my flesh; I can't imagine not breaking into a screaming run. I file Louise's advice in the big box of things I hope I'll never be tested on.

"Come see the puppies," she says, taking me to the nursery. We scrub up like surgeons, and I promise not to touch any of the babies. It's a hard promise to keep. They are asleep, of course, squished against each other, squeaking. Every now and then one crawls away from his siblings, searching blindly for his mother and for milk. Pups in the first litter I see still have their eyes sealed shut, but the next is full of babies with storm-blue eyes. They look at me, unfocused and solemn, before cuddling back to sleep.

Louise Paquet passes me off to Louise Falk, who is doing a puppy demonstration for a TV show. Louise Falk comes running out of the kennels, wearing a dark uniform and a bright big smile. She is followed by six black and brown tumble-bumble puppies, trotting hot on her heels.

Louise Falk runs fast enough that the pups have to really hustle to keep up with her. They follow her into the puppy-training arena, where she leads them through the gate and shuts it behind her. Already, at only seven weeks old, the pups know how to follow her through various obstacles. That doesn't mean they are happy about working. As soon as they are separated from Louise by the wire fence, they start a series of sharp, whining protests that don't let up. She leads them around the ring from the outside, and they follow eagerly through the obstacles. Even though they are still babies, tripping over their big paws, they work a puppy course that is a replica of what the big dogs must master, complete with tunnels and steps, mazes and bridges and wobbly balance boards.

The pups do very well, protesting all the while—*Yip, yip, yip! Yip, yip, yip!*—but then one little fellow goes into a maze and can't find his way out. He goes ballistic, yodeling and yipping, as the other pups whimper encouragement and dread, running after Louise but looking over their shoulders at their slow sibling. Louise gives him a minute to figure it out. When he doesn't, she circles her whole pack back and guides the lost pup back to the pack. He quiets at once. When she's done, she enters the arena and praises the puppies for a job well done.

At Innisfail, I also get to see the puppies tested. I am one of very few civilians ever permitted to witness the first test that the puppies must take. The handlers warn me beforehand not to interfere in any way. There are four trainers to administer the test. One handles the pups, and three observe and score. These tests are critical in determining whether these roly-poly pups will become someone's pet or elite members of the police dog force.

The first test the pups take is at seven weeks. This litter is a distinct group of six fuzzy puppies, some brown with black markings, and some solid black, all of them rotund, bumbling, driven to explore.

First, each pup is separated from its siblings and brought in a crate to the entrance of a strange room. Will they enter the room boldly, or will they hang back, fearful and whimpering? The first pup on deck is a black female, strong and solid on her oversize paws. She trots into the room, curious but unafraid. Already, she moves like a winner.

"Look at her ears and tail," says one of the trainers. "The ears and tail are the barometer for a dog's emotions."

I look. This girl's ears are perked, her tail up, alert, wagging— she frisks around, tugging at the kennel attendant's trouser leg. I would love to hold out a hand, to pet her, but this test is serious business. I put my hands behind my back, just to keep them out of petting range.

The first pup passes the next round of tests beautifully. At this point in her life, she has no name, just a number she was assigned at birth. All puppies are given a number for tracking. They will receive a regimental number later on, if they pass and become police dogs. The regimental numbers are like an officer's badge number, and those stay with the dogs for their working career. They will also be given names, of course. Twelve of the pups born this year will be named through the national Name the Puppy contest, where school children in Canada send in names that are then selected for the new police dogs. Other pups receive names directly from the kennel staff.

The next test is to see again how this first puppy responds to stress. The handler picks her up and holds her off the ground, making no eye contact with her. Does she struggle, or does she submit? The RCMP wants a dog that is not submissive, and this little girl struggles valiantly, paws churning the air as she fights for purchase. Next she is flipped on her back and held down for thirty seconds. Again, the test is whether she will fight to regain her footing, or just give up.

This girl's a fighter. She scrabbles and whines and licks the trainer's hand frantically, not giving up for the whole thirty seconds. When the pup is released, she's scored on how quickly she recovers. Will she sulk or avoid the handler, which would indicate a loner personality, one that is hard to train? Or will she return to the man that pinned her, tail wagging, jumping on him, showing she's not cowed, that she's ready to rumble?

Immediately, this puppy jumps right up, shakes herself off, and trots over to the trainer for more. She licks his hand and jumps on his arm. She's clearly recovered and ready to interact again; although she didn't appreciate being pinned, she doesn't hold a grudge. "Let's go!" she seems to be saying. "What's next?"

The tests continue: the trainer blows up a paper bag and pops it, testing the pup's fear response to unexpected loud noises. She looks up, but doesn't lose her cool, and when he crumples the bag and throws it, she follows and fetches. This is an important skill for a future police dog, perhaps the most important skill of all. How a dog fetches and chases, how much hunting drive she has, is the best barometer of how she will do as a tracking animal, and police dogs at the RCMP are prized above all for their ability to track.

The puppy has to chase a rope on a stick. The test measures how long she will pursue the rope. How fiercely will she shake her head and fight when she gets it? Does she give up easily when she can't get what she wants? Not this pup. Once again she passes with flying colors. Her drive is intense and relentless. She's only seven weeks old, but she has every sign of becoming a police dog.

"Females tend to score better at first," the trainer tells me. "They mature faster and test better, but then around adolescence that advantage drops off."

This echoes what other trainers have told me. While fewer female dogs make the cut, those that do are exceptionally good.

Out of the six pups, two pass with flying colors, and two pass with reservations, while the final two don't make the cut at all. This just doesn't seem fair. How can one test at seven weeks determine their whole future?

Whether I like it or not, though, these tests have proven remarkably accurate in predicting which pups will become successful police dogs. The pups that don't pass will quickly be adopted by members of the public; there is a waiting list for every single one of these talented puppies, even those who aren't quite up to being police dogs. Those puppies that do pass will soon be sent to live and work with police officers across Canada who have taken the puppy training course, and who want to become police dog handlers. These police officers prove their dedication by volunteering to raise, train, and love these puppies for a year. After that, they have to say goodbye and send the pups back to Innisfail to be matched with their new handlers. It is a lot of work and sometimes a lot of heartache for the volunteer puppy handlers, who have to practice loving and letting go.

Tom coaches me about what goes into the art of matching a specific dog to an individual handler. "It is of the utmost importance that the dog and handler like each other," he says. Trainers like Tom Smith and Eric Stebenne try to match canine and human personalities, and avoid putting a very dominant dog in the care of a soft handler, or vice versa. If a trainer identifies a team that is not bonding, they can be rematched during their time at Innisfail. A solid bond is the essential base upon which everything else is built.

◾

My week is done. I'm eager to go home to my comfortable life, eager to see my family. I've had too many meals at the Red Deer Buffet, all you can eat Chinese and Western food, and I'm ready to get back to Vancouver. But I'm sad to be leaving, sad I won't get to follow the teams for their entire training period. As Tom drives me to the bus station in Red Deer, I write notes madly, trying to get every detail I can about the training program. "How many handlers drop out once they get to Innisfail?" I ask.

"Not many drop out. It's rare. Those who leave usually have been injured during training. But we've had guys complete the course on a sprained ankle or a stress fracture. They just grit their teeth and pull through, because the alternative is coming back a year from now," says Tom. "The course takes approximately eighty-five days, so that's a setback they will avoid."

Eighty-five days of living in a hotel. Eighty-five days away from home and family. Eighty-five days in pursuit of a dream. Whether dogs are raised in Washington State by trainers like Suzanne Eviston of Von Grunheide Shepherds, in Indiana at Vohne Liche Kennels, or in Alberta at Innisfail by the Louises and Eric Stebenne and Tom Smith, they will have a similar start in life. Most of the processes and much of the philosophy behind shaping a puppy into a police dog are similar. Whether they are called Police Dog Services members, as they are in the RCMP, or K9 teams, as they are in most of the USA, they are part of a network that transcends borders. (Interestingly, the abbreviation K9 has been used since at least 1876 in London, though it was popularized by Secretary of War Robert Patterson during WWII.[1]) Working dogs tend to move all over North America, and sometimes across the world, with dogs born in Germany, Poland, or Canada ending up in law enforcement in the U.S. or Paris. Passports don't matter to a police dog. Raising and training these dogs is both a science and an art, a dance between animal instinct, human intelligence, and the bond between humans and canines. Innisfail gives me that solid base of understanding that informs every future interaction I will have with police dogs.

■

The young dogs and recruits at Innisfail are the chosen few. But before they ever are selected, potential dog handlers for the RCMP must prove their dedication and drive through volunteering for years as puppy trainers. Constable Nathalie Cuvele is one of those volunteers. With dark brown hair, serious eyes, and just the hint of a French accent, Nathalie embodies a quiet confidence. She lives on Vancouver Island with her wife, Michelle, and their baby daughter, and is

Constable Nathalie Cuvele and Eryx in training. (Rachel Rose)

raising police dog in training Eryx. Although Constable Cuvele is a police officer, she is not yet a dog handler. That's the dream, and she pursues it single-mindedly. She knows it will take time to make this dream a reality, and she is willing to give it all the time it takes.

When Nathalie was a little girl, there were always police dogs in the yard; her father, Corporal Didier Cuvele, was a police dog handler. Nathalie's goal is to follow in her father's footsteps and be a police dog handler herself. At almost a year old, young Eryx has passed every test so far, but he's not a police dog. Both dog and officer have many hurdles to pass before they can claim their respective titles.

It's mid-winter when I take the ferry to Vancouver Island. I drive from Victoria to Nanaimo across a twisting highway. The cliffs on the side of the road are shot through with frozen waterfalls. At the hotel, I check in, fortify myself with black coffee, and stuff a chocolate bar in my bag. At eight o'clock, Nathalie calls me to tell me she is waiting outside. I don't know what the heavily pregnant desk attendant thinks when I smile, wave good-bye, and step into a full-sized police van, but I hope she notices that I am going willingly.

Nat drives me back to the Nanaimo detachment, where I sign a waiver saying I'll behave myself, and identify my next of kin in case I get killed that night. I look up hesitantly, my pen hovering over that section, thinking of the kids at home, brushing their teeth. Nat sees my hesitation and smiles warmly. "Don't worry, Rachel, I won't let anything happen to you," she says, holding my eyes.

I sign and head for the washroom, through the women's lockers. One wall is covered by female police officers' heavy black boots. Taped on many of the lockers are the photos of their babies and children, watching over Nathalie's mothers, as they go about their duties. The contrast is striking: combat boots and laughing babies. I see two different pictures of Nathalie's daughter, one on Nathalie's locker and one on her wife Michelle's. Michelle is also a police officer, but she has no intention of going into the dog section. They have arranged their work so that their daughter doesn't need to go to daycare, so that one of them can always be with her. No matter how tired they may be after a night shift, they are there for her.

I will never know what it feels like to be up all day with my baby and then up all night on the road with my dog, wearing the uniform and the badge, cruising around looking to prevent trouble and keep the peace. I've been tired as a mother before, but that must be a whole different level of exhausted.

Nathalie shows me what she carries on her belt. I've never closely examined a Taser before.

"You get Tasered, don't you, as part of training?"

"Yes. And it *hurts*."

I had just recently learned that police recruits often get Tasered on their initial RCMP training course in Canada. Although it was optional, Nathalie took it upon herself to get Tasered during her training. I don't think I would have. I've been shocked by enough electric fences during my childhood that I have no desire to be Tasered.

We step outside and get Eryx from Nathalie's truck. He leaps around in the cold, clear night, frisky and full of energy, but when Nat opens the van he hops easily into his kennel in the back. Eryx is nearly full size, but still a puppy at heart. When he came to Nat at eight weeks old, he cried for two nights solid in his outdoor kennel. He wanted to come in and curl up by the fire with their family dog. But Eryx is not a pet. He is a police dog in training, and standard training policy for RCMP police dogs is that they sleep in kennels when they aren't working. If he passes, he won't be curling up by the fire until his working days are through, in another decade or so.

I peer into the van. There are two holding compartments in the back, both of which have reinforced steel seats. I climb in shotgun and Nathalie takes the van out on the road. We circle the town. The hills are bright with a thin layer of snow. A call comes in from the dispatcher about a man who had taken speed the night before. "He's concerned now," says dispatch. "He says, 'Poison is coming out the end of my fingers!' That's what he says." Another patrol takes the call, with an ambulance in attendance, but we mosey on by to check all is well.

"This is a building known to police," Nathalie tells me. "We get lots of calls here."

I see a couple of officers heading to the waiting ambulance, but even though I want to, I do not see the man or his poison-leaking fingers.

Our next stop, I'm relieved to find out, will be Starbucks. "Please, let me buy you a coffee," I say. But at the window, when I hand over my twenty dollars, the cashier says, "Oh my goodness, I almost forgot, the person in front of you paid for your drinks."

*Wow,* I think. *I wonder if this happens often.*

"Only the second time in seven years this has happened to me," says Nathalie, as if she's been reading my mind. We sip our coffees in silence as she drives. I don't know how she can read the computer that is bolted on the dash between her seat and mine, listen to the dispatcher, and steer a full-sized van over icy roads while typing in license plates and drinking coffee. But she does it all effortlessly.

We drive slowly down the street, and a tall, thin female wearing a very short skirt, very high heels, and bare legs despite the icy night, gestures for Nathalie to pull over. She pulls the van to the curb, rolls down the window and asks, "Is everything okay?"

"Fine," says the woman, as she stumbles toward the van through the snow. She puts her hand in the window, in my space. She must be freezing. It's clear she's not fine.

"Do you have a card or anything?" asks the woman. "In case I need help?"

Nathalie hands her one. "There's my number, right there," she says. "Thank you, thank you so much," says the woman, and Nathalie smiles.

We drive out to an elementary school and let Eryx run. As soon as we hit the frozen ground, he has his nose in Nathalie's pocket, rooting for his favorite orange ball.

"This one knows how to unzip my pocket to get what he wants," Nathalie tells me. Nat throws the ball about ten times farther than I've ever thrown anything in my life. Eryx runs full tilt into the darkness to retrieve it. He streaks up the hill toward the dark trees like a joyful wolf. The parking lot shimmers, the street lights illuminating its crust of snow. I'm shivering and happy.

The next day, I visit Michelle and Nathalie at their house to see where Eryx lives. He has a big kennel in the back, with a cozy doghouse lined with straw for him to sleep in. Eryx barks when I arrive, but settles down right away. I come in for coffee while their daughter naps.

"All my time raising Eryx is volunteer time," says Nathalie. "I don't get paid. For me, it's play time, not even work—I go outside, I just have fun. I love the outdoors and I love animals. My status now is as a quarry with the police dog section. I started as a quarry in 2010. I approached the handlers. I said, 'I'm interested, and I would like my career to go toward dogs.' I did two years of volunteering with the handlers. In April I went through the puppy course. I got Ev, my first puppy, in May. We have to do at least twenty-four months with a puppy in the yard. Ev didn't make the program. She was kicked out early. I knew she didn't have what it takes. She was sold as a pet.

"Now every Wednesday I help the police service dogs train. I lay tracks for them. I put a scenario in place. Maybe a home invasion, I'm the bad guy. I reenact that I left in that direction. Half an hour prior, I start. It's a planned track, maybe I run through town for two or three kilometers. Then the dog comes and sniffs out the track, sniffs out the human scent. The dog will eventually find me, then there's a bite at the end."

"I don't know how she does it," says Michelle, joining the conversation. "Sometimes I call Nat and she's out hiding. She says, 'I can't talk for long, the dog is going to be here in a few minutes.' She's so calm!"

It's definitely not a situation where I would be calm, crouched in a ditch somewhere, waiting for a dog to find me, attack me and shake the stuffing out of me. But the police dog handlers I know have a different relationship with adrenaline than I do.

"As a quarry, you're probably going to get bit once for real," says Nat. "For me it's just adrenaline. It just takes that type of personality to go out there and hide and be a big chew toy. I think it's the best job in the RCMP. There's a big board in Alberta somewhere with all the names of the quarries across Canada. I'm now at the bottom. Slowly you'll creep up the list, and you'll eventually get picked. It can take four years, seven years. There's no magic number."

"How about Eryx? How long will he be with you?"

"You never know when he gets called. To know I've raised him from eight weeks to where he's out fighting crime on the streets, I'll be proud. I grew up as a kid from very young having huge police dogs in the yard. To me they were never scary. I knew what the dog did, what the dog's responsibilities were. As a teenager I put on the arm"— the protective arm pad made of jute—"and my dad set the dog on me. I was part of it all. I've always admired my dad for doing that job. To me, my dad was the coolest guy around. I'd go out with him, put out some tracks, it was just the coolest feeling."

■

"My older brother is a paramedic and a firefighter. Mum was a stay-at-home mum, we got to have her all those years. Then she was a teacher for special-needs kids when we went to school."

"How did you decide to go into the RCMP?"

"The summer I was graduating from university, I was in Idaho, doing my whitewater program"—for river guides. "I thought, I'm just going to put my name in and see what happens. I was having fun in school. Dad was in the RCMP, his career was great, so I thought, I'll just see. In 2006, I got the call saying 'Okay, you're going to Depot.'"

Depot Division is where all the RCMP cadets go to become police officers.

"I spent six months in Regina with thirty-two other people. Until you do it, you have no idea. I played competitive hockey. All my life I've played structured team sports. Depot was very structured. They get you ready for the streets. You learn to march. You learn everything from firearms to basic file work to discipline to commitment, ground fighting to boxing. You learn to drive emergency vehicles. I learned how to push myself. Sometimes you think, 'this is my limit!' but really it's not. Depot pushes you almost to your extreme, because if I'm in the middle of an alley fighting someone twice my size who is drunk or high, I want to know that I can keep going, and that I'm coming home at the end of the night."

"So what's a typical day for you with Eryx?"

"Usually around six thirty, I get him out, run him for a good twenty minutes. He just plays, that's his fun time, and he does his business. I throw the ball and play tug-of-war with him. Then we do some stress-free exercise in the airport, jumping on chairs and counters, getting him comfortable. I also do alley walks on a twenty-foot-long leash, past cats and other dogs. You want the dog to get familiarized so he'll just blow by smells. I walk him through with a ball and toy and just make it fun."

"How would you describe Eryx, personality-wise?"

"Eryx, he's independent. He's like, 'You're cool, but I've got better things to do.' He's not focused just on people. You can definitely tell how smart they are at a very young age. They know more than you think, and they are capable of more than you think. He's still young, but learning very quickly."

Eryx is not a big dog, and he's kind of skinny. If he doesn't start gaining mass, he's at risk of being cut from the program. Nathalie has spent a lot of time researching how best to help him put on some muscle.

"I'm feeding him three times a day so he can catch up a little bit. Feeding these dogs is a science in itself."

"What do you think people don't understand about police dogs?"

"A lot of people ask how we train the dogs, if we use a lot of discipline, a lot of force. When I took the puppy course, everything was built around love. If you love your dog and your dog loves you, they'll do pretty much anything for you. People worry, 'Oh, are you sure the dog's happy?' They get a whole lot of care from us, and they learn. It's so different from raising a pet: you don't want to be overpowering a police dog. It's a balance: they have to be Alpha. Your dog is your partner for life. If someone's going to save you, it's going to be your dog. You're usually ten to fifteen feet behind your dog, who is running after somebody dangerous. He's going to do whatever it takes to save you. He's gotta know you've got his back, too—that you feed him and love him, that you are there for him."

The last time I see Eryx is on a wintery day. Again, I take the ferry from the mainland and drive to Nanaimo. There is a dusting of snow, and it's very, very cold. Nathalie and Michelle meet me at the small Nanaimo airport where they train Eryx. Michelle is carrying their bundled-up baby daughter in a sling. Retired police dog handler Corporal Didier Cuvele, Nathalie's father, is there as well.

While Didier's wife and Nathalie's wife stand near the van, talking and keeping the little one warm, Nathalie and Didier run Eryx through his paces. Again and again, Didier challenges Eryx, lunging toward him, shouting and waving his arms at the young dog. Again and again, Nat sends Eryx in for the attack. Although he's young, and not yet full grown, Eryx is still intimidating. I stand close to Nat, hoping that Eryx will know which of us to attack when she gives the command. When Eryx catapults himself across the frozen field, I repress the urge to point at Didier and shout, "Not me! Him! Get him!" But I don't need to bother. Eryx is completely focused on the corporal. I might as well be invisible. Even with the wind blowing the snow around, I can hear the solid impact of Eryx's body striking Didier. I notice with some relief that he lets go immediately when Nat commands him to.

Nat is an attentive, thorough trainer. As Eryx does his attack scenarios, the cold sinks into my bones. It is a relief when training is moved into the warm airport. This is one of Nat's regular training grounds, a place where Eryx can get used to working with different challenges. A police dog must be able to address any environment, whether it's searching an airport locker or navigating slippery counters.

Eryx responds well to everything Nathalie asks him to do, except jumping up and climbing onto bathroom counters. It's comical to see him scrabbling all over the slippery counters, like a dog on ice. Nat praises him for overcoming his fears, takes him away to do something easier, and then brings him back to the dreaded bathroom counters again. Nat asks a lot of this young dog, and Eryx is willing to give it.

Even though I only visit a few times, I get to know Eryx and Nathalie and her family pretty well. Nathalie's parents seem to live at a different energy level than most people. Although they are retired, they are about to leave on a six-month backpacking trip through India. The rest of the time, they live on a boat, fishing, sailing up and down the coast, and generally grabbing life and shaking it like a bear shakes a salmon. When Didier retired, it was only so the full-time adventures could begin.

"There was never a gender role with my parents," Nathalie tells me. "How we were brought up was, 'you are brother and sister, now go do what you want to do.' We were always outdoors. My brother got a fishing rod and I got one too. It was never I got a butterfly net."

It is a bittersweet day for Nathalie. Eryx, the dog she'd had since he was only eight weeks old, is leaving soon to be matched with his new handler. He's put on the weight and growth he needs and he's working well in all that will be required of him as a police dog—even dealing with slippery counters. "On the one hand, I'm happy, because this is what it's all about for him, this is what we've been working toward, and on the other, I know it's going to leave a hole." It is even harder because just the week before she'd been told Eryx would probably be with her until the spring. But then a handler needed a new dog, and Eryx was that dog. It's hard, the loving and letting go.

"He's doing really well in his training. There's nothing holding him back," she says. "His tracking abilities are very good, he does really, really well in that. His aggression is not a weak spot, but there's a few quirks that need to be worked out."

I am glad to be there on what is supposed to be the last day Eryx will ever train with Nathalie. He does a great job. First he runs some trails, trying to find a scent he's been told to follow. He crosses the bare pavement, losing the scent briefly, but picking it up again. All around us, the wind lifts little sparkling puffs of snow. We are all focused on Eryx, and Eryx is entirely focused on his task. "If he sticks close around," says Nat, "I'll see him again, but if he's shipped off to Nova Scotia, who knows? You're just preparing yourself for letting go: seeing him leave and me getting another one just brings me closer to my goal of having my own, and it's heartbreaking but good at the same time."

Nat has only a little more time with the dog she loves. I learn that he will go back to Innisfail, to be matched with a new recruit. As the months go by, Eryx will become a police dog, passing all his levels. Nathalie and Michelle will have another baby, a little boy. She will bring home a new little police dog puppy, Hemi. And with Michelle's support, Nat will submit her name once again and follow her dream—to go to Innisfail for eighty-five days, leaving her family behind so she can immerse herself in the world of dog training. There is no doubt in my mind that Nathalie's unwavering drive and determination will pay off. She's been around police dogs all her life, and done a great job raising Eryx from a fuzzy puppy into a successful police dog. It's only a matter of time before Nathalie Cuvele will become a police dog handler, with a dog of her own.

# 2

## Situational Awareness and Public Perception

It's two a.m. on a winter night, and Darrell, Cade, and I are out tracking a fourteen-year-old runaway. Her boyfriend called the cops after she took off. We're out in Maple Ridge, a suburban area of big quiet houses and empty streets, and of course we don't have any of her clothing or any way to know where she might have gone except to start from the point where she was last seen and go from there. Darrell swears a couple times as he straps Cade's tracking harness on. I'm allowed to track with them, because what's this girl going to do, even if we find her?

We start at the point she was last seen, a house that is indistinguishable from all the others in this suburb. Cade picks up her scent right away, and we're off through the silent streets, past sleeping houses, our breath billowing in the frosty air. Then Cade loses the scent and we circle. I try to keep out of their way, so I won't hinder the track or tangle the long lead, but then I have to hustle to catch up, running hard, my stupid purse slapping against my leg, my bad knee throbbing. I have faith in Cade's nose, but the task seems impossible—what fourteen-year-old girl would be outside here, in the bitter cold, where there's no shelter? Cade is swerving all over, in and out of yards, ducking around fences, pulling one way and then the other. It's hard for me to tell if he even knows what he's looking for. We keep moving, covering block after block. I want Darrell to give up. I want him to call it a night.

Just then, Cade turns so fast I lose sight of him. He bolts down a side yard into the darkness beside a garage. There is a sudden scream. It's the girl, running away in terror. Darrell shouts at her to stop, which she does, instantly. Darrell's holding Cade, and I am afraid Cade's attacked her, even bitten her, because that's what he's trained to do. But no; she's unhurt, just absolutely terrified.

"What's your name?" Darrell asks, as he pulls Cade away. His voice is gentle. He praises the dog, and asks the girl—let's call her Kayleigh—for an item of clothing, something he can give as a reward to Cade, something he can chew. Kayleigh doesn't even have a coat or gloves. She has nothing but the hoodie she's wearing, and she holds it tight to her shivering body. Darrell praises Cade, throws him a Kong to chew, tells him he's the best.

"You okay, Kayleigh? You got a lot of people looking for you," Darrell tells her. She covers her face with her hands, shutting out the world, shutting out Darrell. I see her bitten nails, the chipped dark purple polish. I stand close to her and try to talk to her while Darrell radios the other cops.

"I wish I had a blanket to put around your shoulders," I tell her. "You must be so cold."

She starts to cry. "I don't want to go home," she sobs. "I can't. I can't go home."

"Why not? What's wrong at home?" asks Darrell, but whatever it is, she's not telling. Her long hair falls over her face as she stares at her feet. Another cop comes up to talk to Kayleigh, but she doesn't talk to him, either. Darrell's already packing up and ready to go, ready to leave the paperwork and whatever emotional cleanup there will be to the other cops. He and Cade have found the girl; their job is done. Just then Kayleigh's dad pulls up, driving too fast. He jumps out of his truck and storms toward her, mad as hell.

Darrell and Cade intercept. Darrell steps in the father's path, polite but solid as a brick wall, Cade at his side. "Just give them a minute," Darrell says, blocking the way, as the other cop leads Kayleigh a little distance from her father. "I know you want to see her. I know how you feel, I've got kids too, but just give them a minute so she can answer a few questions." The dad is enraged, but nobody gets past Darrell and Cade.

What will Kayleigh say? Nothing. The cat has got her tongue. For a minute, the dog loosed it, but the fear of speaking is too much: Kayleigh shakes her head, covers her face again, tears spilling through her fingers. Finally, the other cop gives her a number and gestures to her father to come and get her. Darrell nods to me. His work here is done.

"She was behind the Dumpster there, all curled up in a ball," Darrell tells me, as we begin the long cold walk back to the truck.

"Amazing that Cade knew not to bite her," I say.

"Yes, I was a little bit worried about that, actually," says Darrell. "But he did good."

"I hope she has a good life," I say as we drive away. "I hope she's okay."

"Yeah, she didn't seem like a rat kid. She seemed like a good kid. I tell you what, she needs to get away from that boyfriend."

What does Kayleigh need to get away from? She won't tell. I can guess, though. There aren't too many possibilities, and all of them are ugly. And we sent her back to face them. We sent her back.

■

Some months after finding Kayleigh, I'm heading out with Darrell and Cade for another night. Every time I leave home to go to the dogs,

I feel sick to my stomach. I know that I can't anticipate what's coming, but that it will likely involve terrifying, gut-wrenching chases at high speeds and at least a couple of moments where I wonder if I'll make it home. At the same time, perversely, I always feel my spirits lift when Darrell agrees to take me out. As a chronically anxious person, there's relief in knowing that my life will be in someone else's hands for a while. There's no therapy like speed therapy. It shakes the cobwebs off my spirit.

When I first started going out with the cops, I worried about finding enough to talk about with strangers for eight or ten hours at a time. I shouldn't have worried. The cops I ride with are natural storytellers, and most of the time I just sit back and listen. I could ride along with them for months and never hear the end of their adventures and their observations about human nature.

Darrell also takes time to answer my questions about what he has learned over the years of being a cop. He drills me in situational awareness, in learning to pay attention to my surroundings. It's an interesting process. As a poet, I am acutely attentive to certain things in my environment—animals, trees, emotions—but I learn that I am entirely oblivious to other things: cars (including model and make), directions, what people are wearing, the passage of time.

This time, Darrell has told me to meet him in the upper parking lot, so I cut across through the rows of parked police cars, some with lights on. Clusters of cops are talking. Other cops walk to their cars, staring at me.

I linger a moment too long in the parking lot, waiting with my backpack full of books and my cell phone in hand. I linger just long enough to attract their suspicions.

"Can I help you?" demands one, but his tone says, "Could you please get the fuck out of here?"

"I'm waiting for Constable Moores," I say.

"Then you should go wait in the reception area."

"He told me to wait here. He'll be here at seven o'clock." It's 6:59. I walk up the hill away from the detachment to give them some space. Situational awareness tells me this is not a good situation in which I ought to linger. Someone I think must be part of the Emergency Response Team (ERT) walks to the bushes behind me with a long black semi-automatic gun, which he loads. I am jumpy and am just about to go back to wait in my car, when I see that unmarked dark truck drive up and hear Cade's booming barks ringing out through the twilight. I grin and run back down to the parking lot. Darrell reaches across the seat and opens the door for me.

"Hey, Cade! How's my guy? How's everything, Darrell?" But Darrell can't hear a thing over Cade's barking, and he just smiles at me and raises his big hand in welcome as I climb in.

We drive off, windows open, evening wind in our faces, Cade barking at deafening decibels at our backs.

"Cade! Knock it off!" Darrell yells, and pounds the metal cage, which he's left open a crack. A black snout appears through the mesh opening, and then a black scrabbling paw, big as a wolf's.

"Just let him sniff you and he'll calm down," Darrell advises, so I offer my hand to Cade. He sniffs, licks, closes his teeth against my coat sleeve and tugs, scratches against my arm with that massive paw. "Hi Cade. Hi buddy, remember me? We're good, you're good," I say. "It's all good." Cade settles down, and we head out to make our first stop, at Tim Hortons, for coffee and sandwiches.

On the way, Darrell tells me a little about his family. His son's teacher has said that the boy might have attention deficit disorder. This pisses Darrell off, because there's no way he's going to put his boy on drugs to settle him down. Darrell has learned to channel that restless energy that his son must have inherited, and if he can do it, his son can, too. In fact, Darrell has the perfect job for some-

Rachel and Cade. (RCMP Police Dog Handler Darrell Moores)

one who gets bored with routine, and enjoys the challenge of things coming at him from all directions. Even though it makes him swear, he loves it.

We pick up our fast food fuel from Tim Hortons and get back on the road.

"You get to know the dispatchers," Darrell tells me. "Candy's one I like. I even came and brought her a coffee this one time. I don't know 'em all, though. Some of the voices in Burnaby I know."

*Some of the voices in Burnaby I know.* To know a disembodied voice, to trust your life to her to get you the information you need at the right time. The 911 dispatchers are mostly women, women like Tom Smith's wife Roxanne in Red Deer, women who want to guide the officers they work with through danger but can only do so much from a distance. The dispatchers develop an extraordinary sense of situational awareness, but can only go by the information they have. If you've ever called for help, you know that it will be a woman's sure voice guiding you through what may be the worst moments of terror in your life. They tell the cops where to run and who can provide backup. They demand the cops check in and let them know they are all right. They can hear shots being fired. They can hear everything as a collar goes down—or goes horribly wrong. They have high rates of trauma, listening to violence in real time, and not being able to intervene.

It is fascinating to listen to the different channels on Darrell's radio, emergencies and interventions unfolding all across the city. There are always several voices competing for our attention. I stop midword to listen to a female cop radio for all available units to assist as her assailant attacks. The radio clicks off as she engages in the fight. We are too far away to reach her, and I hold my breath until she checks in again: suspect is in custody before anyone had a chance to come to her assistance. It's hard to focus. Everything sounds urgent, and I'm constantly distracted.

"Darrell?"

He turns to me.

"I just want to thank you for taking me out. I keep showing up and you just keep taking me out again. It's great."

He grins. "It's no trouble to have you here. Makes the time pass, having someone to talk to."

We meet up with Claudio and Jeremy, other dog handlers who work the Lower Mainland. Claudio and Jeremy are buddies. Physically, there's a similarity in their lean, compact frames, though Claudio's darker, Italian, more of a joker with a shaved head and an easy smile, and Jeremy's blond, with penetrating icy blue eyes and an electric intensity. Neither of them really wants to talk to me, especially not Jeremy. Jeremy grudgingly gave me a ride down a mountain once after a group training session. "No offense to you personally, but I don't trust journalists," he said. "They have a way of twisting your words. I've seen it happen."

"I'm not a journalist," I tell him. "I'm a poet." But today when I say, "Hi," he says, "How're you doing?" with his quick smile. Maybe one day he'll talk to me.

The guys share details about various tracks and police disasters, and I listen. They get riled up, talking about when cops they know have done stupid things but somehow gotten away with them.

"Don't mistake good luck for good planning," says Darrell. "Just because things turn out okay doesn't mean you did the right thing, it might just mean you got lucky."

I know wisdom when I hear it. I write the phrase down: *don't mistake good luck for good planning*. I'm the luckiest person I know, sitting here at Tim Hortons at eleven o'clock at night with three monumental cops, listening to their stories of survival. A call comes in. It's not even clear if it's one for the dog handlers, but Darrell, restless as ever, wants to check it out.

"Do I have time to use the bathroom?" I ask, and he says, "Oh, sure."

But even though I'm fast, by the time I'm out, the atmosphere in the room has changed completely.

"Good-bye, goodnight," I say, and grab my books and run, run to the truck, where Cade throws himself against his cage and barks like he's ready to rip my face off.

"Jesus, Cade, knock it off!" shouts Darrell, pounding the mesh cage. He picks up the radio and tells dispatch that he's on the way.

I press my hand flat against the grille, and am rewarded with a sniff and a swipe from Cade's incredibly long tongue. "Hey, Cade, it's me," I whisper, holding on to the door handle as we pick up momentum. I force myself to exhale while Darrell drives and talks on the radio and reads the computer screen *all at the same time* as he's fly-ing the car. It's impossible, and yet he's doing it, and I swear we are only inches away from kissing the concrete highway divider good-night, sweet dreams.

Someone says, "Suspect is wearing dark jeans, a dark hoodie, and a dark baseball cap."

"Oh, *that helps*. In other words, he's dressed just like every other friggin' person we'll see out there," says Darrell, irritably.

We tear down the road. I lean back in my seat the way I do when I'm in an airplane at takeoff. We are accelerating so fast I think we will actually leave the ground. One stupid move from any of the cars in front of us, blocking our way, and we could crash.

Just like that, the cars brake and Darrell, cursing, pulls us into the left lane, the wrong side of the road, into oncoming traffic, and ma-neuvers around them. I close my eyes, feeling sick as we hurtle down the road. We cross a bridge and the cables zip past us in a blur. Then Darrell stops the truck. We are blessedly still. I want to roll out of the truck and kiss the dirt. Darrell leashes Cade up, reminds me what to do if something really bad is happening outside and I need to call for help: "Push and hold the red button, speak into the mic," and then he and Cade are gone into the night and I'm alone, my breath still coming in gasps.

My heart pounds in my ears. It's a strange thing, watching a chase from the truck. It's like seeing a movie behind glass, a movie with real actors and real weapons, but where much of the action takes place offscreen. Cade has gone stealth, quiet as a hunting wolf. I hear in real time the dispatcher checking in with the cops as they give chase.

Someone says, "He must be cut up pretty bad on that barbed wire."

I see someone wearing exactly what the suspect is supposed to be wearing, dark jeans, a hoodie, baseball cap. Should I press the button on the radio and call for help? If I make a mistake, will that be the end of my ride-alongs? Should I burrow down below the seats so he won't spot me? I try to make myself invisible, but the lights reflect my skin in lurid flashes of blue and red.

And then the guy I think could be the suspect enters a nearby apartment building, and another guy wearing something that also looks like what the suspect is supposed to be wearing crosses the street. In the time I wait, I see three or four guys all wearing more or less what the suspect is supposed to be wearing, and I start to feel ridiculous. A little situational awareness can be a dangerous thing, without the knowledge and experience to evaluate it. How quickly I start viewing everyone on the street as a potential suspect.

When Darrell gets into the car, I hear about it.

"A fucking comedy of errors," says Darrell. "They don't really know where the suspect was last seen. They couldn't tell me definitively if the area was secured or not."

Police dog handlers hate to lose. They are extremely driven, competitive people. Not getting the suspect keeps them up at night. But in fact, it's very hard to catch a suspect unless the information is good, and it is a given that there will be many failures. Criminals now use cell phones and have accomplices waiting to pick them up. They get lucky all the time. But if they don't get caught this time, they might get careless or unlucky down the road when they do their next crime. Sooner or later, their luck runs out.

*Don't mistake good luck for good planning.*

We roll to a stop outside a deserted house, and Cade and Darrell hop out to do another search. "Radio's right here if you see we need backup," Darrell reminds me, and he's off before I can ask him to please show me again how to use it. I see the flashlight beams penetrating the wooded ravine behind the house. Once again, I settle in and wait. It's nearly three in the morning, and the adrenaline's worn off, leaving me limp with fatigue.

It's impossible to feel so afraid and so tired at the same time. The heat is blowing full blast into my face, and the sirens from the other cars are swinging red and blue arcs as I scribble my notes in the half light. Finally fatigue wins, and I drift.

As foreign as the world of police dogs is, there is something deeply familiar to me that I relive every time I'm alone, waiting in an empty truck for a K9 team to return. Because I was the daughter of the only doctor on a small island, the siren songs of emergency were the lullaby of my childhood. The ambulance lights, the helicopter lifting off, blood and fear, the groans from the stretcher, my mother's busy hands, me watching everything unfold and being helpless to intervene, the feeling of being forgotten and thus at peace, drifting in and out of sleep in the eye of the storm, curled up in hospital waiting rooms imagining the end of the story. And now, waiting in the warm truck while cops outside do their dangerous work, I feel drowsy as a baby.

It's difficult for me to fully wake up when they come back. Cade's had a good run, and Darrell's pissed that the suspect got away, but there's nothing he can do about it. I am incoherent with fatigue. It's still the thick of night, without even a whisper of light on the horizon, and I just want to be horizontal somewhere with my eyes closed. Later I learn more about the adrenaline dumps from high-speed chases, and the resulting fatigue. The release of adrenaline makes me alternate between hyperalert and near-comatose. But back then I don't quite know what's wrong with me. I bite my tongue, swallow my yawns, fight to stay awake, and then rifle through my purse to find some mint gum. I pass the pack to Darrell.

"You saying my breath stinks? Oughta give some of that to Cade!" I reach my hand back against the grille and feel Cade's warm breath chuff like a bear's on my skin.

Darrell drives us to an industrial park. Long, low deserted buildings hug the dark manicured lawn. We get out to run Cade. The air is crisp. I hope it will wake me up.

Cade leaps out of the back as I step down from the truck, and before I've got my balance, he jumps up to greet me—a huge exuberant black beast cavorting in circles. He grabs my coat sleeve in his jaws and pulls.

"Cade, get over here!" shouts Darrell. He throws the Kong way across the length of the dark lawn. Cade speeds after it, and emerges out of the darkness to drop the rope at my feet. He dances in front of me, ears pricked, big tail wagging expectantly. "I'm not good at throwing," I say, winding up the rope as hard as I can. I send it crashing a few yards away.

"That was a *terrible* throw," Darrell says in amazement. "Here, try it like this. Spin the rope and then let it fly out underhand when you let go."

I hurl the Kong again. It goes straight up in the air, then drops, vigorously smacking the lawn a few feet in front of my feet. Cade looks at me with his head cocked, as if he's saying, *What the hell?* Still, he bounds across the grass and retrieves the Kong. In a couple of leaps he's back, ready for more. Darrell doesn't even try to hide that he's laughing at me.

■

Another night I am out with Cade and Darrell and it starts to snow. We are called up to Burnaby Mountain for a break-in at the Simon Fraser University Campus. It's maybe two a.m. and we fishtail up the mountain road, the snow blowing across the windshield, for what appears to be a false alarm. On the way back Darrell takes Cade to romp at the Kinder Morgan site in Burnaby. Based in Texas, Kinder Morgan uses its extensive network of pipelines to ship petroleum products across the U.S. and into Canada. Although it is under twenty-four-hour guard, the cops have a deal where they can run their dogs in this big, open, protected area. Strange, to have such crystalline purity, such untouched snow, on one of the most environmentally contested sites in the province. Cade romps and jumps like a giant black jackrabbit across the snow, boomeranging to get the ball Darrell throws, then racing back, kicking snow up with his snout, leaping on me. I don't know when I've seen him so happy. I don't know when I've been so happy myself, playing outside in the snow in the middle of the night with this handsome, wild black dog.

The problem starts when we are all three back in the truck, Cade panting happily just behind my head. Darrell starts the truck but it can't gain traction in the snow. We skid, then skid further, and start to slide alarmingly down the slope. I grip the door as Darrell lets loose a string of curses, twisting the wheel this way and that as he accelerates. The truck tires spin uselessly. Suddenly Darrell changes tactics, and puts the truck in reverse. It works. We drive backward at a speed faster than the one I usually use for driving forward, bumping over the snowy fields and back to the main road. I make a mental note: when you're stuck, sometimes the only way out is to reverse course entirely. It is this situational awareness that I am learning. When things aren't working, don't accelerate into failure. Back up.

Another night I am out with Darrell and Cade when the U.S. border patrol calls to tell us a guy has gotten through from their side, and has made it into Canada. Darrell asks dispatch to plot location and time, but they get back to us saying that U.S. border officials can't, or won't, share that information. Darrell is frustrated.

It's not possible to track and guard an open, unsecured border that runs for miles. The only way someone will be apprehended tonight is if Cade gets lucky. We drive past the fields where, if you are dropped off at the right point, you can run through the night, through the wet pastures and the brush, crossing under the barbed wire, and make it into Canada. Only the desperate make this run.

"I kinda feel sorry for them, whenever I pick them up," says Darrell.

The man we're after makes it through undetected. We'll never know what he was running from, or what he is running toward. We'll never know the end of the story.

Cade is barking at something in the night, out of our scent range. My left ear is ringing like a phone off the hook from all his barking. We drive back toward the city, the wipers beating wet flakes of snow off the glass. I know I'll pay for this tomorrow. I'll stumble around in a fog that feels like jet lag as I get the kids to school. But right now life is sweet. My family is safe at home, fast asleep. I don't know exactly where I am or where I'm going, but it doesn't matter. We're just going to keep driving, see what comes next in these last few hours of the night.

"How old was Cade when you got him?" I ask as we drive.

"Eight weeks."

"Wow!"

"I could put Cade in a lunch box when I first got him. He was only eight pounds. I didn't know he'd be my guy going through, though. You never know how the pups are going to turn out or who they'll end up with."

"You've been his dad from the beginning? Lucky." Most police pups are matched with their handlers at around a year old. But not Cade.

Darrell grins. "Oh, yeah. Some dogs you can be leery as to how they'll act, but with Cade I've never been concerned he'd go crazy or any of those other things. I see him as such an easygoing guy, but when he's in the truck, he's totally different. He doesn't say 'Boo!' at home in the kennel. It's 'cause he knows he's not working. Cade always knows. He knows more than I do."

■

It's December 31, the last day of the year, and I am hoping for an uneventful daytime ride-along. I'm not up for any high-speed chases. I just want to catch up with Darrell, see Cade run a bit. I have twelve guests coming for New Year's in a few hours. I figure a day shift during the holidays will be dead quiet, but it's been hopping, and we haven't even had a minute to stop for Cade (or me) to pee, let alone time to grab a bite of lunch. Cade whines in the back, restless to get out and run. I sneak him a chicken treat, and he snuffles it up neatly, politely, through the grille. Darrell is listening to the usual channels from dispatch, but he's also got an earpiece that I can't hear, connecting him to priority air to track a convicted felon wanted on new charges of child assault. I keep forgetting that Darrell's got the other earpiece I can't see, and then suddenly he'll go silent right in the middle of a sentence, and I realize he's tuning in.

All day the cops have been staking out a very bad guy who has given them the slip more than once. This suspect has already served time for aggravated assault, assault with a weapon, and child abuse. He's now assaulted his new girlfriend's young kid badly enough to make himself a serious police priority.

"We'll just pull over here and see if Buddy comes out," says Darrell. "I doubt it. He's probably spooked."

I hear this term, "Buddy," a lot from the police in Canada, when they refer to suspects. We stake out the apartment where he was last seen. Watching for a suspect to emerge is a perfect opportunity for Darrell to tell me some good stories.

"Once I was after this stolen car. The suspect was going up the street. I was going down. I was out with Claudio. There's a general duty member between us. So the member gets the spike belt out, lays it on the road. Buddy drives over it and comes by me with his tires deflated, *bu dup, dup, dup.* It's two thirty in the morning. We stayed with him until finally he spins out—sparks are flying. The GD members come up. They've got him on the side. Then doesn't he start gunning it to spin loose again? So Claudio came on one side and I came on the other. Just like that, we pinned him."

"Why was he running?"

"He was high in a stolen car, out to do more crime. They all incorporate stolen cars. A stolen car is not just a joyride anymore, like when we were kids. Now they are stealing them to do crime. You don't do a home invasion in your own car. People go, 'Oh we should never be chasing cars.' But most of the time in these cases, we're looking at more crime than just a stolen car."

I nod. Darrell is not the first cop to tell me this.

"You'da been proud, I tracked this kid from Mission," says Darrell. "He had no coat, we were worried about his well-being. He took off from his mom. I go there, we hook a track down a road, up a barn and there he is. I wasn't going to bite him, but we found him."

I could listen to these stories of rescue all day long. But Darrell's restless—there's no proof they actually saw the suspect there, and if there's one thing Darrell hates, it's sitting around doing nothing. After three quarters of an hour or so, he lets dispatch know we'll be on our way.

"I wish I were more of a deep thinker for your readers," says Darrell, thoughtfully.

"Yeah, well, I wish I could do what you can do," I tell him.

He grins at me, and is about to say something, but interrupts himself, touching his earpiece. "Priority air. They're just giving me an update." I hold my breath. He turns his truck around, and I brace myself.

"Oh, *Cade*! He fucking *farted*!" Darrell rolls down his window to let the clean winter air sweep through.

"You and Cade are together all the time. Do you get annoyed with him?"

"When am I not?" Darrell laughs. "Tell you the truth? Nothing gives me a moment of rage like when I see Cade licking another dog's pee. That's what dogs do. I know that, it's their bulletin board. But because he's a working dog, I grit my teeth. I think sometimes I forget he's a dog. I *literally forget* that Cade is just a dog. I'm around him all the time; he's my partner. I start to think, 'You know better than that!' So I think, 'What are you doing, Cade?' That's what makes me so mad. *Don't fucking lick piss!* He's never been allowed to lick piss. He knows I don't like it and he's not supposed to do it. But again: *he's a dog.* When I tell myself that, I can calm down. But what makes me have that rage moment, I think of him as a human who is doing something he's been told not to."

Something is unfolding in New West. Dispatch announces that a guy has holed up in a shop, announcing to everyone around him that he's "gonna put wings on pigs" and that he's "gonna shoot people as they go by."

Darrell takes this as a teaching moment. "We deal with so many people where after a situation they say, 'Why did the police shoot him? He was sick, he was off his meds.' Take this situation—we don't have the luxury of sitting down with the guy to discuss it. He's outside threatening to shoot people. People say, 'That poor guy! It wasn't his fault, he was sick.' *Right.* Same as this fucking clown. Sure, maybe he's crazy, maybe he is sick. But basically we have a guy quoting a guy that just killed two policemen in the States. Obviously we do a risk assessment. But if we're there, if he pulls something out of his coat: Is that a gun? Is it a cell phone, is it nothing? We're there, we react to what's in front of us, and we're criticized for it.

"Here's another incident. We were called to three males in an alley in Burnaby. One has a black handgun. I'm looking at it. That's a gun; is it real? I have no idea. He's showing it to the other guys. We go in, guns out, and we prone 'em out. They're just kids, but we prone 'em, arrest them all. We find this BB gun. Two of the kids are black, one is Asian. The mother comes out screaming, 'You're racist, you fucking cops!' If you really think I go to work and say, 'I wanna hurt someone today'—that's *crazy*. We screen those people out when they apply. Those people do exist, don't get me wrong. Nobody's against being accountable, we get it that someone has to keep everyone in check. But put yourself in my shoes just for five minutes."[1]

"Well," I say, "I'm trying to do that, to put myself in your shoes. I know there's prejudice against cops. But at the same time, you know, we don't hear cops condemn other cops in public, on the record, when they do something wrong. Not all of the bad ones are screened out, whether we're talking about excessive use of force or racism. When you see those videos of black youth being shot in the U.S. we don't hear that public denunciation."

"I denounce it. I *denounce it*! I went after dirty cops when I was in ERT. They gave us all a bad name. When you break the trust, you are far out on your own. We're stuck with your mess. We've been in on a couple files where it was corruption circumstances. I *loved* those ones. I don't relish taking down criminals half as much as I do dirty cops.

"Everyone loves the dogs, you know. But they don't see us. We're not like cops in the movies. In movies you are either a dirty cop, a tough cop, or a bumbling idiot. You're never a normal person, never just a cop who does his best.

"I'm sure there are people who believe we lie and cheat. I just laugh," says Darrell. "It seems to me the criminals' rights are respected more than your right not to be victimized. You didn't read him the charter correctly. We're going to release this person so he can go victimize the next person. Release these guys, they get back on the street, they can do more crime, victimize more people. Their right to be free is given heavier weight than your right to be free."

Darrell stops at an empty lot so Cade can get a bathroom break. I'm jealous. I could use a bathroom break myself. Cade jumps around, happy to be free. I pick up his spare lead and he bounds over and grabs the dangling end: just like that it's *on*. Playing with Cade is like tug-of-war with a bear. He throws his big head around and I brace myself against his weight so I won't be knocked over. I feel the skin on my hands abrade as Cade pulls the lead through it. I rock back on my heels and Cade power walks me to the truck.

"Okay, let him win here, let him have it," says Darrell, and I do. Cade shakes the lead one more time to make sure he's really killed it, then lets Darrell take it away. He flashes his wolf grin at me, and jumps in the truck. I sneak him another treat from the front seat.

"Certain cops are hunters, they look for stuff," says Darrell. "I do that. I like to be proactive."

I'm about to ask if I can get dropped off and go home—I've got to get ready for New Year's Eve—when out of nowhere Darrell slaps on the siren and hits the gas. With the first wails of the siren, Cade goes off like a bomb, barking.

"That stakeout in Surrey, they found the guy. They need additional members in uniform for the takedown," Darrell explains. I'm astonished. I didn't catch the dispatch request at all. How could I have missed it?

"It's the encrypted channel. HRTT, the High Risk Target Team, they are all under cover. They want a member in uniform," Darrell explains. Once again I've forgotten the private dispatch channel in

Darrell's left ear. We pull up. Cade is barking furiously. With a terse, "Stay with the car," to me, Darrell leashes up Cade. Darrell says two words to Cade in a deep whisper: "Quiet. *Quiet!*" It works. Cade moves low to the ground, straining against his harness but silent as a black panther. I watch from my seat as they go around the side of the building, where they disappear from my sight. In two minutes, it's all over: the guy is out in handcuffs, scruffy in sweatpants and a hoodie, surrounded by men who look just like him. The undercover cops who guard him look like the kind of guys I'd cross the street to avoid. Only Darrell is recognizable as a uniformed police officer, with Cade leashed up beside him. The bad guy's not even mad. He's got a little half smile on his lips as he calmly answers questions.

Darrell comes back to the truck and drives us away. "Why was he so calm?" I ask.

"Guys who are in that life, it's just another part of the day. He knows he's gonna be picked up eventually. The first conviction of assault of a child probably wasn't as bad as this one. I don't know that for a fact, but I do know that if that team's going after him, it's because they really want him caught."

I'm glad they got him. I don't know what he did to that woman's child, and I don't want to. I know this suspect will be out soon enough to do more harm. I wish I didn't believe that. But for today, he's been caught.

Cade settles quietly in the back of the truck as Darrell drives the long stretch of highway that will take me back to my car. Darrell's gone overtime, after having been up since before it was light, and he has a two-hour drive ahead of him to get home.

"It was good to have Cade there," I say.

"They didn't need us, but you never know. It's better for the public to see that we are there. Cade, he's just a spaz. He's not a mean dog, though. He's got two personalities: when Dad's around it's, *Okay,*

*I'm supposed to be working, I put my game face on.* The rest of the time he just turns it off. It's like he flicks a switch. When you say okay, let's go, he's BOOM! Then he's done. More than my other dogs, some of whom were high strung all the time, others just very soft. Cade does everything you ask him to. He doesn't balk at anything generally, even new stuff like going through a window, or going through tunnels, something that would cause a dog stress, Cade is like *Oh, you want me to go, I'll go.* Cade will keep coming back to me in a building, coming back, like, *Hey, Dad, what's going on?* I love when he looks at you with those, whatever they are, brownish eyes. It just kinda pierces you, like he's looking right through you."

Darrell's kind of a poet after all. He drops me off, and I get in my car and follow him out to the freeway. For a couple of minutes I think I can keep up with him on the long drive, but I'm fooling myself. Darrell flashes those red and blue lights once to say good-bye, and he and Cade are gone. There's no way I can drive like he does.

It's the last night of the year. That old Nina Simone number drifts into my mind on my long drive home:

> *I'm just a soul whose intentions are good.*
> *Oh Lord, please don't let me be misunderstood.*

I did not expect to feel protective of the cops. They are tough guys, sure, and they don't really need my protection, but at the same time they are misunderstood. I've met a lot of cops, and a lot of what I thought I knew was dead wrong. I can't defend the cops who use the power of the badge to hurt civilians. It sickens me when I see those videos of white cops killing black men, those videos that pop up across the U.S. I know there are some cops who are racist and power hungry and cruel. But those cops are polar opposites of the cops I know. The cops I know are the ones who will go overtime without a thought to make sure a man who has assaulted a child gets taken down.

A New Year will begin in a few hours. Darrell will go home to his wife, Nat, who is also a cop, and their two boys. He'll let Cade out into the yard for a last pee and a run before he kennels up for the night. Cade will greet the New Year from inside his kennel in the backyard of a house in Squamish. He'll curl up in the straw in his doghouse, looking at the stars glittering above the mountains. If anyone wanders drunkenly home in the early hours, Cade will go nuts, hurling himself against the kennel and barking. If they are needed, on New Year's Eve or any other night of the year, Darrell and Cade will hit the road, Darrell forgetting sometimes that his partner is not human, Cade taking every opportunity to remind him that he's actually a dog. Probably this night will be like all the other nights when Cade's not working; he'll wait, head on his paws, guarding his dad's house, his dad who raised Cade from an eight-week-old obsidian black ball of fluff.

◼

Iowa City K9 Officer Brandon Faulkcon is not an easy man to reach. During my months in Iowa on a fellowship for writers, I've left phone messages for him at work, but Faulkcon doesn't return my calls. I have more than enough to keep me busy, and the weeks slip by as I give readings with writers from Afghanistan to Nigeria, Cuba to Mongolia. It is the first time since I had children that I've pursued my dreams with everything I've got. For the first time, I've left Isabelle behind, left the kids and Dandy the dog behind, and I miss them like an ache, but I'm writing fiercely, with everything I've got. Isabelle and I talk every night, and even though we're in different countries, the closeness between us grows. We both know that this will be the final test, this shift in our relationship and our roles.

I really want to learn about what it's like to be a K9 officer in this small, football-loving university town. Normally I never call someone more than twice, but I know how busy cops get, and I also know a lot of them are guarded about talking to writers of any kind. But my calls go unanswered, and I worry that it would be rude to keep calling. Finally, I resign myself to accepting reality: Officer Faulkcon is not going to talk to me, and there's nothing I can do about it. But just when I give up, he leaves me a message saying he hopes he didn't miss me and that he would be available to speak with me the next day if I'm still around. Of course I contact him right away and set up a time to meet.

We have a lot to talk about. Officer Faulkcon is the first African American police dog handler I've ridden with, and parts of the U.S. are incandescent with rage at shootings of African American men by white police officers. I want to know how Faulkcon sees things from the driver's seat, and how he personally navigates these minefields.

I also really want to meet Rakker. This K9 is locally famous. It was during Officer Faulkcon's very first week of patrol with Rakker that they tracked and arrested two thieves who had robbed a restaurant at gunpoint.

I don't have a car in Iowa, so I walk to our meeting place. It's a warm dark night, and Officer Faulkcon is waiting for me. I settle into the Iowa City Police Department cruiser. Faulkcon doesn't have a truck like most of the K9 teams I've been with. A solid man with a generous mouth and warm brown eyes, Faulkcon smiles at me, his eyes searching mine as if to assess my character as I buckle up for the ride.

"You are the first person I've allowed since I had a news writer ride with me. I asked her, 'Do you want to see what really happens, or do you just want to do a ride-along?' She said, 'I want to see what really happens.' She told me she'd let me check the quotes. She didn't. I got burned."

"Thank you for giving me a chance," I say. "I didn't think you would, but I'm so glad you did. I want what I write to be accurate. You can check your quotes before I publish them."

"Thank you," says Faulkcon. "I appreciate that."

"Hi there, Rakker," I call to the dark shape in the back of the cruiser. Rakker doesn't answer. This dog is not a barker, which is nice, but I won't get much of a sense of the kind of dog he is until he gets out. "So, did you grow up here in Iowa?" I ask Faulkcon.

"No, I grew up in Detroit, in one of the worst neighborhoods. I have five brothers. Definitely at that time Detroit was the number one worst place to live. My mom worked hard, really hard. She kept us out of trouble. My real father, he left when we were young. Even though he wasn't there, he was always a phone call away. He left; it was for the better, I get it."

"Six kids. Wow."

"Six *boys* on top of that. I went to sleep to gunshots. I woke up to gunshots. That was an average day in Detroit: drugs, gangs, and a police force that did not have the backing to do anything about it. We had metal detectors at my school, and they didn't work. I remember the principal grabbed this one kid and a gun fell out of his pants."

"That's *insane!*" I say in my polite Canadian way. "How did you survive that kind of childhood?"

"I created a different life for myself because I wasn't okay with settling for the life everyone said I was supposed to live. My entire life I was called white, especially because I'm light skinned, because I listened to country music and I didn't want to grow up ghetto. I played basketball for high school. I was popular. I never got into any fights. I was well liked. At the same time, I guess I was always an oddball. I liked cowboy hats, cowboy boots. Whenever I showed up, I stuck out. My stepfather came into my life when I was a teenager. He was an awesome, awesome guy. I really looked up to him, to his work ethic.

He always saw something in me that I saw in myself. He would not let me settle for less. He was a cable installer. He would go to these different places for work. Sometimes he'd get lost, so he'd call and make me read the map. I could *not* read a map. I used to get him so turned around. He would not let anyone else give him directions. It had to be me. He was teaching me how to do it. Do you know that Western movie, *Tombstone*?"

"No."

"Well, there's this line in it, my stepfather would always say to me, 'You're the one, Wyatt. You're the one.'"

"Why you?"

"I was just a little boy who knew he was different. I begged my mom to marry that man. At first he was just brother Derrick from church. He wound up being exactly what we needed."

"Why did you want to go into policing?"

"It was my childhood dream. When we were younger, we used to play cops and robbers. All the other kids used to be robbers. I was the only one crazy enough to want to be a cop. Where I lived, there was no respect for law enforcement at all. Once at school there was a fire alarm, and the students wound up letting the air out of the officers' tires who came to the call. I'm the first in my family to get a college degree, the first to become a police officer. All along, my stepfather kept saying, 'You're the one, Wyatt. *You're the one*.'"

"It's a lot of pressure to be the one, isn't it? To always be different."

"I thrived on it. Being different meant I was able to be me."

Faulkcon worked hard at whatever he did. At age sixteen he was a crew manager at McDonald's. "I decided if I'm going to work at McDonald's, I'm going to be the best there is. I used to live in Las Vegas. I was a bartender. I wanted to be the best bartender. Right now I'm a K9 handler. My goal is to be the best K9 handler ever. I'm never gonna stop training, I'm never gonna stop learning about dogs."

"What do you do when you come up against racism on the job?"

"I just don't see it. A lot of my family says I'm naïve. I *refuse* to see it. I enjoy breaking every stereotype possible. So I feel that if you were to meet me, you are not going to judge me by the color of my skin. Once you put that in your head it starts to consume you. You start making excuses for why your life is the way it is."

"Can't you do both? Can't you strive to be the best and also call people out on their racism?"

"My fear is, if I was to let that into my life, I would allow myself to make excuses, and be content with things, like, 'That's just the way life is.'"

"I hear what you are saying," I tell him. "And I agree with most of it. But what about those videos I've seen—and they are everywhere out there—where white officers shoot African American men? They're brutal."

"You're trying to tell me out of nowhere cops just decide, 'Hey, let's go kill people?' I have *never* put myself in a situation where a cop would even think about shooting me. Does someone deserve to get shot? No. But I'm a police officer and if a cop stops me and says, 'Come here,' I say, 'Yes sir, okay, no problem.' If you falsely arrest me, I can sue you. I can put in a complaint. *People need to calm down.* They need to relax. What about all the white people we kill, too? Doesn't it matter if they're white? People say, 'It's against the law to be black.' Well you know what, I do pretty well. I'm not out on the corner of those streets, I'm not in a situation where cops even have to talk to me!"

I'm about to break in, but Officer Faulkcon isn't finished: "I know there's racism out there. I know that it happens. If a person literally told me, 'You didn't get this job because you're black,' I'd say 'Huh, I'm gonna reapply.' *Don't deny me.* I'm gonna reapply. I'm gonna get better."

Officer Faulkcon looks at me intently, to make sure I understand. And I do. I have understood that pressure to be better, to let no one deny me. As a lesbian mother, I know that some people see me as abnormal, or as harming my children just by being their mom. When Isabelle first became my partner, gay marriage was illegal, and discrimination against lesbians was not unusual in Montreal, where we lived. Sometimes it felt like everyone was judging us. Especially at first, when the kids were young, I felt I had to be perfect. I spent a lot of time trying to make other parents like me. Whether or not I even liked them was beside the point—I had a lot to prove. I just wanted people to look past the stereotypes and see what a great family we were, even if we didn't look like the typical family. But the years, and my kids, disabused me of holding on to that notion of perfection. My friends' lives were messy and so was mine, and we loved each other anyway. Maybe we loved each other more because of it.

I know that I had choices Officer Faulkcon never did in terms of interacting with people; he was always African American; I was only sometimes identifiable as a lesbian mom. But that armor he wore? I've worn it, too. Mine just had more chinks in it than Faulkcon's.

"So when I show up to arrest you, it's because you're a black man? No, it's 'cause you robbed a store and there's a warrant out for your arrest."

All the time he's been talking, Faulkcon's driving slowly around downtown Iowa City. Faulkcon speaks with force, as though willing me to understand exactly where he's coming from. "My wife is white, I'm black, my kids are mixed. We get along so well. I govern my life by that."

It's an intense conversation. I think we are both relieved to stop the car and let Rakker out for a run. He's a wiry dog with calico markings: black, tan, and a patch of white on his chest. Rakker's not a big dog, and he doesn't exude attitude. I have no hesitation about giving him a pat when Officer Faulkcon invites me to. Rakker sniffs my hand with marginal interest. It's a warm autumn night in Iowa City. The ginkgo trees are in full gold bloom, wafting their carrion stink into the air. The Hawkeyes won their football game a few hours earlier. Now the streets are full of groups of shouting, drunken students and football fans wearing yellow jerseys.

"Can you tell me what you thought when you first met Rakker?"

"I thought he was gross. I did *not* want this dog. After my first dog, Becky, passed away, I got Rakker two days later. I wanted a big bear of a dog. The trainer at Vohne Liche Kennels in Indiana said, 'You need to try this dog.' I saw him, I said, 'I don't want him.' I thought he was ugly. He was also thirty-seven pounds and horribly skinny. I said, 'He looks like a hairy Dutch shepherd.' I didn't like Dutch shepherds to begin with. He said, 'Try Rakker, I think you guys would be a good match.' He goes, 'Brandon, let me tell you why you need this dog. This dog is advanced.' Rakker started to work and I said, 'The dog knows how to work. I guess he's okay.' I still wanted a bear. Rakker was still such a puppy. I said, 'All right, let's do it. I'll take him.'

"I worked him for one day. It was the weekend so I took him home. He met the family. That was big for me. I wanted to make sure my kids and my wife were okay with him. It was a good fit. Rakker's still a small dog, but he's powerful. He's got boundless energy. Right now he's sixty-five pounds, maybe seventy.

"After the second week I came back and they said, 'Hey, I've never seen a dog create a bond that quickly.' Going through training was hard."

"What was the training like?"

"Best training experience I've ever been through, hands down.

At Vohne Liche, they pretty much train you to train your dog. They explain it, and you teach your dog to do it. Rakker didn't know how to do an interior sniff for drugs. He had to learn everything."

Vohne Liche Kennels, in Indiana, is one of the largest police dog breeding and training facilities in the United States. They are known internationally for their K9 work. They also made headlines when they welcomed a Parisian K9 police officer to their facility. When one of the police dogs in Paris, Diesel, was shot and killed during the Paris Bataclan attacks, Ken Licklider, the owner of Vohne Liche Kennels, flew Diesel's handler Joss out to give him a new police dog. This dog was donated by philanthropist Caesar DePaco. As Licklider said to Diesel's handler, "We're brothers now. Whether you're a dog handler in New Jersey, Indiana, or France. We're all the same." [2]

"When I took the dog to certification, I told the breeder, 'I will win every single certification.' He said he's never seen it happen, but we did, we took every single one."

"Do you trust Rakker with your kids?"

"Absolutely."

I understand why. Rakker doesn't give off an aggressive vibe. He is totally attentive and attuned to Officer Faulkcon. This is a dog who has found the leader of his pack, and is fully invested in pleasing his handler. Rakker is now four years old, a dog at his peak.

Rakker gets back in the car and we continue down the road in the cruiser. There are people falling off the curb into the streets, stumbling drunk. Iowa City's university has a reputation as a huge party school, and tonight it seems richly deserved. As we drive, I watch Faulkcon decide which drunks to deal with and which to ignore. Policing is as much an art as a science. A cop must constantly call upon his own discretion as to when an intervention is required.

"If they see me and move off the street, I'll let it go," he says.

We head to the freeway. Within a few minutes Faulkcon has

pulled over a car with no taillights on. Rakker and I stay in the cruiser. I notice with interest that Faulkcon just goes straight up to the car to talk to the driver. RCMP members call in the license first and do a background check before they even leave the car. Faulkcon sets up a mic for me so I can hear the conversations. It helps, though the man he has pulled over, a white middle-aged man, answers in such a low mumbling monotone I can't make out most of what he says.

Faulkcon talks to the guy, then comes back to the car to give his verdict. "He's drunk."

"Did he admit it?"

"No. I didn't even have to ask him. Some things are kind of flags. He wouldn't turn his head to look at me, wouldn't make eye contact. You could just smell all the alcohol on him. I'm just gonna call for backup. Here in Iowa City, we always have another unit coming. There are always two cars."

When backup arrives, I watch the two police officers invite the driver to exit his car. The suspect looks like a smaller, drunken George Clooney. His pale face gleams under the streetlights. His eyes are at half-mast. His teenage child and his wife are in the car, and I can see his son thrashing in the backseat even from here.

This man cannot walk a straight line. He cannot balance with one foot in the air. He stares at me with his flat eyes as the officer puts him in cuffs. When his wife gets out, she's speaking shrilly, obviously very worked up. Officer Faulkcon says to me, "If she can't keep their son in the car, I'm going to end up arresting him, too." The other officer speaks to her quietly. "Is there someone you can call to drive your car? I can't let you drive it," I hear him say. She doesn't contest the fact that she and the kid have also been drinking.

"I'm very upset," says the woman after her husband has been taken away.

"I understand that. He's going to jail. Even if you bond him out, he's going to have to return."

"How much to get him out?"

"A thousand dollars. To bond him out, it would have to be cash, a thousand dollars cash. They don't accept credit at the jail."

Their son is still in the car, cursing and slamming his fist into the ceiling. But whatever his mother has told him works, and he doesn't get out. Officer Faulkcon gets back in the cruiser to wait until their safe driver can come. It's one in the morning, and I'm sure whoever it is isn't happy to be called at this hour, but he still makes it within twenty minutes or so.

"Their kid is pretty worked up," I say.

"I can guarantee you, all I've done is put hate into his heart against the police. He's still in there banging on the dashboard. He's probably drunk, underage, his parents probably feeding him alcohol."

"So you don't think he'll come out of here saying 'It's terrible that my parents were driving drunk, and putting me at risk'?"

Officer Brandon Faulkcon turns to me and grins, the biggest smile I've seen from him yet, as if I've said something adorable. "I don't think he's gonna say that. He's gonna say, 'I hate the police, we weren't doing nothin', it's so unfair.' I can guarantee you, if her son gets out of the car, he's going to jail. And the thing is, now it's all my fault."

But the teenager stays put. Their driver comes and moves the car to a restaurant across the street. We drive away.

Rakker has been quiet throughout the arrest. I ask if Faulkcon ever worries about his own safety, or the dog's.

"No. Every time Rakker's out of the car, I feel more safe than going out with a team of guys. He's never gonna go so far without saying, 'Hey, are you okay?'"

"What's your favorite part of being a police dog handler?"

He laughs. "I get to talk in my car, and not feel like I'm talking to myself."

"You better watch out if he starts answering back," I say.

"He and I have very real conversations. Rakker's favorite thing to do is play ball. If I open up this cage, he loves to push my hand until I pet him."

Faulkcon continues: "We keep track of every time the dogs are deployed. So far this year we've had ninety deploys. I've never had to apprehend. Most people hear him and they give up. I believe people are more afraid of Rakker than they are of guns."

"I believe it," I say. "I tell you, the first time I had a dog coming at me—that was Cade—I was really, really scared."

He smiles. "I've been bit so many times, I can't tell you. I started my decoy work after I was a police officer. I just started to take an interest in training. I started to research, to read books. There are so many different ways to train."

"It's kinda like kids," I say. "There are so many methods and philosophies."

Just then, a man drives down a one-way street the wrong way. Officer Faulkcon puts on his lights, pulls him over and runs his license. Rakker stays in the car; no need to bring the K9 out without a good reason. Faulkcon lets the man go.

"I love doing this job," he says as we drive away. "Rakker, he's awesome. I love working with him, but just like any partnership, it gets annoying at times. Our first week, the barking was too much for me, so that was it."

"How did you manage that?"

"I went to our park and I corrected him with an electronic collar. Now I do not have to correct him. After that first week, he realized, 'I can't bark while he's in the car.' It took me about two days. There are times where, if I go Code 3 to a call, he gets louder. Sometimes I put myself in his shoes and realize that I can't hammer down on him all the time, because he's excited about what he's doing. You don't want to take that away from a dog."

Code 3 is when a call is urgent enough to require lights and sirens. Many dogs learn, in a very Pavlovian way, that lights and sirens mean something major is going to happen, where they will be called into duty. It's tough for them not to respond.

Yet another car is going the wrong way on another one-way street. We pull up. There's a teenager driving, and he is agitated. Rakker goes off barking, so even with the mic on I can't hear much from my shotgun seat.

"I'm just lost. I'm just *lost*, okay? Now there's a dog in the car!" says the driver in wounded tones.

"Don't worry about it," says Officer Faulkcon calmly. They talk for a few minutes and he lets him go with a warning.

"That was a good interaction back there, ending with, 'Thank you very much, I'm sorry about it,' and me saying, 'That's okay, take care.'"

"There are a lot of drunk college students out tonight," I say.

"The University of Iowa is the number two party school in the nation.[3] It was really bad when I first started. Now it's not bad at all. I try to average a minimum of five stops a night; tonight I'll probably do more. I think the only way to find drugs is to stop cars."

"What is Rakker trained to scent?"

"Meth, ecstasy, heroin, crack, and marijuana. We put a lot of stress on these dogs. I do my best to calm him down."

Literally moments after we pull away, we spot yet another car going the wrong way on a one-way street. With lights on, Faulkcon pulls him over, a tall, young white kid. Faulkcon is very polite.

"How's it going? You were making a left on a one-way street."

The driver gives him some attitude: "Okay."

Faulkcon doesn't rise to the bait. He issues another warning, and we drive away.

"How did that one go?" I ask.

"He was a bit apprehensive, but he had a clean record. With what's going on in our country right now, that's why."

"Well, a good interaction can shift that a little."

"Yes. Unfortunately with a lot of the African Americans we stop, they are all apprehensive, 'Why you stopping me?' I love interactions like that, because of all those stereotypes I get to shatter. No, we're not out there to mess with people, we're just out there to do our job. I think this right here is the purpose of a K9 car, to make as many contacts as possible, to get the dog to work. I am not out there to ruin anyone's life, I'm out there to save a couple."

I settle back in my seat as we drive. Iowa City's a small city, and we cruise the main streets several times. I wonder if I'll run into any of my writer friends at the international writing program, and what they'll think if they see me. It's such an incongruous idea—that my writer friends would come out of the Fox Head bar with their arms around each other's shoulders (which is how we walk when we need a steadying influence after a beer too many, or when we are home-sick and just happy to be together) and see me waving at them from the passenger seat of Officer Faulkcon's cruiser. How would I explain myself?

Before he joined the police force, Faulkon tells me, he was in the Navy. "I joined the military because of 9/11. When I got back I wanted to still protect my family and do it the right way. I don't think there's anybody who can protect my family better than I can."

"What was it about 9/11 that made you take that step?"

"I personally felt attacked. I was just out of high school, and I literally personally felt attacked."

"On 9/11 I was flying home from France with my partner," I tell him. "Our little son was sleeping between us. We were told we couldn't land, but we weren't told more than that, except that all the airports in North America had closed. We thought there'd been a nuclear war. It was like the end of the world, to see the stewardess walk by in tears. That silence, it was like nothing else. And our families couldn't locate us. The airlines had lost track of our plane." There is a moment of silence.

"I wonder sometimes about the life of my grandchildren, what they will experience," says Faulkcon.

"I wonder about that too."

Faulkcon is reflective. "We are not heroes. Every police officer has come to grips with that. Our stories don't end with praise and 'hip hip hooray!' When we deal with people, they are already at their worst. No one is happy to see us. It's very unfortunate. The fire department shows up, puts out fires, they're heroes. Not us. We're the people that everyone wants our help, and no one wants our help. I've just come to live with that."

"What would you say is the biggest misconception about the police, about who you are?"

"The biggest misconception is that we're not human. We have real-life problems just like everyone else here has. The only thing is we stand up and say, 'Okay, you're having a problem and we'll try to help you with your problem, even if we have to put our life on the line.' We're going to stand up and we're going to do it. It's our job. We are asked to correct people's actions and not too many people can take correction."

It's true. Not too many people can take correction, even if that correction is taking away their keys so they don't possibly kill themselves, their wife, their teenaged son, and maybe innocent bystanders, by driving drunk on the highway. Not too many people can take correction, even to save their lives.

"Another misconception is that what you see on TV is what you are supposed to get in real life. Everyone thinks that every time I pull up, I'm letting my dog out on them. That's not how it works. We take it one interaction at a time.

"If we get a K9 call, you'll see me talking, making jokes, bringing that tension down. I have more negative experiences with my own race, unfortunately. If I show up, most people are happy to see me. They think a black officer will understand."

A headlight on a truck is out. The other patrol car pulls up first, and we pull up behind. Something about this truck has made the other officer suspicious. He gets consent to search and Faulkcon brings Rakker out. The driver, a young African American guy, and the passenger, a girl from the Middle East, stand at a slight remove from each other. They are both texting intently, heads bent over their phones. I follow the dog team around the car. Rakker sniffs quickly and thoroughly, but finds nothing. The two are told to pack up their stuff and leave the car, because one of its headlights is out. All night, I've seen Faulkcon give more warnings than tickets, but this truck will be towed because it has no insurance.

The driver who comes to pick them up is fuming, loud.

"The guy who picked them up was very upset. People who get the most upset are usually the ones who don't have anything to do with it. The girl who owned the car, she and her dad, they weren't upset. You can't drive without insurance. That's the law. It was the guy who picked them up who was causing trouble."

I'm glad we left when we did. The driver was ready to explode. "What are some of your best adventures with Rakker?" I ask, changing the subject.

"I'll tell you the story of that first week, of the track we did. A guy robs Gumby's Pizza at gunpoint and then takes off. There's snow on the ground. We have one footprint, just one. They say, 'Hey, let's get the dog!' I realize, 'Oh crap, that's me. Oh boy.' So I get there and pull him out. They show me the footprint and say he ran that way. The footprint disappears. It's all on Rakker now. He tracks to this building. He won't leave. I'm like, *Come on, everyone's looking at me.* "This is embarrassing," I tell the other officers. At this point I'm feeling like I'm a failure. It's my first week on the street. You know what? The guy was up there, hiding out in the building. Rakker tracked right to the right place. That showed me to just trust my dog. I was already telling him, 'You're wrong, you're not doing what you're supposed to do.' That made me need to learn more about what he's trying to tell me. He was saying, 'Hey Dad, there's something here.'[4]

"Two weeks later Rakker tracked a guy who stabbed his mom. The guy jumped the fence and was hiding in an old lady's storage shed. Once we got there, I saw the storage. There was snow on the ground, we saw the footprints lead there, and we got him."

*Trust your dog.* That's the refrain I hear again and again from the men and women who work with these animals. Things may look implausible, but your dog's nose knows what it knows. Listen to your dog.

It's a busy night. Rakker is pressed into service once again for drug sniffing just a few minutes later. Officer Faulkcon asks me to stay in the car while he and Rakker check over a big red pickup. The girl stays in the truck, but the driver, a slow-moving man, stands to the side. They are both young, both wearing jeans, both with that white-blond hair I see all over Iowa, hair that seems to shine even at night. I can't get a read on the driver. His words come out impossibly slowly. Faulkcon tells the girl not to be scared. "Just hang tight for a second, k?"

Rakker sits and stares pointedly and fixedly at the back of the truck. There's no mistaking his signal. Officer Faulkcon checks in. "My dog alerted on your car. Any reason?"

"No, it's my mom's car. There's nothing in it."

"Nothing in it," repeats the guy, slowly.

"Okay, we're gonna search it."

"There's nothin' in it."

"In just a few minutes, we're going to have a female officer come to pat you down. So tell me honestly if you've got anything on you."

"No. Nothin'. Nothin'."

Faulkcon and Rakker search the truck while I wait in the car. A female officer arrives and does the pat-down behind the truck. She's a young blond ponytailed woman. She gives me a quizzical look. I smile.

There are no drugs in the car. Sometimes a dog alerts on cars where there were drugs at an earlier time, and sometimes we humans will never know what caused them to alert. We leave the other officers to finish the call. He'll be taken in for driving drunk. As we drive away, the young man turns toward us, his head moving slowly up from where he's been studying his shoes. The light illuminates his pale face.

"So many times, it's like this," says Faulkcon, as we head back into town. "The driver is drunk, and there's a sober passenger in the car. It doesn't make sense."

I turn to Faulkcon.

"Thank you for letting me spend time with you and Rakker," I say. "You've given me a lot to think about."

Officer Faulkcon gives me one of his rare, dazzling smiles. I like it when he smiles; his whole face lights up like the sun. "No problem! Me personally, I would like to go my entire career without having to shoot somebody, without Rakker having to bite somebody. I complain about this dog nonstop. I wouldn't trade this dog for any dog in the world."

■

Cade has always been special to me. Maybe it's his winning personality, maybe it's because he was the first dog to attack me, or maybe just because I've probably spent more time with him than any other dog, but he's one of my favorite K9s. Cade has two clear sides to his personality: his badass side, where he's ferocious and furious, and his watchful, mellow side, where he knows he's off duty. At those times, Cade is relaxed, and just has a genuine capacity to engage with whatever happens.

Too much time has gone by since I've gone out riding with Darrell and Cade. I've been away on my writing fellowship in Iowa, and before that, I've been busy with my kids over the summer break, busy launching my new book of poetry. When I call Darrell to see if I can hang out with him and Cade, he tells me that he's leaving the K9 unit and moving to Ontario at the end of the month. I'm speechless.

"I hope to take Cade with me," Darrell rumbles. But that will depend on the judgment of Senior Trainer Eric Stebenne. Cade's five and a half, and still has a couple of good years of service in him, so it would be against protocol for the RCMP to not keep Cade on as a working dog.

"Oh, you have to, you just *have* to take Cade," I say. They've always been together. This is when it hits hard, that these dogs don't belong to their handlers, that they can be removed by the Force and reassigned to someone else. I can't imagine Darrell out on the road without Cade. But Darrell's mother is sick, she's alone in Ontario. Family comes first.

When we finally connect, though, Cade has already been matched to a new handler. Senior Trainer Stebenne has decided that Cade is much too valuable to the RCMP to let him just retire at the peak of his career. Darrell and the new handler will spend a few sessions together to make the transition easy on Cade, and then Darrell will say one of the toughest good-byes of his life.

"I got a sweet deal," Darrell tells me. "I get Cade back when he retires." I know Darrell's holding on to that. If all goes according to plan, Cade will put in his last couple years of service and then spend his retirement with the man who had him since he was eight weeks old. He'll run and track until he can't track anymore, and then he'll come in and find a place to rest by the fire.

My last day to meet up with Darrell is the first day I get to meet his family. I drive to Squamish in the pissing rain, in a fog so dense even my headlights don't cut it.

I meet the family as they are packing to leave and driving the boys to hockey. Darrell decides to take us all to one of Cade's favorite places to run. It's their last day as a family, and it means a lot to me to be included.

I climb in the police car, and Darrell's wife Natalie follows in the family car with the boys and their family dog, a sweet blond Havanese called Phoebe.

Cade is barking at full volume as we drive, and Darrell yells over him, "I won't miss that!" We are on a long road through the trees to the place where the dogs like to run. Cade and little Phoebe cavort around us. Darrell keeps Phoebe in his sight. The eagles chortle, and huge ravens call nearby, and she's at risk of becoming an eagle's dinner. A light mist of rain soaks us all as we stand around.

"What are you going to do with all the time you have, without all the dog stuff?"

"It's been probably ten years of having a dog to take care of. I won't have any regrets. I think I would if I didn't leave and my mom passed away with no one there. At the end of the day you have to do what's best for the family. It's easy to say but tough to do. A job's a job, it won't be as satisfying but it is what it is."

Darrell's wife Natalie is busy that day. I wonder how she feels about the move, and about having shared her husband with K9s all these years. She's also in law enforcement, but I don't get much time to talk to her—she's packing up one house to move to another, shepherding the boys to and from hockey, and Darrell's going to be gone all night on his last shift with Cade. I make a plan to meet them at Police Dog Services headquarters in Surrey when Cade has to say good-bye to Darrell.

At three a.m. Monday morning, I get up in the dark and drive to Surrey. It's full dark and the streets are quiet; it's so easy to drive an empty highway. By four thirty in the morning, I'm at headquarters.

"The last shift was a bust," says Darrell, stepping out of his truck to meet me. Cade barks from in the back, then comes leaping out, snarling and menacing me. There is a moment where I think he may attack. Flashes of thought: protect my face, cross my arms, turn my body. He jumps and Darrell is right there shouting, "CADE! NOOOOO!" Cade retreats. The blast of adrenaline is like sticking my finger in a socket. Cade grabs my sleeve and tugs, and then grabs my backpack and pulls, hard.

"CADE, KNOCK IT OFF!" yells Darrell. And then Cade sniffs my backpack and sits, staring fixedly at it. He's indicating on my backpack, indicating that there are drugs, a gun, or explosives inside.

"What you got there?" Darrell rumbles at me. "You got drugs or something in there you want to tell me about?" I shake my head. I stare at Cade. Cade stares at my backpack.

I'm clean but I don't feel clean. It's a disconcerting feeling. Cade's teeth clap and chomp the air as Darrell leashes him up. What the heck did he smell? I shake my head, wishing, not for the first time, that Cade could talk so he could explain himself.

Cade's new dad, Officer Rempel, arrives. Rempel is a guy of medium build, fair-haired and direct. He shakes my hand and Darrell's. He's already had Cade twice, first for a weekend, and then for a week, but this time it will be until Cade retires. There's a hand-off of gear: kibble, leash, harness, a training collar with chain and spikes, all of it stuff that Darrell no longer has any use for.

Cade plays with Darrell, a couple of quick tosses of the ball, a couple swings in the air. "Good dog, good dog," he says. "I'm gonna make this short. Easier on both of us." He gives Cade a final thump on both shoulders.

Cade barks his head off in the truck. "I know you're going to use the electric collar on him," says Darrell, "with that barking."

Rempel laughs, but doesn't deny it. Darrell drives away to a new life, a life he never anticipated even a year ago. Cade settles in to the truck of a new handler. He barks furiously for a moment, then falls silent. It's the end of an era, the end of my time with the team I know best.

■

But what is certain is this: I'll see Cade in a couple of weeks, and Darrell will see him again in a couple of years. Cade's with a good, experienced handler, and he's got so much drive in him before he gets to move. Darrell and Nathalie have bought a country house in Ontario, on five acres, with the boys and Phoebe, the Havanese, and a place waiting for Cade.

■

The first time I met Constable Rempel, I didn't get a good look at him. Our meeting was obscured by the darkness just before dawn, as Darrell said good-bye to Cade, and handed him over to his new dad. Rempel's come to meet me on his day off. His light hair is cut short, his blue eyes are friendly. He wears jeans and a gray hoodie. We hop in the truck. As usual, Cade is barking like a maniac. I hold out my hand for him to sniff through the grille, and he calms down.

"Just so you know," I tell Constable Rempel, "I'm going to take notes on my computer while we talk, but I won't get everything. And of course when we're outside or whatever, I'll just type things up from memory, so it won't be word for word."

"No problem. You can make me sound smarter than I am. Give me some big words," he says with a comfortable grin.

Cade's now been with his new dad for more than two weeks. They've just passed the intensive recertification course together, the one that Tom Smith and Eric Stebenne run.

"They made me *work* on that course. Cade and I both lost a few pounds. I was running up and down through the brush, running until I was throwing up. But we passed."

Constable Rempel came to policing late. He was selling advertising space at hockey rinks when 9/11 happened. "I remember not going to work that day. I was in awe and shock in front of the TV. I talked to my girlfriend. I said, 'It's not fulfilling what I'm doing. I've always considered being a police officer. I want to try it.' I was older, twenty-eight years old. I had life experience, education. I applied, and my friends said it would take a year or so before it all happened. But in less than five weeks I got hired."

"Very cool."

"I'd always known if I were to be a cop I wanted to be a dog handler."

"Why?"

"I always just imagined how amazing it would be to work with a dog, and to have such an amazing partner. I've always been fascinated by dogs. I love dogs, the way they work."

"I get it."

Roger Rempel is the first cop I've ridden with where I don't have to ambush him with poetry when he's a captive audience on a midnight ride-along. He tells me he and his oldest daughter searched out my work on the Internet. "We found some of your poems online, listened to them online together. She said, 'Daddy, she's really pretty!'"

I immediately wish I had a few poems appropriate to a curious seven-year-old. Why do I have to write so much about sex and love and death and politics anyway?

"Does that poet gig of yours take up a lot of time?"

I nod. He's talking about my poet laureate position for the City of Vancouver. As poet laureate, I promote poetry and community, give readings at official events, and work with a team of poetry ambassadors to edit an anthology that will also raise funds for refugee and low-income families. "It takes about as much time as I have to give it. But I love it. I love the people I've met through it. I love what we're doing."

"Sophie, my oldest daughter, she wants to be a writer when she grows up."

"Tell her to send me a story," I say. "I'd love to read it." I tell him about a poetry contest for children and youth in foster care I've just been invited to judge. One of the best parts of what I do is encouraging kids to write poetry, to speak their truths.

Constable Rempel has three young daughters: Sophie, who is seven, Mae, who is four, and three-year-old Vivienne.

"What does your wife do?"

"My wife, Alicia, she's a mom. She was a director at the Leukemia and Lymphoma Society. Then she quit and stayed home with the kids. It's so good to have Mom home after school. Sure makes my life easier! When I was training I could concentrate on the training, if I have to sleep after, I can sleep. She does before- and after-school care every day, brings a bit of money home."

"Did you grow up here?"

"I was born in Brazil. I grew up filthy poor. But *never* was our house not clean. We never had garbage lying around. That's why I have so little time for that excuse. Just because you are poor? You can still take the garbage out. Do something for yourself. My mum always kept a clean house. We had food on the table. We didn't have a lot of things that other people had, but we had pride."

"Do you still have family in Brazil?"

"Yes, my grandma is there. My dad had eleven brothers and sisters, and they are all still there. My dad did construction here. We came to Canada on a Saturday. On the Tuesday he was already working on construction. It worked out all right; he raised three daughters and me. I thank him all the time for coming to Canada. My life would be quite different if we stayed in Brazil."

"Did you grow up speaking Portuguese?"

"No. I didn't speak until I was four, actually. I turned four in March the year we left. We came to Canada in October. My sister turned one on the airplane as we came over. I remember the flight attendants gave her a bib on the flight.

"I've been back several times. It's always been a bit depressing, the poverty and the corruption. Brazil's a tough place to make a good living. There are a lot of rich people and then a lot of very, very, very poor people. Not a lot of middle class, that's what makes a country prosper. My family was refugees in Brazil. They're Russian Mennonites. Everything was going great in Russia until communism and persecution. So we left Russia and ended up in Brazil.

"There are a lot of corrupt cops in Brazil. I got no time for corrupt cops. Corruption makes me so angry. We were going to Paraguay, and the border guards accused us of taking the car and trying to sell it, because I had a Brazilian passport. I had an eighteen-year-old soldier holding a gun to my head. My uncle tried to negotiate with them. In the end we had to give them a hundred and fifty U.S. dollars to let us go. I was so angry, but what are you going to do? A lot of people in Brazil are sick of getting extorted by the police. Now they are videotaping the extortions."

"Well, that's good," I say. "I hope videotaping this stuff will make some of it stop, bring the corruption to light."

"Did you ever hear about the death squads in Rio, the police that kill the kids?"

"Yes, I heard about that. It makes me sick," I say. I feel the revulsion rising within.

"I went to that church where the kids were shot. It's unbelievable. They're eight years old, twelve, thirteen years old, no family to be had that you know of. They pickpocket you, they've got their scams, yeah, but it's survival, and you do what it takes when you are a kid. Of course you're going to steal."

Police killing of homeless children in Brazil has been going on for a long time, but has gotten even worse prior to the Olympics in Rio. The United Nations has accused Brazilian police of executing street children in order to "clean the streets."[5] As tools of the state, police have so much power. Even a few corrupt or racist or sadistic police officers can cause an incredible amount of damage in a community, anywhere in the world. The public trust is destroyed when the state turns against its own people.

I shift to a lighter subject. "So, how are things going with Cade?" I ask.

"Things are good, things are going really good. The first time I met him, I could tell he's a confident dog, but he's got some edge. He's not a little shadow in the alley. I wasn't going to pet him that time. I was going to make him come to me if he wanted to come to me. I took him home for a week. Once I got to know him a little bit then I realized, Cade is an edgy dog. He's a nice dog with edge. If you know that line, he's easy to handle. I'm not going to bring him to a schoolyard, I'm not going to take him into a classroom. My old dog, he was the kind of dog you could let loose into a kindergarten class. He just lay there, never growled, never barked, but out on the street he was there for me. I trusted him in a kindergarten class *and* in a dark alley.

I think I need to be a little more careful with Cade. Introducing my family to him is a slow process. I tried introducing him to my three-year-old, Mae, and she came to pet him. I told Cade to lay down and he growled at her, which in my opinion was unacceptable."

"That's no good."

"No. So it was right away back in the kennel. They say hi to him. Every day they go to the kennel, the gate, they say, 'Cade, no barking!'"

Oh, Cade. Constable Rempel's assessment matches my own. Cade's like the friend who is always up for a good time, the friend who is good-looking and super fun to be with. Part of what makes him fun is you don't really trust him and aren't really sure what he's going to do next.

I know him better than any police dog. I really like him. I think he's the handsomest dog I've ever seen, but I don't trust him.

I love hanging out with Cade, but when he jumps back in the truck and I move too close to the open door, Cade snaps at me. I step back quickly.

"See, that's manners, that just comes down to him being a prick. He didn't bite you, did he?"

I shake my head and climb in shotgun.

"So here's what I wonder about," I say. "How did you manage your very first few days with Cade, right when you took him home but before he knew you? That's what I'd find intimidating. Why would he listen to you?"

"That's an excellent question. Especially at first with a dog like Cade, I went in there like I owned the place. I walked him into the kennel with the leash. I closed the gate and filled the bowl with food. I made Cade eat out of my hands, made him eat the whole dinner like that. I controlled his food. Then I took it away halfway through. Cade showed no aggression. I did this for a week. At that point I thought, him and I are not going to have an issue. It's going great. I keep sending Darrell texts to say how nice of a dog he is." As we drive around New Westminster, Constable Rempel takes me to various crime scenes.

"This happened four years ago. There was a stolen truck, driven by a male, and a female passenger. A cop went to talk to them and they took off. I happened to be on a training day. I chased the truck a little bit, and then I was told to call it off. I pulled over by the Fire Hall, and just then someone said, 'There's been a crash, a collision with an oncoming truck on the Queensborough Bridge.' I was very close, I was at the crash scene in forty-five seconds to a minute. It was their truck. The pair jumped over the fence. I checked over the other driver, and he was in my opinion dead. (It turned out he wasn't dead, but I didn't know that at the time.) I got my dog, Gunner, over the fence; we jumped and landed on a trailer. Gunner doesn't want to leave the spot, so I knew we were close. He was looking up at me, circling this truck and barking. Then a guy yells, 'I give up! I give up!'

"I say, 'Step down.' We're in a huge lot full of trucks. I can't see his hands. It's dark in the truck, and now he's not listening. He won't come out. I send Gunner up. Gunner grabs him by the foot and drags him out. My dog ends up biting him in the head as I try to arrest him. He got eight years in prison. We found her too, laying on top of one of the trucks. My dog went to the odor so quick. Out of all those trucks, he found him. The guy had only been hiding for five minutes. My dog wouldn't leave that truck. He continued to bark; his barking made the guy semi–give up. That was nice to see, this training stuff does work."

"Oh, I've been there!" I say. "That's the place with all the thousands of smashed cars, right?" It's an eerie place. So many of those wrecks were so obviously not survivable. "We did some group training there where the dogs had to drag someone out of the car who was resisting arrest."

"We do a lot of training in that ICBC lot. A lot of good lessons in that yard."

"Have you been in a life-or-death situation with a dog?"

"A lot of times it's hard to know. Really I don't know, would the guy in the bushes have shot me? One big file I was on, coming back from Burnaby, I see the guy get out of the car, somebody I assumed was the driver going into the gas station."

As Constable Rempel talks, he drives me to the gas station where it all went down.

"So I parked in front of the car right there and started getting out. I thought the car was empty, but he was actually hunkered down. Next thing he's ramming my truck, ramming me, but my truck's not moving. I'm calling it in. He's trying to get out, but eventually his car gets stuck on the curb. All of a sudden a Mountie comes up from behind, a couple of officers from New Westminster arrive as well. I go to smash the window out to rip the female out of the passenger seat. I go to grab the female and I hear shots being fired. I remember yelling at my dog, Banks, to lay down. I didn't want him to get shot. I was just hoping he'd lay down.

"I tell the girl, 'Don't move.' I throw her out the window and hand-cuff her to a tree. She was the girlfriend. Then I grab the officer I saw who shot him. I say, 'What happened, are you all right?' He says, 'Yeah. He pointed a gun at you.'

"He sees Buddy pulling a gun on me, at that moment two people shoot him. The Mountie shot him through the headrest."

"What did the girlfriend say after?" I ask.

"I think she was cooperative. The guy had another incident earlier in Vancouver. He had a gun and was holding it to his head. He wanted the police to kill him. He was a typical dirtbag, doing dirtbag things. I remember seeing his family at the coroner's inquest.

They were not police haters as a result of what happened. They knew what their brother and son was into."

The gas station looks so ordinary. Banal. This is the place where a troubled guy makes his last wrong move, and his girlfriend spends the worst moments of her life handcuffed to a tree as her boyfriend dies in the driver's seat a few feet away from her. I shiver. Cade whines against the grate that separates him from us.

"Can we go somewhere you can take Cade out one more time before I go home?"

"Sure. My first dog, Banks, I never had that middle gate closed with him. Cade is another story. Did I tell you this one with Banks? It was the middle of the night in Ladner." (Ladner is a small city near Vancouver.) "I was called to what started out as a break and enter. But then the guy went into the daughter's room. She was twelve. She woke up and he was in her room. She screamed, he ran out, and the family came in and phoned 911. I got out there with Banks. I was so mad. We tracked for half an hour, got the guy. Banks bit him in the leg."

It is easy for me to imagine the girl, waking up to find a strange man in her room.

"I'm glad you got the guy."

We drive to Deer Lake to the RCMP detachment and find a quiet grassy place for Cade to hop out of the truck. Cade is more relaxed than usual. I can sense the change in him. He comes up to me, wagging his big tail, and I give his head a rub, then rub down his shoulders. He closes his deep amber eyes, like a black bear in the sun. It is the closest we've ever been, as he sits next to me, soaking in the bright spring sunshine.

Cade has a thick, strong black tail, the thickest I've ever seen on a dog. As he sits, waiting for Rempel to throw him a ball, that tail thumps the ground with the force of a paddle hitting the water.

We all get back in the truck and head back to New West.

"So what are your hopes and plans for Cade?"

"To catch as many bad guys as I can. These dogs love to work. I love to work. I also want to give Darrell his dog back, healthy, happy, and with a couple more bites under his belt. For me, it's tough. If he is my last dog, I'd definitely consider keeping him. It makes me a little bit sad. I'm kind of renting."

"I think Darrell's holding on to that, that Cade's coming back."

"I might phone him the day before and say, 'Sorry, bud, I'm keeping him.' My plans for Cade? To make Darrell proud. How 'bout that? But selfishly? Just to catch lots of bad guys. I'll make Darrell feel as bad as possible to give him up: 'You're going to rip this dog away from my kids who love him.'"

I smile. "Can I go out again with you and Cade?"

"Sure, any time."

I say good-bye to the big guy in the back, the dog I've spent more time with than any other. Life is full of change, and dogs have to roll with whatever comes, just like people do. Cade's rematch to Rempel is a good one, though. I am glad to know he's in good hands. Cade's big tail thumps hard against the truck bed, and I head to my car for the long drive back to ordinary life.

# 3

## Outlaws and Outliers

I drive south, crossing the border into the U.S. to meet Deputy Jason Moses, who works out of Mount Vernon, Washington State, with his K9, Espo. Deputy Moses is an athletic deputy with military-short brown hair and a chiseled face. Espo is a two-and-a-half-year-old black-and-tan German shepherd with a black mask, golden eyes, and awesomely expressive eyebrows. Like his handler, Espo is in his prime working years. We meet near the train station, just outside the sheriff's office. It is not until I am in the deputy's car that I realize the brick building I've parked next to is a jail. I should have known by the narrow slits it has for windows, just enough space to let in light. But I have learned, since I started riding along with the dogs and their handlers, that, while I am attuned to people and animals, I am spectacularly unaware of cars and buildings. My situational awareness is limited. I've been in Mount Vernon many times over the years, and never even knew there was a jail in this town.

"This jail, it was built for eighty-two prisoners, but it typically holds a hundred and eighty to two hundred. We have to let a lot of criminals go. We can't house them. The good news is, we got some funding for a new jail, should be finished sometime in 2017, a four-hundred-bed jail with room to grow."

Deputy Moses knows I've been working with police dogs in Canada. "Espo was actually born and raised at Innisfail," he tells me. "It'd be cool to know more about his parents, more about his first year of life." I tell him I'll find out whatever I can. But all I know so far is that Espo is a dual citizen, like me. Like so many expats, Espo's made a good life for himself in the USA. Deputy Moses tells me he's trained with some RCMP police dog handlers, and knows Constable Jamie Dopson and his dog, Chrisa. Chrisa is one of the few female police dogs I've ever met. It's a small world, the world of K9 handlers.

Like many of the handlers I get to know, Deputy Moses has always been drawn to high-intensity work. He was a volunteer firefighter for fifteen years before he became a K9 cop. His wife is a paramedic.

"Our first dog bite, she was the paramedic that was dispatched. The ambulance came for a dog bite on a suspect, and it was her. It was a single puncture, nothing too bad. Espo did really well, he immediately let go upon command."

"Is Espo your first K9?"

"Yes. He's doing great. I'm also on the SWAT team, and my hope is to integrate him in. I'm always working with him. Even if I have to spend my own time, it pays off to have a dog doing well. This is one of the most rewarding jobs, and also one of the most frustrating. I can't read his mind; he can't read mine. He's doing what he thinks is right. He does things usually for a reason. It could be something he thinks I want him to do. It's learning how to read him."

"How do you qualify to be a K9 handler here?"

"It requires four hundred hours of basic training minimum before you qualify to take the accreditation test. It took us two times to pass. The first time we just weren't ready. The second time we passed with flying colors. We focused a lot more on the obedience portion, made a few little changes. A couple of my trainers, they laughed after we passed: 'Why doesn't Dad smell like stress anymore?'"

"Hey, the guys at the RCMP also refer to themselves as their dogs' dad!"

"They call themselves Dad in Canada too? That's cool."

Along with all the usual computer screens, GPS devices, and radios, I see another device in the car I can't recognize. It looks like a mini–vacuum cleaner, and when Deputy Moses sees my puzzled look, he says, "That's my Cool Cop. You like it? You can stick that right into your uniform after doing a track. It cools you right down, gets all the hot air off of you."

"Nice."

Moses is a man with grit. He's determined to get better at whatever he does in life. "We basically do the same thing the SWAT team does, but while SWAT might take an hour to plan an approach, we just go in. K9 handlers are eight times more likely to be in a shooting. It makes sense, because we are going in after the guy. If he's armed, if the seriousness of the crime and all of the factors we need to meet for the use of force are set, we go in.[1]

"About two months ago we had a call in Sedro-Woolley. The guy was inside a house. He had felony warrants. We yelled for him to come out. Then I told him I was going to send in the dog. He yells, 'Okay! I give up!'

"When I pulled the dog back he charged the door and slammed it shut. He dead-bolted it. A couple guys ran to the front. He goes running out the back. We tried to chase him but the scent was too fresh. It typically takes ten to fifteen minutes for the scent to lay down, or the dog can have difficulty finding where it's at.

"I tried a few times to watch his place. I set up a couple guys from the sheriff's office and the city police. When I went to the front door, he again ran out the back. He jumped over the fence and our guys were there and caught him. Later I went up to talk to him in the jail. He told me exactly where he ran that first time. He said he watched us the whole time we were searching. It was kind of eerie that he was watching us."

I shiver. I can only imagine how it feels to know after the fact that the criminal you were hunting was lying in wait, watching you, and you had no idea where he was. Little do I know that in a few hours, I will know exactly how this terror-fest feels.

We go to an empty field so I can see Espo in action. First Jason Moses lets Espo run off some steam and retrieve a ball a few times, and then he calls the big guy over for some bite work. Moses and Espo are the only K9 team in his unit, so he has to train solo a lot of the time, although he makes it a point to train with other teams from across the county on a regular basis.

I watch Espo run toward Deputy Moses. I watch him leap into the air and bite. He's a dog who attacks without hesitation but can stop on a dime and is completely attuned to his handler. Finally, Deputy Moses calls time, so they can catch their breath.

Espo sits happily beside his dad.

Deputy Moses surprises me when he asks if I want to take a bite.

"No, not really," I say. The memory of Cade's impact is still strong. In fact, I will never forget it. "I already took a couple bites, and it was not fun. I could barely walk after. I ended up having to take a couple months off writing this book, just so I could do physio. I really don't want to go through something like that again."

Moses tries to reassure me. "You won't. I'll hold Espo close, and he'll release right away. Come on, you want to take a bite?" Moses asks again.

Just thinking about the attack makes me light-headed with adrenaline. I can feel my heart race. *Don't do this*, I tell myself. *You really don't have to do this.*

"Sure, I'll give it one more try," I say to Deputy Moses.

I put on a bite sleeve—it's a soft one this time, a training sleeve, which is alarming. With Cade the bite sleeve was hard and I still got hurt. But when I voice my worry, Deputy Moses says he uses the soft sleeve to protect Espo's teeth, and that makes sense for Espo. Claudio's dog Chuckie has two gold teeth because his canines have been broken in fights. It remains to be seen whether a soft sleeve makes sense for me, though. Deputy Moses keeps Espo on a short leash and commands him to attack, and just like that, Espo leaps up and bites my arm. Espo's not coming from far away and Deputy Moses is right there standing next to me, but I feel those teeth bearing down. Those are definitively thick, strong canine jaws biting my arm. I can't think of anything else but that. Even though the pressure hurts, it's nothing like what I experienced with Cade, which was not about the bite but had everything to do with force. A heavy dog like Cade coming

Bite work with Espo: the embarrassing evidence that I closed my eyes.
(Deputy Jason Moses)

at you at full speed from fifty feet away is something else entirely, a quick and dirty lesson on torque and leverage.

I'm relieved that I took a bite and found it survivable, so I agree to take a couple more. At the last one, Deputy Moses snaps a picture of Espo biting me. I would have sworn this wasn't the case, but the proof, the humiliating, photographic proof, is irrefutable: when Espo launches himself at me, *I close my eyes*. I'm braced and ready, the bite sleeve on one arm, my other hand balled up into a fist, and *my eyes closed*.

It's embarrassing. Now I know what I would do if I were facing a deadly assailant. I'd dig in my heels and close my eyes.

At least I stood my ground. At least Deputy Moses didn't snap a picture of me running away, with Espo in pursuit.

Another little known fact: you never know how bad the fit of your bra is until you are braced, every single muscle in your entire body contracted, with a dog leaping on your body. That's when you'll know if you have adequate support. I'm just saying.

After biting me a couple of times, Espo is totally relaxed. He sits on his haunches next to me, tongue hanging out, beveled penis protruding like a hot-pink lipstick in a fur-covered case. That dog, I swear, is laughing at all of us.

Deputy Moses tells me to expect a quiet ride, and I tell him that's fine by me. I've just had all the excitement I can handle with Espo's attacks, and I'm hoping a few hours of quiet county supervision, with maybe a drive-through McFlurry somewhere on the road, will bring my heart rate down to normal and dry the sweat that is trickling down my back. I relax into the seat, content to listen to Moses talk. I should know by now that there is no way to predict what a shift will bring.

"Do you find the night work difficult?"

"I like the nights. The hardest part is they want me working our busiest nights, Friday and Saturday. So my social life is basically gone."

A call comes in. "Squatters in a vacant home," says Moses. "I'll go to that." We speed up.

"Do you have many requests for people to come for ride-alongs?"

"Not as many since I got the dog. I love riders, though. When I first started I got to do ride-alongs. It was super exciting for me, so now when I can, I get to pay it forward."

We intercept the potential squatters next to their truck outside the abandoned house. They are a couple, a young white man and woman in an old red Ford truck. She has a high blond ponytail and smiles a lot. I watch as Deputy Moses runs their plates. He comes back, talks to them. They laugh, the young woman throwing her head back as if Deputy Moses is telling the funniest story she's ever heard. Another deputy meets us. For some reason, Espo goes off like a machine gun when he arrives. My head rattles with ricochets of barking. Another guy in a white T-shirt stands between the deputies and the two in the truck, arms crossed, bullshitting to beat the band. Deputy Moses comes back and fills me in with what he thinks is going on. Apparently the couple are just helping out their friend, the guy in the white T-shirt, who used to live there. The bank has foreclosed on his house. The question is, does he have rights to this stuff? "There's no history of criminal behavior. It seems like a hard luck case," says Moses.

It's sad. The guy just wants to load up his lamps, his boots, his framed painting of a bald eagle soaring over the sea. Then he comes over and says he's actually not taking his stuff away. He wants to store his things in what used to be his house, putting it under the roof of the place that is now bank-owned, in this little corner of rural Washington.

I catch snippets of the conversation. "I'm pissed at the bank," he says to Moses. "Actually I do appreciate your coming out."

Moses comes back to tell me the guy in the white T-shirt could be arrested for not providing identifying information. "He was like, 'I don't have to provide this.' Well, actually you do. We're here for a legal reason."

Is he taking stuff out of the house or putting it in? It's unclear, at least to me. We may be watching the world's slowest robbery unfolding right before our eyes. It doesn't feel right. I feel my vulnerability, sitting here. They match the guy's appearance, they think, to another guy who has done a lot of break and enters, and decide to press him a little more, get his ID. Turns out he has given them the wrong date of birth.

"I could arrest you for that," says Moses. He is being polite. "We just want things to check out. We want things to make sense." Finally the guy hands over his ID, and they run him and let him go. I'm relieved to be back on the road. "It's irritating when they give us a false name," says Moses, "but at the same time it's kind of fun, it's a challenge to find out who they are."

I ask why the man wasn't arrested—not because I want him to be, but because I want to know how they decide on who to bring in.

"For squatters right now, it's a misdemeanor crime. Our jail is so crowded right now that we book and release them on the scene. It's the same for DUI or petty theft. We have to call our jail and ask them if they'll accept that new warrant."

I'm shocked that drunk drivers can't be jailed because the jail can't hold them, but what can I say?

"Here's a story for you," Deputy Moses says as dusk turns to night. He switches on the headlights. "It was Christmas morning. This was about a month before I got Espo and the K9 car. There was a med call down a little bit aways from here. A guy showed up at someone's house. He had scratches on him. He appeared to have been assaulted. Fire and aid are staging to make sure the scene's safe. The guy barely speaks any English, just enough to let me know what was going on. He said it was black magic, there were witches after him. He's wearing a T-shirt and he's shivering. I want to remove him from the scene. I go to put him in the back of my car. Then I step behind the car. I'm talking to his wife who had just showed up. She was saying he had a bit much to drink. From the back he's able to manipulate my middle window. He crawls through and takes off in my car. He drives right for me! I jump out of the way so he won't hit me. He wrecks the car into a tree. The car is totaled."

"Why did he do it?"

"He was drunk and he thought we weren't going to help him. He wasn't under arrest, he wasn't in handcuffs. We just put him in the car to keep him warm."

We are heading to a domestic dispute. Dispatch says the wife complained she's being harassed. By the time we get there, the wife has left. The husband is with his mom. He comes out and he and his mom explain the situation with such sad faces. From what they say, it's a situation of mental illness and chemical dependency, and he has custody now of the child. Deputy Moses tells him how to take out a restraining order. Finally the husband says, "My daughter is in the house. I'm going inside."

"The one who leaves is usually the one with something to hide," says Deputy Moses. But I wonder what the wife's side of the story would be, this mother who wants to see her daughter, who claims harassment and then disappears.

The shift's been busy. At eleven at night, when things seem to be settling down, a call comes in from two police officers requesting the K9 unit. We drive deep into the dark countryside, navigating these narrow roads at top speed. I concentrate on breathing so that I don't throw up. I count the blessings of my long and eventful life, in case this should be my last night on earth, and I try to beam love toward my family, asleep as they most definitely are at this hour, safe in their beds.

There are two cops at the scene when we arrive. They found the car, parked by the side of the road, stuffed with stolen goods. The engine is still warm and the keys are still in the ignition. The man's wallet is on the dash. Why has he left the car like that, just minutes before the officers happened to drive by? Is it one of those lucky (or unlucky) things? Has he stepped in the woods to answer nature's call? When they call in the plates, they see the car belongs to a convicted felon, a meth-addicted criminal who is responsible for a number of break-ins. It is so odd to see his car, abandoned here on the roadside in the middle of the dark woods. They walk around carefully, peering in with flashlights, unwilling to touch anything. The police officers are exceedingly careful, debating like lawyers whether or not they have probable cause to go inside the car. "There's a holster, a gun holster on the seat and it's empty," says one. This is obviously bad news.

"There's a sword in the backseat," says another. "One of the houses that was broken into this week, I saw it had two samurai sword holders, but one of them was empty."

Still they restrain themselves from actually opening up the vehicle. I sit in the car, willing my stomach to stop churning, and wondering where the hell this felon has gone. Is he watching us right now?

Deputy Moses comes over and taps on my window. I roll it down and he looks me in the eyes. "Would you be afraid, going into the woods in the middle of the night after an armed felon with a warrant out for his arrest?" he asks. I nod, my heart thudding. "'Cause *I'm* afraid," says Moses, and he gives a sharp, sardonic laugh.

"We'll be back as soon as we can," he says to me. "I'm sorry to leave you here, but we've got all the lights on, and there's no way he's going to come back to the cruiser. This is the *last* place he'll come."

*Right,* I think. *Unless they're wrong.* The suspect's car is next to the cruiser; his keys are in the ignition; all he has to do is pick his moment and circle round. I sit there alone in the dark, hunched down in my seat, afraid even to have my phone on because he might be drawn to the light. I try to breathe silently. The blue and red sirens light up my face; there is nowhere to hide, nowhere safe to exist. All the other cops have been swallowed by the forest.

"Rob-BURT!" Branches crack. "Come out now or you could be bit! Robert, *Rob*-BURT! Come out *now* or you're gonna be bit by my dog!" I shiver in my seat as the night closes in. The minutes tick by as my heart thuds in my chest, so loud I think Robert can hear it from wherever he's hiding.

The guy is out here somewhere, but where? Finally, they decide to call off the search. One of the officers stays with the car until the tow truck can arrive, and Deputy Moses takes me back to my car, so I can get a few hours' sleep before the sun rises.

We are talking about nothing important when the officer's voice, the one who has stayed behind with the car, breaks in on the radio. Deputy Moses holds up a hand, every muscle suddenly tense. He knows how to read every nuance in this man's voice. "Dammit, answer him," he says, in the long pause before the dispatch replies.

"Suspect in custody," reports the officer. "I'm bringing him in."

As I'm falling asleep that night, I shiver again, thinking of the officer waiting in the woods for that tow truck to arrive, sometime after midnight, when suddenly the felon returns, sneaking back to his car. I think of the fight, witnessed only by the trees, a fight that could have gone either way: two armed men in the woods. This time, the law won.

■

Two days later, Sheriff Gene Davis and his dog, Gunner, pick me up in my motel near Winthrop, Washington. It took me almost ten hours of driving through some of the most stunning, rugged scenery in America to reach this little Western town. This morning I'm keyed up, wondering what the day has in store. It's only eight in the morning, but scorching hot already as Sheriff Davis pulls up in his truck with Gunner in the back.

Our first stop is to the training facility where Gunner works out. Just like any guy at the gym, Gunner has to practice his climbs and work on his ladders and his jumps to stay fit. We drive up a gravel road to a locked training course. The heat, when we step out of the air-conditioned truck, is instantly oppressive.

It's not until he hops out of the truck that I get a good look at Gunner. Born in Poland, he's a four-year-old black German shepherd with tan front legs. Gunner's not scary. His energy is different than Cade's; Gunner seems like a basically friendly dog. He kind of smiles at Deputy Davis as they work, and I can tell how bonded they are. I follow through the terrible heat as Gunner tackles the training equipment. He moves easily through his paces, doing everything that Sheriff Davis asks of him with steady focus and good will. We can't do much, though. This intensity of heat is hazardous to man and beast alike, and soon enough we are back in the truck with the AC blasting as I ask questions and Sheriff Davis patiently answers them. Behind our seats, Gunner's head turns from one of us to the other as we talk, watching us intently.

I ask about the dangers of the job.

"For K9 teams, one out of one hundred have a lethal encounter with a firearm; for the average police officer, it's one out of one hundred thousand. We go in to track people, usually felons in the middle of committing a crime. For me," continues Davis, "the biggest thing is my backup when I'm running a track. A lot of times I have to stop and wait for my backup officer to catch up with me."

We drive through the city of Okanogan, and Sheriff Davis stops

Sheriff Davis gets some love from Gunner. (Rachel Rose)

in at the Okanogan County Sheriff's Office, where he introduces me to a number of city officials, from deputies to a homicide detective. It's lovely and cool in the building, which contains both the jail and the detective and sheriff's offices. I drink in the air-conditioned air.

As we drive away, I see a group of prisoners sitting together outside the building in the hot shade of the jail, all shackled together. They wear green-and-white striped prison uniforms, and are all smoking cigarettes. "These guys are the jail cooks," says Sheriff Davis. "They've earned this privilege." This scene looks like it could be from a hundred years before—the silent men squatting or sitting in the dust, garbed in their striped prison jumpsuits, smoke from their cigarettes rising into the white-hot sky.

Although Sheriff Davis heads up a team of three K9s, he and Gunner work in isolation most of the time. Okanogan County, where Gene Davis lives and works, is a huge terrain, the largest county in a very large state.

Sheriff Davis tells me that it wasn't until the mid-1980s that the state started regulating K9 units more. "It used to be that if you had a dog and you could train it, you had a K9. Most police dogs were pretty friendly, not like city dogs who've been in a lot of fights. You'll see the difference."

"I already have," I tell him. The difference is huge. Working dogs in their prime, like Cade, have been choked, kicked, punched, and yelled at by people they've been commanded to attack. Dogs like Cade, who've lived through a lot of action, have developed a basic mistrust of anyone but Dad. Fighting urban crime has roughed him up.

But dogs like Gunner (and Espo, too) are friendlier. In my time with Gunner I sense a basic difference in demeanor, in the vibe he sends off. It's a general friendly curiosity.

We drive to check on a house broken into and invaded by squatters. Since I was a kid, I've roamed the streets of Vancouver's Downtown Eastside, a tough, impoverished and drug-ravaged but still often startlingly beautiful and resilient community with an average life expectancy that was recently lower than that of Calcutta. But what I see in this old house with its beautiful stone walls and deep fireplace is like the wreckage of a human tornado.

A room that was once a nursery, with teddy bear wallpaper, is torn apart, strewn with piles of filthy clothes, broken glass, and the remains of crack pipes. A car seat is stashed in one corner, a baby's pacifier in another. I can't picture a baby in this filth, and yet one was here. Drawers have been pulled open, doors wrenched off their hinges. I move curiously toward the fridge, but Sheriff Davis stops me firmly. "Don't open that," he says. "I made that mistake once. Everybody makes that mistake once." The smell, he says, is almost unbearable, and hard to escape once it's been let out.

I back away from the fridge. Sheriff Davis was called in because the squatters had reportedly returned, but nobody is around when we arrive.

We drive slowly through the massive Indian reservation belonging to the Colville Confederated Tribes. It's the burial site of Nez Perce Chief Joseph (Hinmuuttu-yalatlat) who refused to sign the land of his ancestors over. Despite his great skill as a negotiator and peace-maker, Chief Joseph and his followers were never allowed to return to Idaho, and were hunted and killed by the U.S. Army nearly all the way to Canada, before being forcibly resettled in the Wallowa Valley, Oregon, on land that belonged to other tribes. We are driving through a desolate place scarred by a terrible history of colonial brutality and appropriation. I feel that I don't belong here. Today the Colville Reservation covers 1.4 million acres in Okanogan County, Ferry County, and Chelan County. Sheriff Davis tells me that the reservation has its own police force for non-felony crimes. They have their own K9 team as well. The poverty here is profound, shotgun shacks with broken windows, rusted cars stacked in front yards. It's too hot for people to be out in the streets, I know, but the reservation seems deserted, empty of people and bereft.

"We work with the tribes quite a bit, doing enforcement," Sheriff Davis tells me. "Under the law, if a suspect is tribal, they go through tribal courts. The FBI comes in and helps them out for major crimes. Their court system only deals with misdemeanor crimes. If a crime goes beyond that they go to federal court."

We pass some tumbledown buildings tagged by graffiti, and a store selling fireworks. "The reservation is just like any other town," says Sheriff Davis. "There's some graffiti, like everywhere else. At least they're getting a little better at it. A big population of migrant workers lives here, also guest workers from Jamaica."

As we leave the Colville Reservation, Sheriff Davis tells me about the people he deals with, mostly poor white people like the squatters who busted up the stone house we had inspected. We pass cherry orchards as we drive. "Our products probably would not be picked if we relied on locals."

"Why not?"

"They don't want to work." Again, I flash on that baby seat, flung in a dirty corner. We drive and we drive. I unkink my legs. The sun is glaring even with sunglasses on.

Tumbleweeds, huge and fragile, roll across the highway, bouquets of lace and air.

I ask Davis about support for the K9 team. In Okanogan county, Gunner was entirely paid for by private citizens, he tells me. The purchase, care, and training of a K9 can be expensive, especially initially, and Okanogan County is not a wealthy place. But the fact remains that police dogs are not a priority in the state budget. As Sheriff Davis says, "We were in a recession here way before the recession even hit the rest of the country. We get our funding from property taxes, so if houses aren't selling, we're affected."

We drive through golden hills covered with blowing wild grass, shimmering in the heat. Sheriff Davis pulls over to show me one of many new marijuana farms, a fenced-in acreage just off the road. "Our biggest revenue now is agriculture—apples, cherries. But marijuana is taking over, it will be our second biggest crop in five years."

This hardscrabble, beautiful place is pinning its hopes for economic revitalization on pot smokers in distant rich cities. The police will be indirectly funded by drug money.

"I disagree with the decision to legalize marijuana. As law enforcement I know it is a gateway drug. It's very scary. Our dogs used to be trained on marijuana, but now they can't be, since it's legal."

I ask how the K9 program got going in his county.

"There was a woman around here, her daughter was an attorney for hockey players in NYC. This daughter, she got murdered and killed. She had so much money in the estate. The mom decided to donate it to us for police dogs in memory of her daughter. That helped us a lot."

This K9 team of Gunner and Sheriff Gene Davis owe their existence in part to a violent crime, and a grieving mother's resolve to prevent other such crimes from occurring.

The day rolls on. When a call comes in about a stolen ATV, we fortify ourselves with junk food and cold drinks at McDonalds and prepare to head across the county. It's a hard life for K9 cops, on the road all the time, eating whatever they can get, and yet required to be as fit as the most elite athletes when the call comes in and they have to track.

The drive to the stolen ATV is more than an hour away. Sheriff Davis calls for backup and we meet up with a local officer en route. The suspect who has been seen with the ATV is known to police.

I sip my huge, sweet iced coffee and watch the miles slip past.

Gunner snoozes in the back. Like Deputy Moses, Sheriff Davis is training Gunner with the SWAT team. "Not every dog can be a SWAT dog." But Gunner can. "A SWAT dog has to be quiet, obedient. You are using them as a search tool. You don't want them to be noisy.

"Out here, we work really well with the other cities. We are almost like one police department 'cause we have to be, but often I'll go to a call, wait for someone to come so I can track."

"You must have to wait a long time out here."

"Yes, I do. You have to be really patient. Gunner was really immature when I got him. He was pretty young, pretty handler-sensitive. Unfortunately a lot of European dogs are trained a little bit harder than we train. Sometimes with the European Schutzhund, it involves more forced training to make them do something."

We stop for gas, and Sheriff Davis shows me a video of his five-year-old son watching Gunner play in a sprinkler. As Gunner twists and turns, leaping through the spray and biting at the jet of water, the little boy shrieks with laughter and turns to the camera. "This dog is hilarious!" he chortles. Sheriff Davis smiles at the footage of his boy, his only child. "I want to make it fun for him. You hear so many stories of cops' kids, how they are so strict." The miles slip past. "We waited too long to have kids," says Davis quietly as we drive.

As an hour slips by, the landscape changes. The low, open hills rise into treed mountains, and we climb into coolness. Sheriff Davis turns off the AC and opens the windows. My nostrils fill with sweet, redolent pine, pine and honey. I've never smelled anything so incredible in my life as the Okanogan County mountain air. A bluebird whisks past us, and then a mother black bear and her small cub hustle across the road in front of our truck.

"Training is critical," Sheriff Davis is saying. "Bad guy reaches for a gun and the dog is on him. Rookie cops try to shoot around the dog, but seasoned cops shoot through the dog. Nobody wants their dog to get lost or die in the line of duty. *Nobody*. But I would rather go to the family and say my partner died, the dog died, but he brought your husband home."

I think about this as we drive, about having the discipline to shoot through your dog. How do you shoot your partner, the one who always had your back, the one who would save your life and become part of your family?

Outside the weather abruptly changes. The sky goes gunmetal gray. Lightning dazzles the hills. Suddenly we are driving through torrents of rain, beating down on our truck so fast the wipers can't keep up.

"I'm pro-second amendment, pro-gun," Davis continues. "I've been shot at two or three times." I don't say anything. To me, the proliferation of guns in America poses the greatest possible threat to democracy. But I want to listen.

"I'm also a crisis negotiator." He pauses. "To be honest, ever since I had my kid . . . I don't want my son to be raised up without a dad. It's hard."

We drive through pine forests and old logging roads on our way to the ranch on Pontiac Ridge where the stolen ATV has reportedly been taken. Pontiac Ridge, Sheriff Davis tells me, is a place where people move who want to be away from other people, particularly law enforcement.

I ask if that includes sex offenders. "Sex offenders? We deal with them all the time. They are registered in a state database. The way the severity goes is a scale from one to three. If it's number one, only law enforcement is involved, number two, schools and daycares are notified, and number three, the general public is alerted. If you are homeless and a sex offender you have to report weekly. Your level jumps up." Davis pauses.

"I saw the rape of a child," he says abruptly. "We waited until she gave birth to press charges. It was her mother's boyfriend. The girl came in to the hospital having had no prenatal care of any kind. She was twelve years old."

I say nothing. I have nothing to say. Or I have so much to say that I can't speak. It's obvious that witnessing the crime had an impact on Sheriff Davis.

Some people travel to other countries in search of adventure: strange lands, exotic worlds, people with customs and morals very different from their own. But going to the dogs taught me that I didn't have to go away to find the outlaws. All I had to do was shift my focus and my company. There are outlaws all around, people living on the margins of society up in the hills of the remote counties, or out in the bush and off the grid, or even in the heart of the city, if I know where to look. There are outlaws hiding in plain sight, other worlds unavailable to most citizens. We lack situational awareness, but whether or not we see them, they are there. Sheriff Davis arrested the man who raped that twelve-year-old girl, but waits until after she gives birth to do it. I shudder to think of her going through labor, of the shock of the pain. I suppose justice was done in the legal sense of the word when her rapist was arrested, but what kind of reparations can make up for the loss of that girl's childhood? And how can society possibly make amends to the baby she birthed?

"A lot of sex offenders move into our area to hide, from all over the country. I don't know if they have a forum, 'Hey, come to this area, it's nice!' All over the north end, it's the area to get away from big city society in general."

Remote doesn't begin to describe what we are driving through. We pass homesteads composed of two old school buses under a blue tarp.

"There's no electricity here, it's all generators. It's off the grid. Most of them run on wood heat in the winter. They don't want to live by society's rules. They respect us more because the sheriff is elected by the people, constitutionally appointed by the people. But a lot of times they don't like us. Most people are human beings and if you just talk to them and treat 'em by the Golden Rule it goes a long way."

I nod in agreement.

"A lot of it is knowing when to walk away. We will get people when we have to. When we come back with the cavalry to go arrest 'em, we will win. We always win. But we have to think it through."

There have been no homes, no people, for miles now as we drive the pine forests on logging roads through the heavy rain, and then we reach the crest of the hill, and there we are. The other officer has followed us up the dirt road, which is now sluicing water in torrents. There's a barn and a fenced-in garden on the side of the hill. Three calves outside bawl at the onslaught of rain. A beat-up trailer with one shot-out window hunches under a tin roof, and the rain ricochets like buckshot. The other officer is in a cruiser, not a truck, and they pull over to discus how he can get back if the road washes out. They move up the driveway on foot and leave me in the car with Gunner. I watch the two of them step out in a blur of rain to talk to some of the extended clan, see if they can find the suspect. They are instantly, spectacularly, drenched.

I'm jumpy. Almost certainly these people are armed, and there is nobody who could help us, who could even discover us, for a good long time. I sit in the car, trying to see them through the clattering sheets of rain. I'm relieved when Sheriff Davis climbs back in the car, shaking off water.

"They say the suspect's up on the hill with his father. His mother doesn't deny he stole it, but says it isn't here. I believe her."

We drive further on to another pile of rusted cars and shacks. As we drive, the rain shuts off like a tap twisted closed. The sun stretches its rays across the hills, and I open the window to breathe as much honey and pine as I can.

We climb through a pine wood, still driving on gravel, and pull up to a house made of many different materials: half a wall of log poles, half of plywood, some of which is papered over with tar paper, some of which has metal sheeting on it. A ladder leans against one wall, and parked nearby are four or five broken-down trailers. A friendly black lab comes out to greet us, tail wagging, which sets Gunner off to barking in the back.

"Oh, I've been up here many, many times," says Sheriff Davis. They approach the house and a skinny, grizzled man comes out, a white man so sun-beaten and weatherworn that he's the color of jerky. He wears a baseball cap and holds a can of beer in one hand, a cigarette in the other.

Sheriff Davis gets out of the car and has a polite talk with this father. He and the other cop poke around the place, but the father tells them right away that his son has just run off. Nobody's saying where the four-wheeler is hidden. I overhear the father explain all the places his boy and that ATV might be hiding. He just slips down the mountainside and is gone. I have ended up on another planet. I've been in the truck for five hours straight. My hips hurt from sitting. We drive away. There will be no ATV showdown today.

"How is Gunner with your family?" I ask on the drive home.

"My wife is not a big dog person. It's kind of ironical, her whole family is kind of standoffish around any dog. I've always had a dog, growing up, so it's second nature to me. They are cat people. I like cats, too. I use my cat as a tool to get Gunner social to housecats. You don't want him to chase that cat. Gunner's been sprayed three times by skunks at our house. Out of the blue, he goes after them.

"My wife likes Gunner, but if I bring him in the house he would be constantly searching to get his reward. He'd be looking all over. He's too high drive. He'll run through a fence to get his ball."

"Did you have Gunner from a puppy?"

"When I first got Gunner, he was eighteen or twenty months old. I flew to Michigan on a Saturday, and we were training on Monday. Gunner was looking for bonding, he wanted to bond really bad, you could tell. Naturally I grabbed him, gave him a bath in the hotel where we were staying, then we went for a walk, played ball, then hung out in the hotel room. He was looking for a master, somebody to be his partner. We did dope work, learned how to do drug detection.

"Gunner is so tuned in on me. I can do verbal outs with him." (A verbal out is when a dog attack bites, then releases on command.) "I don't know how he'll do on the street yet. Is he going to engage? They say if a dog's a good muzzle fighter, they'll engage on the street. But with Gunner, any muzzle fighting, muzzle work, he's not keen on that yet."

"I don't know what muzzle fighting is," I say.

He explains. "Sometimes with dogs they get in the habit of attacking the equipment and not the suspect. With the muzzle, the decoy doesn't wear any equipment. The dog's fighting with them directly. You can see the frustration. It gets to the point with Gunner that he's constantly trying to fight the muzzle. It's more of a deterrent."

"In Canada, they call a decoy 'quarry,'" I say.

Sheriff Davis nods. "Ultimately, what will ruin a dog is your decoy. You have to find the perfect decoy to do it. I love decoying, it's the best thing in the world, you can bring a dog into prey drive, or throw him into defense."

Gunner's not yet been in a situation that tests whether he will attack ("engage") when needed. An officer can only be sure of their dog after he's proven himself fearless in attack situations two or three times. Sheriff Davis doesn't yet have that certainty.

The hours have slipped by, hour upon hour of solid driving, from one end of the county to the other, up mountain passes and into sage brush scrub where rattlesnakes blend in perfectly with the rocky landscape. Working with Sheriff Davis and Gunner is a radically different experience from working with K9 teams in urban settings.

Back in Winthrop, Isabelle and the kids have driven all day to meet me. We are going to stay overnight and explore the old Western mining town of Twisp. Sheriff Davis welcomes them all with great friendliness. He poses with Gunner for pictures with the kids. I give Gunner a final pat, and snap a photo as he and Sheriff Davis play in the tall grass behind our motel. I know Sheriff Davis and I see the world differently. We don't agree on gun control, and we probably have other political differences, but it's been an easy ride in his courteous company.

# 4

## The Thrill of the Chase, the Whim of Destiny

I have to go to jail to see the first K9 I'll get to know in Santa Rosa, California. I hand over my ID, get a visitor's badge, pass my purse and cell phone to my Aunt Sue, and head in for an afternoon behind bars.

Sasha is a small short-haired Belgian Malinois. At only two and a half years old, and fifty pounds, she's a young, energetic dog, wiry and feisty. When I first hold out my hand to greet her, she lunges toward me with a growl and a snap. It's a warning, not more than that. Still, I pay attention and give her some space. Her handler, Deputy John Cilia, has been working with Sasha since she was fourteen months old. "Drug dogs don't have much obedience training at all," he says. "Apprehension dogs need to have obedience, but dope dogs work on their own." Sasha is the first K9 I've met who is a dedicated jail dog.

Cilia is a heavyset man with a ready smile who manages to make me feel relaxed at his workplace—the Sonoma County Jail. Officially known as the Main Adult Detention Facility, this jail is the largest detention facility for men and women in Sonoma County. I haven't been in a jail for nearly twenty-five years. A lifetime ago I spent a couple of months volunteering in a GED class at the jail for women on Alder Street in Seattle. That was a difficult experience of witnessing and trying to connect with one broken life after another: so many young women, almost half of them pregnant, caught up in the drug wars of the time.

I hadn't known until yesterday that going to jail was on the agenda, but I go wherever the dogs take me. I came to California because my aunt and uncle, who live here, have a family friend who introduced me to Deputy Greg Piccinini. Piccinini welcomed me and set up my whole week. Going to jail is a bit of a surprise, but at least I know we won't be doing any high-speed chases today.

What strikes me first about this jail is how bright it is. The walls are painted a light cream. The wide hallways gleam. Deputy Cilia takes me to booking first. There's a waiting room where those who can control themselves sit quietly on chairs in front of a television until they are booked. Inside are a number of individual cells that hold those who are so troubled or intoxicated (or both) that they can't contain themselves.

"They are a lot more comfortable sitting there, watching television, than they would be over there," says Deputy Cilia, gesturing at the cells. Inside the first one, I see a heavily tattooed white man who has taken his shirt off so he can thrust the naked slab of his chest against the window of his cell. He gesticulates obscenely, leering.

"Sometimes the wait here is up to twelve hours," says Deputy Cilia. I follow him over to the withdrawal unit, where those inmates who are coming off of drugs and alcohol are taken immediately after booking.

"This is a tough job for the corrections officers. It's like taking care of a child, a sick child. The inmates stay here a week. They get medically checked every four hours," says Cilia. This wing looks like a hospital, with a central station in the middle that looks just like a nurse's station, and small cells around it, most of which are open.

I see no people, though. They are out of sight in their cells. Though they have the freedom to move while they get clean, nobody's moving.

"It wouldn't be good for them to be coming off whatever and stuck in their cell the whole time. We want them out and moving around," says Deputy Cilia.

Sasha tugs on her leash, eager to get to work, but we don't enter the detox unit. "Sasha knows how to alert to heroin, cocaine, meth, marijuana, tobacco, and pruno," Cilia tells me.

"Pruno?" I ask, wondering what new drug this is, and whether it's smoked or snorted or injected.

"Pruno is jail-made alcohol," Deputy Cilia replies. While we observe the detox station, he tells me this is where Sasha made a find that could have killed her.

"It was last year. We were looking for drugs in this unit. We were doing a snatch-and-strip-search check in that cell right there," he said, pointing to the third cell in the row. Sasha found a stash of liquid heroin under some papers. She kinda jumped back as she found it. I saw it splashed her on the nose and in the mouth. Dogs don't react the way people do to these drugs. They can be fatal to dogs very fast. So I picked her up and we got out of there. We went Code 3 to the vet."

"How long did it take to get her there?"

"About three minutes."

"That's good."

"Yeah. They gave her meds right away to counteract the heroin. I called them here to test the drugs, and they ran a test that found that the heroin was also laced with methamphetamines. After they gave Sasha the drugs to counteract the heroin, we just monitored her. She was real quiet. She was real low energy for a few days, but in the end she was okay. For three nights after I brought her home, I slept on the floor with her so I could watch her. I didn't have to, but I wanted to."

I've heard it before. Deputy Cilia is not the first K9 officer to sleep on the floor next to his dog when his dog needs him.

"What happened to the guy who had the drugs?"

"He got charged with possession. On the streets, it's a misdemeanor. In jail, it's a felony. Plus, he got one strike. Do you know what a strike is?"

"Yes, I do." Three-strikes laws have been passed in a number of U.S. states, beginning in Washington State. If a criminal gets three strikes, he's jailed for life, with no chance of parole.

"The guy had a needle up his rectum as well."

After a pause, because I can't think of a response to the needle-in-the-rectum factoid, Cilia continues, "We've got tons of drugs coming in. These inmates, many of them keep working in jail. They have to work. They have to move drugs to support their families. Drugs go for five to ten times the price in jail as on the streets."

"I guess that keeps Sasha busy," I say. "What kind of reaction does she get from people in here?"

"They think she's a bite dog. She's a fifty-pound female! But we don't give them any information. It's none of their business."

"How are all these drugs getting in?"

"A lot of the guys are on crews, work crews. They work at the fairgrounds, and set up drug drops. We try to intercept that. We search the vans when they get back to jail. We find knives, cigarettes, tobacco . . ."

I follow Sasha and Deputy Cilia to the female module.

"We tend to find less here," says Cilia. "Here we do a lot more urine tests."

"Why? Is that because women use less?"

Deputy Cilia gives me an appraising look. "Females are made to be better at hiding drugs."

"*Oh.*"

Some of the women are outside in a unit open to the air, playing basketball. Many more mill around. They are young, nearly all white, and seem very curious about what we are doing standing there, watching them. One woman with long blond dreads smiles at me. I smile back.

We wait to be buzzed into the next module, which is segregation.

"Why would someone be taken here?" I ask.

"If you get in a fight and you are not cooperative after, or if you assault a correctional deputy or detention staff. You have to be violent to get in here. We're not petty about it. Based on the inmates' behavior, they can work their way out of segregation."

The cells are small, with long narrow windows. I see a couple of faces pressed against the windows, but I can't get a good picture of them.

"Used to be there were no windows, but the psychologists said that was too much for them, to be isolated like that. Now they can see out."

Seems to me it wouldn't take a psychologist to figure that out, but I say nothing.

"Sasha's done six hundred and forty-eight searches since March to the end of December."

I follow Deputy Cilia's broad shoulders out to the loading dock, where Sasha will do some detection work. He puts her in the car while he hides the drugs, and then gets her out again. Sasha's in overdrive, her haunches quivering as she jumps out. Cilia commands her, in German: *"Such!"* (It's pronounced "Sook!")

Sasha zooms across the parking lot. It takes her no time at all to find the first hide, a little paper dipped in pure heroin and hidden in some crates just outside the jail. Cilia praises his dog, clapping her on the side. Inmates are hard at work beside us, unloading food from a van. One of them stops to watch us.

"You can search this before I bring it in," he says. "That way we both know it's clean."

"Sure," says Deputy Cilia. He leads K9 Sasha over. Sasha gives the crate a cursory few sniffs. There's nothing there, and the inmate grins and gets back to work. Sasha moves immediately to the next hide, finding it as quickly as a well-shot arrow finds a target.

"Good DAWG!" says Cilia, throwing her the chew on a rope, praising her hugely. Sasha wags and frisks, loving every minute of it. "What a good DAWG!" he says again.

"Working dogs," Cilia tells me. "They'll cheat, but they'll never lie to you."

"She did well today," I say. "No cheating and no lying either. Does Sasha live in the house with you?"

"No, she has a kennel. I can't punish her for jumping up on things in the house when I want her to do it here. I've got three kids, so it would be hard to have her in the house."

Cilia takes me to see photographs of all the stuff Sasha's found—tobacco, a twelve-inch knife hidden in the sac crew van, a long nail, lighters, razor blades, needles, a tattoo kit.

"Are there a lot of fights in here?" I ask.

"Not as many as you would think."

"How did you choose Sasha?"

"She was going to be used for breeding. We wanted a K9 that wasn't a big food-motivated dog. She doesn't care much about food. Her personality with me is very lovable and very assertive. She knows she has a job to do. She will do whatever she can to make it work. Sasha has more drive than any other dog I've seen. For her it's a game. She puts in all the work. She doesn't know how important she is to this unit."

"Is there a policy for what breed of dog to use?"

"No. We have Malinois, German shepherds. Recently we've been going to this breeder in Mexico, that's where we've been getting all our dogs."

I want to give Sasha a pat before she's kenneled up in Cilia's cruiser and I leave the jail for the day, but I don't. This tough little dog has made it clear she is nobody's pet. Sasha leaps into her kennel and settles quietly, and I head back through the jail and out into the blinding sun. I say good-bye to Deputy Cilia until tomorrow night, when we'll meet up for group training. He passes me along to Deputy Greg Piccinini, who takes me out of the jail and shows me around the rest of the department.

Deputy Piccinini is the reason I'm here at all. He knows friends of my aunt and uncle, and when I asked to come and observe, he wrote to me right away and extended a big warm welcome. Deputy Piccinini was originally going to take me around for a ride-along with his dog, Yakk, so I was disappointed to hear he'd been transferred out of the K9 unit to work in Sexual Assault. It's hard to rise in rank in the K9 unit, and it often involves a transfer, which is what the deputy has decided to do. For Piccinini, this means separating from Yakk, his K9 companion. The deputy is a large, cheerful, ruddy man, who looks as though he's put in time working in the sun. Piccinini is Italian in background, like many of the original settlers of this wine region.

I follow him around the buildings, and examine The Bear Cat, an armored rescue vehicle that is used in collaboration with the SWAT team for hostage situations and other major crisis events. The Bear Cat has a Kevlar blanket behind which men can situate themselves. It is equipped with a spike that can pierce a house, and a container that can then pump gas into the dwelling. The Bear Cat can hold four or five guys and two dogs. A medic is always part of the team.

The Bear Cat had been brought out last year, during a thirty-two-hour hostage standoff.

"Me and Yakk did eighteen hours in that situation, then Santa Rosa Police Department SWAT Team relieved us. I went home, took a nap, then came back and took over the scene. Finally the guy shot himself in the chest."

"What happened to the people he took hostage?"

"We got them out early on."

I can't imagine a thirty-two-hour standoff inside a tank. I did less than an hour on a stakeout with Officer Moores in Surrey, BC, and let's just say it was not for me. It's being trapped, being scared and, at the same time, being so bored that you kind of hope something terrifying will happen.

Piccinini takes me to the narcotics wing of the detachment. I'm not allowed inside. There are too many restricted substances, and if any of them were to go missing, anyone who had been in recently would be a suspect. He calls one of the detectives out to chat with me instead. Between me and the detective stands the larger-than-life statue of Santa Muerte, posted outside their door. Deputy Piccinini introduces us, as I've never heard of Santa Muerte before.

Santa Muerte is one scary Saint. She's a skeleton in a black dress, wearing long beaded necklaces and carrying a machete. Later, I learn she's a personification of death itself, but symbolizes protection and healing. Santa Muerte's cult is growing across the U.S. and Mexico. This one was removed from a local Mexican drug cartel during a raid and brought to the office so she could be on the side of the police, and help them win.

It is jarring to see Santa Muerte looming over the entrance to the narcotics lab—this bright, efficient, modern police academy has enlisted the protection of an effigy of death, the saint of their worst enemies in the endless, deadly war on drugs.

"You heard of Jesus Malverde?" asks Piccinini, and I shake my head. "He's the patron saint of drug dealers." Who knew that narcos have their own saints? Later, I look up Jesus Malverde and find he has his own feast day, May 3, and is the patron saint of robbers, outlaws, smugglers, people in poverty, and Mexican drug cartels.

As we are leaving, Piccinini takes me to a small room where all the body cameras are stored. All the cops and deputies are now required to wear recording devices at all times while they are at work.

"That's a direct result of the Andy Lopez case," says Piccinini. "Maybe you've heard about that case?"

I have. Andy was a thirteen-year-old kid who was shot after refusing to drop what appeared to be an AK-47. It was a toy, but did not have the orange tip that all replicas are required to have. When Deputy Erick Gelhaus called out to Lopez, demanding that he drop the weapon, the boy turned toward the two deputies, weapon in hand. He was shot seven times and died on the scene. Seventeen seconds passed between Andy Lopez's initial contact with cops and his death. I pull up his face on the Internet: he's a dimpled, bright-eyed kid, earrings in both ears, his face still round with baby fat. He smiles directly at the camera, a dazzling, insolent smile. Next to him are photos of the fake rifle, which looks terribly real, and Andy's friends and relatives, sobbing at his grave.

"Now we all have cameras on, all the time," says Piccinini. Every single deputy I spend time with in Santa Rosa brings up the Lopez case. I have questions, but they are the sad kind of questions for which there are no answers I want to hear. Questions like, why was this handsome, bright-eyed child walking on this street with a fake machine gun made to look real? What happened after the officers realized how young he was, and had to drive home to their own families, their own kids? Who broke the news to his mother?

My ride is waiting. Piccinini walks me to the door, and we step out into the hot, bright afternoon, where my aunt Sue and uncle Tim stand. Piccinini makes a point of introducing himself. He talks to us about how hard it was to give Yakk away, even though, with his new handler working nearby, they get to see each other pretty often. I notice that Piccinini uses the present tense, as though Yakk were still his dog, still with him all the time.

"Policy here is paws before boots. But I spend more time with my dog than I do with my wife and kids. The worry is never ending: Did the AC turn on in the truck? Because it only takes twenty minutes for a dog to die. Did I just send my dog in on a suicide mission?"

"It must be so hard," I say, adopting the same present tense.

"I broke cover on a scene once. We sent Yakk in, and I have an e-collar on my dog, so I sent him a signal to come back, and nothing. I sent a stronger reply, and still I got nothing. Then I broke cover. The SWAT guys had to settle me down.

" 'I'm going in. That's my dog in there,' I said.

" 'That's your dog, not you,' they told me."

I say goodnight to Piccinini, and my aunt and uncle and I go out to dinner at a nearby Italian restaurant. This part of California was settled by Italian families who knew how to grow grapes and make good wine. They farmed and policed and opened restaurants.

It's a warm evening, and the air is sweet. I feel that same brief flash of gratitude you do right after recovering from an illness. There's nothing like spending a few hours behind bars to make a good meal taste even better. I'm free, I'm sitting in an Italian restaurant drinking a crisp local white wine, and tomorrow I go back to the dogs for more adventures.

Back at my aunt and uncle's house that night, I check a couple of facts online about the Sonoma County Detention Facility, and I come across a Yelp review. I didn't know posting reviews of prisons was a thing, but why not? Here's a Yelp quote from Michael T.:

> *I only give it 4 starts* [sic] *because . . . well . . . it is a jail. Check it out in your free time . . . or drive drunk . . . or commit a crime . . . or don't pay your dog license . . . or what ever else you can think of to get you in! They take pretty much anyone. They're not picky.*

Here's my favorite jail review, from Fat Pat O.:

*. . . an All Inclusive resort! Beautiful stucco building with views of the Santa Rosa foothills in the distance. Extremely CLEAN place with minimal intrusions. This place allows you to become one with yourself and reflect on your life, it doesn't get more relaxing than this! Minimal privacy allows you to interact with other members of the community. You will most likely share a room with another person of your same caliber and stature. Food and clothing are provided when you stay at this wonderful facility . . . the one piece suit is comfortable and exquisite. I wish they sold them in the gift shop! Room service is provided 24/7 and showers occur at the same time each day. Relax, and enjoy your stay at the Sonoma County Jail.*[1]

Deputy Piccinini invites my aunt to come along on the group training session the following afternoon. "That would be great!" she says, her bright blue eyes shining with excitement. "I can help Rachel take notes." Aunt Sue's an animal person. She loves dogs and cats and horses. She's spent a number of years breeding and showing Peruvian Pasos, beautifully gaited horses famous for their smooth stride and long, flowing mane and tail. She is as curious about the animal-human connection as I am.

The next afternoon, Sue and I are both prepared, dressed in layers for when the sun goes down, and ready to spend a few hours following the K9 teams through their training. We meet Piccinini and the teams at a Starbucks near the airport, and then follow the line of patrol trucks and cars down the back roads of the airport to an area that is reserved for police training and was once used as an Air Force base during WWII. This part of the airport is all tarmac surrounded by flat grasslands, rippling softly in the wind, full of singing birds.

The troops gather round. There are no women on this division, no minorities that I can recognize; all the teams are white men. Piccinini runs the training, dividing the men into groups—some for narcotics searching, following Deputy Cilia and Sasha, some for bite work. It's all business. Everyone is moving on to their post when Deputy Piccinini's dog, Yakk, catches sight of his former dad, and starts barking. Piccinini drops to one knee. Yakk jumps up, puts both paws on Dad's shoulders, and then the two of them lean in toward each other, pressing their foreheads together, dog and cop in a moment of pure connection. Yakk's hug with Deputy Dad seems to stop time. There are some bonds that run so deep that no words are necessary. I can't resist snapping a photo. When I do, Yakk turns my way and I swear that dog grins at me.

Piccinini has mentioned that a helicopter named *Henry 1* will be coming to do some tactical work, but at the last minute, *Henry 1* has been pressed into service rescuing a lost hiker. Piccinini had been planning on doing a K9 training mission to get the dogs used to helicopter flight, but of course the needs of the community take precedence.

Deputy Cilia gets Sasha out so she can run the narcotics search. Sasha seems relaxed, happy to be out here. Maybe being away from the jail is a break for her. Even so, I talk to her, but don't try to touch her.

I meet Dan Negri and his dog, Scout, at the training. At twenty-five, Deputy Negri's the youngest K9 deputy I've ever met. He looks like a tough guy, with tattoos on his ripped arms, a long scar on his neck, and a plug of chewing tobacco tucked in his lower lip, but he talks like a college kid, laid-back but polite. Scout is as young as his master, still a pup, really, at two and a half. Although he's a Shepenois, a cross between Malinois and German shepherd, he's got the coloring of a Malinois. Scout looks like a desert dog, with his sand-colored coat and golden eyes.

Yakk and Deputy Piccinini's reunion. (Rachel Rose)

Piccinini has the teams warm up with some general obedience off leash, marching, in formation, responding to commands, demonstrating control. Two of the young dogs are brand new to the unit. They've graduated just days before, and are now fully immersed in their first week of training. So it's impossible not to laugh when Piccinini gives the command to sit and one of the young dogs lifts his tail, hunches his back, and shits. The rest of the unit slowly moves away.

"The command was *Sit*, not *Shit*!" says one of the other officers. "Sit! Do you think your dog's gonna do that every time?"

"I'm never gonna live this one down, am I?" says the officer, shaking his head. His young dog looks up at him inscrutably, and training continues.

We don't think *Henry 1* is going to make it, so the excitement when the chopper blades cut through the blue sky of late afternoon is palpable. I meet the chief tactical flight officer, Henri Boustany. *Henry I* the helicopter is the only multimission helicopter in the North Bay region of California. It seems there's nothing this helicopter can't do: firefighting, long-line rescue, search and rescue, aerial law enforcement, and advanced life support air transport.

Today, though, Henri and the pilot Paul Bradley are going to put *Henry 1* the helicopter to work training K9s to get used to being airborne, at the end of a long line dangling in the sky. It is startling to see the dogs and men hanging from the helicopter on the long line. I wish the dogs could tell me what was going through their doggy minds as they lifted off.

It's just after sunset when *Henry I* carries the last of the dog teams through the sky. Even though the noise of the chopper beating the air is nearly deafening, the guys tell me that when they are suspended below the helicopter, they are flying in a cone of silence. It looks so fun—the sun melting in the sky like a box of pink and tangerine crayons on a blue tablecloth—the trusting dogs held close to their dads' chests as they sway in a gentle arc at the end of the cables like they're on the biggest swing in the world.

It's fully night when Piccinini invites me to climb up a ramp to a metal grate about twenty feet in the air. From here, I have a perfect bird's-eye view of the attack scenarios that will be enacted in the building below. My aunt, with her bad knee, elects to stay on the ground, so Piccinini stations a guard to protect her from possible dog attack, and the two of them move to a safe spot. I'm a little nervous that one of the dogs will climb the ramp and come after us. I can tell Piccinini has thought the same thing, because he has himself between me and the ramp ladder, which is on wheels. Piccinini's foot is ready to kick the ladder away if a dog scents us instead of the agitator. It would not be fun to be in a dog fight perched up here, with nowhere to hide and a big drop to the concrete floor below.

The building is a big concrete structure, without a ceiling. It's easy for us to see wherever the dogs go as their handlers bring them in to run the training. Dog after dog strains at the door, lunging and barking, eager to track and bite the agitators hiding within. It's interesting to be above the action, looking down, as the dogs plunge through the gathering darkness, snarling and barking, to hunt for the agitator. Dog after dog finds the fake criminal lurking in the shadows, and drags him out by the teeth, fighting and yelling every step of the way.

Scout and Negri are on deck. They are set to go in after a team that had some trouble with the scenario. The dog wouldn't release; the handler didn't have the upper hand, and the trainers had to intervene. Deputy Piccinini is not pleased.

"I got pinched a bit," said the agitator, which I know is cop-speak for "your damn dog just left teeth marks in my armpit." There's talk of someone taking his place in the bite suit, but for whatever reason, that doesn't happen. He's just going to tough it out. Scout and Negri are on deck. They are one of the last teams in that night. I watch from my position on the grate.

Scout's search and attack is flawless. He homes right in on the suspect. While Negri shouts, "Bad guy, stop fighting my dog!" Scout drags the agitator out and subdues him efficiently. Like a pro, Scout releases the instant Negri commands him to do so. Deputy Negri rewards Scout with a ball to bite, and then he lifts his dog high in the air by his harness for a victory swing. When he puts his dog down, Scout jumps up, ready for more.

I climb down from my perch in the sky. Once I'm on solid ground, I make a plan to meet Scout and Deputy Negri the next night.

"That was amazing! I have never seen or experienced anything like that in my life," said Aunt Sue.

Deputy Dan Negri sends Scout in for apprehension. (Rachel Rose)

"Yeah, it was great," I said. "I'm so glad we got to share that adventure!"

"I didn't take any notes. I'm sorry. I couldn't. There was just too much going on."

"Don't worry about it," I tell her. "It's always hard to take notes at a training session. I try to write things up as soon as possible after. That's about the best I can do."

My aunt and I are too revved up to sleep. In the five hours we've been out, we haven't had anything to eat or drink, or used the toilet. The action was so compelling, we didn't even notice. It's almost midnight. We sit at the kitchen table, whispering like girls on a sleepover, tearing into chewy, tangy California sourdough with sliced cheese.

My final night ride-along in Santa Rosa doesn't start off well. I've planned on riding for at least five or six hours, from six p.m. until midnight or so, but Deputy Negri tells me that he's already done a full shift and he's putting in overtime on my account. He and Scout are ready to go home for the night. He doesn't have to spell it out: he's taking me out as a courtesy.

Negri promises to drive me around for a couple of hours and to do a bit of training with Scout. I'm disappointed. I want the adventure of a full night's shift, where anything could happen, not just the short guided tour. But I know that staffing requirements change often, and everyone has to roll with it.

We get in the car, and I see Deputy Negri's bottom lip is, once again, stuffed full of tobacco. He has a paper spit cup in the dash. He must have caught my look. "I'm sorry. I'll be done soon," he says.

"No, no," I say. "Make yourself comfortable. How was your shift? Do you like day shifts or nights better?"

"Nights. I love 'em. Especially my crew now, they're awesome. They always require a K9, which is good, because we like to work. I have

ADD. If I was doing one thing I was always doing ten different things. I can focus on every one of those at the same time."

Negri fills me in on his history as we drive. "I was born and raised in Sonoma County. I grew up in Larkfield. I have two older brothers, Tony and Andrew. I'm the baby of the family at twenty-five. My dad was a police officer for thirty years. He retired out as captain. My mom was a teacher. I couldn't get away with *anything*." He turns to me. "I started when I was twenty-two, now I'm going on twenty-six—"

"I've never met somebody who has gotten into the K9 unit that fast," I say.

"I busted my ass for lack of a better term. To get in a role like K9 they want to see you can handle yourself on the street, that you have a good head on your shoulders. They expect you to run the calls as well. If you watch me on a call, I slow play a lot of stuff. We don't want to create what we call the exigent circumstance. We don't want to show up to a call where, say, we have a victim and she's been brutally beaten by her husband and he's in the house. We don't want to go force his hand or have him force our hand. That would be unsafe for him and unsafe for us. We do numerous announcements. We let him know that we're not going to leave until he's coming out. No officer or deputy wants to fight anybody, they want to make it home safely. If he's not coming out, I'll most likely utilize my K9. It's safer for the suspect, believe it or not, and it's safer for us."

"I do believe it," I say. "So tell me more about yourself."

"I went to California State University, Chico," says Negri. "My major was psychology. I did a joint minor in criminal justice and"— he pauses to spit a dark glob of tobacco juice precisely into his cup— "women's studies."

I stare at him. "You're the only cop I've ever met who minored in women's studies."

"Yeah. It was a trip."

"Did you know you wanted to be a cop then?"

"Yes, I did. My dad actually recommended I take a course like psychology, that's probably the best tool I have. You're not so one-sided."

"Tell me about the women's studies."

"I took six classes. They ranged from women's health to women's psychology, women writers. The classes were ninety-five percent female oriented, with only a few guys. Immersing myself in that culture, I got that perspective you would never have from hanging out with your male associates."

"Do you think it's made you a better police officer?"

"I do. I think psych more so, but it kind of all wraps into one. On top of that I was a cage fighter for two years. While I was in the women's studies."

"Wow! I can't wrap my head around that."

"Uh-huh, I'm unique."

"What made you who you are?"

"Probably my family. My grandpa was chief of the San Francisco Police Department. He kind of put us through high school, so I could go to that private school. It's on both sides of the family, the police. My mom's Irish, my dad's Italian, so I'm a nice little mix, kinda like Scout."

A motorcycle drives past and Scout, who has been quiet the whole time, goes ballistic.

"He hates motorcycles. I don't know what it is."

"So you're not cage fighting now?"

"I've had too many concussions. I had to stop. I had to make the decision to continue cage fighting or get into law enforcement."

We drive through some areas that look a little run down. We're in the Roseland area of Santa Rosa. There are flowers in the front yards, children playing outside.

"This place has generated most of all our calls for the last twenty years," says Negri. "The majority of calls I go to are righteous victims, law abiding citizens who truly need our help. I'll use domestic violence as an example. Domestic violence is probably one of our top calls, unfortunately, whether it's family related or spousal abuse. Those are tough situations to come into, you're dealing with sometimes ten-plus years of a relationship, and you're trying to get to the bottom of it within thirty minutes. You almost never get the whole story.

"The other day this guy, he calls 911. He says, 'This is where you'll find me. I'll be dead, laying out by my car.' Sure enough, he had committed suicide in front of his car, just where he said he would be, lying there with his legs crossed. The normal person isn't going to see that in their lifetime, God willing, but they're also not going to hear about it. It goes to that catch-22, you get that disconnect between law enforcement and the community. We're out preventing things from happening. We shelter people."

"What you do is invisible."

"A lot of the time, yeah. Why I do my job is to keep people like my mom from having to see those things. If you think about the good citizen, who does their job, raises their family, does everything that they can to stay afloat and abide through? That's who I work for."

"You think those people generally support you?"

"I'm constantly being stopped and people say thank you for what you do, and give us a wave. I'd say that ten percent of people hate law enforcement. I work for the ninety percent. Obviously I get the 'F.U., Pig!' but when I look at who it's coming from, it doesn't bother me. That's not who I'm working for."

"Tell me more about Scout."

"Scout's personality? He's an absolute sweetheart. It's crazy when you have a dog. When I first got him, he was kinda the runt of the litter. We had a strong bond right away. When we go through that ten weeks of school, you're essentially building a bond with the dog. Then you get that bond, and he wants to please you.

"There's obedience and drive. If you spend all your time doing obedience he stops thinking for himself and starts thinking for you. I actually took two steps back in that area just so he could kind of get back to being a dog. He's with me 24/7. When I first got him he was in the kennel all the time, the kennel in my yard on the side of my house. I'd take him out to feed him or for training. He wasn't a fan of people. He'd start growling. Then I started socializing him with my niece. She's three years old. Her name's Stella."

"And now he's good with her?"

"Oh, yeah. All he does is have fun. I'm not spending my time fighting him or correcting him. There's no altercations between us. It's simple."

"What's your normal routine?"

"A normal day for me and Scout? For off-duty days, I'll go for a run, work out, then go train for an hour or two with him, then I'll come back home, do whatever it is I do, then come back home at night. For him it's all obedience work or narcotics work. I want to know he'll do one bite only. I don't want typewriter dog bites. Each bite is something we have to be accountable for."

"You mean you have to document every single bite?"

"That's right. It's the Nortenos gang out here," says Negri, shifting gears, as he gestures to the houses we're passing. I wouldn't have known. It all looks ordinary to me, just people outside on the street, maybe staring a little longer, a little colder, as we pass.

We drive by a motel.

"Motels like this are a stomping ground for criminal activity. Pimping is a huge problem. We view prostitutes as victims. Many of them start at thirteen, fourteen years old. Unfortunately, there's a limit to what we can do, if they don't want help."

"Are the girls from around here?"

"They come from all over. Some of them are trafficked; when they give a name it's not their real name. We don't even know who they are. A lot of time you have to put them in jail to get their fingerprints, but it's a catch-22, because then they are in jail."

He reaches for that paper cup and spits a brown stream, then turns to look me in the eye.

"You hear the mumbo-jumbo that everyone has a choice. That's not always true. Not everyone has a choice."

Negri is on a roll. "One domestic case I had led to the male subject getting prison time for it. She took photographs the day of, and took photographs approximately one week after. She had several lacerations to her face, bruising, a broken nose, and injuries to her ribs because he actually held her down and kicked her. We had a true victim, a righteous victim, and she was willing to testify."

I don't know it at the time, but that phrase Negri uses, *righteous victim*, will come back to haunt me. At first it troubles me: are not all victims righteous? What makes some count more than others, and who gets to decide?

"Often in these cases you take a report, then you take the stand and they claim that you're lying. We have these body cameras now. I absolutely love them. You get a situation where something happens, they claim they never did that, then you pull out the body camera."

Negri turns to look at me for emphasis. "The fact that we got to a point we have to wear body cameras because the public doesn't trust us, that's a scary thing for me. But I'm all for it. I've written a lot of search warrants. I've done a lot of arrests, righteous arrests, good arrests that lead to prosecution. I do a lot of follow-up. I write my own search warrants. I put myself in as many situations as I can so I can learn the job quicker. I want to make sure Scout's successful: one for him, two for the other deputies on the street, three for myself. When it comes time to utilize him, he'll be used correctly. I study case law, when you can and can't utilize your dog, so you can truly know what you are doing and make the right decisions. Knowledge is fifty percent and psychology the other fifty percent. If you can talk to people and read people, you can dissolve a lot of situations.

"I'll take you to Moorland," says Negri. We drive by a vacant lot where a makeshift tent has been set up, with a shrine to Andy Lopez, the boy who was shot.

"Andy Lopez had a replica firearm. The officers went to contact him. He wasn't compliant. He was thirteen and he wound up deceased as a result. I know the officer involved, Gelhaus. I knew him personally. Gelhaus, he's a very good officer, I was in the third phase of training with him. It's one of those tragic situations. In my opinion, no one's at fault."

The shrine is filled with candles, flowers, and handwritten signs demanding justice. When I go home that night I will stare again at Andy's face on my screen, at his mother, bent over in grief, just as I did last night. What was he doing carrying that fake assault rifle made to look real? I turn away from the shrine. There's no sense to be made out of any of this.

"Do you like being a cop?" I ask.

"It's an amazing job. I love it. Even with all the negative publicity out there, I wouldn't trade jobs for the world."

"How do you handle the negative publicity?"

"It's tough. But everyone I work with, they're good people. All they want to do is help people."

"Has Scout bitten anyone?"

"Scout's had two engagements. The first one, SWAT was called out. It was a gang-related subject with a couple of arrest warrants. The perpetrator was supposed to have multiple firearms. The SWAT team deployed flash bangs, which are a loud bang that disorients and wakes everyone in the house so the people know the cops are there. Then they make a PA announcement ordering everyone out. One of the suspects came out of the house and essentially charged the officers. He was high on crystal meth. He made threats. I released Scout to apprehend him. He did his job. That was a successful engagement.

"The other one was for a subject who had a federal felony arrest for possession of firearms. He was a convicted felon, with prior threats to law enforcement. We located him in the house. It was actually a marijuana grow-op building. Three years prior he had tossed a gun and subsequently fought with deputies. This time we saw him in the back. He refused to come out. He's reaching in his waistband. He's saying he'll come out but he's not actually coming out. He makes no attempt to comply. Normally we'll wait a bit longer but because of his prior, I utilized Scout.

"Wait, this is important to note," says Negri, interrupting his own story. "The first one I told you about, he said, as he was reaching into his waistband, he said he wanted us to kill him."

"Why?"

"He was just in that meth psychosis. I talked to him a few days later. Both potentially could have been shootings. But utilizing that K9, it's just amazing because the suspects focus on the K9.

"The other guy was actually hiding narcotics in his anal cavity, which is why he was reaching around. He was also chewing Norco, which is like a painkiller. He wanted to get his last fix."

Again, I wish I had a less poetic imagination. Deputy Negri has painted an image in my mind that I'd prefer to erase.

"Since I've had Scout, I've had thirty-plus opportunities to use him. Thirty-plus surrenders where you could have used your dog but you gave the suspects enough time to surrender. We give them enough time to rethink bad decisions."

"Are you confident that Scout would go into any situation where you deployed him?"

"I am, and at the same time you're never really fully confident until the fifth or sixth bite."

"You must have been in a situation where you were scared shitless?"

"I'm a big fan of training. I take it seriously. I'm able to kind of battle those feelings because I know I'm well prepared."

"I guess you are not afraid of pain, what with cage fighting."

"I'm not, but as I said I'd rather talk myself out of a situation than fight my way out of it."

"What do you wish people knew?"

"That we're not robots. What makes law enforcement unique, is that everyone is different. What we all have in common is why we do the job. We have a strong ethical compass. We want to take care of community and family. Unless you're crazy, that's the only reason why. And it's fun, it really is. Anyone can be a cop. Not anyone can be a great cop."

"What about corrupt cops?"

"There are a few who go in for the wrong reasons. When you hear about cops going on criminal activity, that infuriates us. It's an insult to the badge, to the community that supports us. One bad incident negates a hundred positive instances.

"People forget we're not robots. Someone might be having a bad day. We're expected to put on a uniform and leave all our emotions behind. That's probably the hardest part. They forget we're humans. They think we're something different."

From the back, as if on cue, Scout heaves a huge, dramatic sigh.

"What's your hope for your career with Scout?"

"Scout will be the only dog I run. It's a great opportunity. I'm not going to want to go through that with someone other than Scout. My goal is that me and him make it through that six- to eight-year tenure, so he can retire happy. I'll create a little Hawaiian backyard for him."

"You'll keep him?"

"Yeah. No question in my mind. Once I finish the K9 I will go into detective and promote up. I want to promote up and do it the right way. If you have someone in the top with a negative outlook, that is going to trickle down.

"We're all country boys. If you see me outside of work I'll be in a hat and cowboy boots. Outside of work, I have the idea I'd rather have five close friends than five hundred friends. I have a pretty tight-knit group of friends and I spend most of my time with them, with my family, and with Scout.

"I have time to devote to this job. I want to keep that going as long as I can, but when the time comes I want to be a dad, while still maintaining this job. And whoever that is I end up with, they have to like dogs. If they don't like dogs, they're not gonna like me, 'cause I'm pretty much a big puppy."

We get out of the car and let Scout stretch his legs. He hops around, puppyish and happy, bounding into the air like a jackrabbit.

"What do you and Scout do for fun?"

"We goof around at the house. We play around. We toss each other around. I'm big into yard work. What Scout doesn't do for fun is baths. He hates baths! It's me and a hose and chasing him around the yard."

"Do you feel proud of him?"

"I am proud of him, especially knowing all the work. You're talking thousands of hours with him. It's nice to see the results. As soon as he gets dialed—"

"Dialed?"

"You know, squared away, perfect."

"I've never heard that term before."

"Yeah. Dialed. Scout just surprises you and raises the bar that much higher."

Deputy Negri's the only officer I've met who is a one-dog deputy. Scout sets the bar, and Scout will be his one and only K9. These two young stars will rise together. Although I don't have the chance to do any fast driving after suspects with Negri and Scout, I know they are speeding toward a bright future together.

■

I'm out near Burnaby, BC with Constable Matt Noel a little before midnight. Brawny and ginger-haired, Matt's kind of a serious guy. Blackie sits expectantly behind Matt, big ears alert to every noise, waiting for some action. Blackie's not actually a black German shepherd; he's dark brown, the ends of his coat tipped in gold, and he's one of the biggest dogs in the force. Like Matt, Blackie's quiet and serious, an intensity of drive that, when turned on a suspect, is terrifying.

So far, the shift's been dead, so Matt's been telling me stories.

"I had a guy try to get into my truck once, in a parking lot outside 7-Eleven. Good thing I was in my truck, or my dog would have killed him. I saw him go around one side of the truck, and I was watching, waiting for him to come around the other side. Then I heard the handle on the back door and I was like, 'Whoa, whoa, what do you think you're doing?' My dog was going ballistic."

"What happened?"

"I guess he was supposed to meet his drug dealer, and he got confused. "No drugs and alcohol in this country, and I'd be out of a job," says Matt.

Seconds later, the call comes out. Story time is over. All available members are needed to pursue a suspect known to police and usually armed. A helicopter has his car in sight. Matt hits the siren and the gas in one smooth motion. I settle in for the sickening ride. The speed is terrifying. I lean my head against the back of the seat and concentrate on breathing through my fear. Automobiles spin into our orbit and we swerve out of their way. We hurl around corners, cut across the freeway, nimbly shifting around cars that seem to be deliberately throwing themselves in our path. My self has split, and both sides are chattering. Never, ever, ever do this again, says the voice in my head. If you live through this, I promise you'll never have to ride in a police truck for the rest of your time on earth. (Just one more lie I've told myself.) Blackie whines softly behind me. And then, seconds later, the dispatcher updates the suspect's location, the helicopter chops the night air overhead, and I catch myself thinking, *Yes! Go, Matt! Go, go, go!*

*Hang on, you* hate *this*, I think, gripping the door, as someone from dispatch says something I can't make out. There's something wrong with my ears. I think it's called fear.

They've set up spikes at the next intersection they expect him to go through, but the suspect surprises everyone by turning off on a small road before that. Now there's a big rush to spike where he's headed. Blackie whines again. The dispatcher's voice is tense as she plots his location.

Matt's next move involves a ninety-degree turn on a country road that leaves my stomach back in a ditch somewhere, my hand over my mouth. I brace my feet against the floor. How long can we keep up this helter-skelter through the darkness? I swallow against my queasiness and try closing my eyes, but that's worse. The chopper beats an incessant reminder overhead. It's an open question whether or not they'll have time to set up the next spikes, and God help any car or pedestrian who doesn't get out of this guy's way.

A minute later, dispatch calls out that the suspect has been spiked. Blowing his tires, though, doesn't seem to slow him down. We're minutes behind him but can't close the distance. All the cruiser lights are flashing like a low-class Christmas scene at the mall. But then the road turns. The suspect can't make the turn at that speed, driving on his rims. He loses control and skids, a long, brutal streak of metal on asphalt, before he smashes into some wooden trailheads, snapping them like toothpicks. When the dispatcher announces that the suspect has fled the scene, Matt bounces in his seat. Although it's impossible, we fly even faster. "This is awesome!" Matt yells, flashing me a grin. "We're blocks away," he tells the dispatcher, and it seems like every cop car in the country is racing in front of us or right behind. When they see the K9 truck coming they move aside to let us through.

"Sweet Jesus," I breathe out loud, as we bounce on and off the road, slamming by a crowd of teenagers walking along the side of the road, any one of whom would be dead if they hadn't crowded to the shoulder as half a dozen police cars hurtled past them. Their faces are startled blurs coming at me and receding. Blackie, usually so silent, whines again, eager to get out and track. Unlike many of the police dogs, Blackie's not a barker. This hundred pounds of wolf-eyed dog hunkers down in the back. He shifts and slides, nails scrabbling for purchase against the force of our turns.

We haul ass to the site of the crash. Matt shouts it again, jubilant now, full of fire for the hunt, slamming both hands against the wheel: "This is *awesome!*" He's out of the car before I've managed to peel my cramped fingers off the passenger door handle, and he's snapping Blackie's harness on, swearing in his haste, every second a waste of time.

"Good luck!" I pant. Matt grins at me. "Thanks," he says, and then he's gone. I want like anything to run after him and Blackie. But this is real, and the job I have is to get out of the way so Matt and Blackie can track. At the crash, I watch Blackie take in the suspect's scent with a big whoosh from his powerful nostrils. Then he wheels off, nose to the ground, pulling Matt along. Me, I'm left alone in the truck, breathless, shaking with adrenaline.

All around me, cars pull up, spilling cops. Some of them stare at me. Two of the cops who were first on the scene inspect the ruined rental car, with its air bags deflating slowly inside the cracked windshield. In the back of the car, I can see his cash spilling over the seat, all those bills like play money tossed around by a messy kid. I watch the two cops high-five each other. But my thoughts are with Blackie and Matt as they track through the dark forest. I am afraid for them both. There's nothing I can do but wait, and hope the suspect doesn't have a weapon that he decides to use.

In exactly eleven minutes, they're back. Blackie has done his job. The suspect is in custody, and I'm pacing around, giddy with relief and elation, unable to stand still. I give Blackie a pat because I know Matt will let it slide this time; usually, no one touches Blackie but Matt. Matt grabs a Kong for Blackie to bite. "Good dawg, *what a good dawg*, good boy!" he says, swinging Blackie around in the air by the Kong. Blackie jumps around us, tail wagging, ready for more. It's all just a game to this big dog with the golden paws.

Two officers lead the suspect into a waiting patrol car. He is calm and unscathed, except for a cut under one eye. The guy looks so ordinary: just a young white male, brown hair, and medium build. There's nothing special about him, and yet he's caused all this mayhem. If he had a knife or a gun, it's long gone in a ditch somewhere. The suspect studies me briefly, a flat stare, devoid of emotion. I hold his eyes.

"Ask him if he swallowed anything," one of the officers demands, and someone takes him out of the car and asks him, politely. They are responsible for his physical safety, and if he's swallowed drugs, they need to know about it. "No, nothing," he says. The officer cups a hand over the guy's head to protect him from the doorframe as he guides him into the back of the patrol car.

Matt is already done here. The police dog handlers in the RCMP don't have to stick around to fill out reports; that's one of the things they like best about the job. I'm bouncing around on my heels. I want to stay with the cops who are taking photos of the vehicle, who are counting the plastic bags full of money on the backseat of the car. I want to discuss this case and relive every detail, but Matt's already gotten another call and is ready to roll. I can't believe this is it, that Matt and Blackie just made a major capture and without any fanfare, without any ceremony, without even a coffee break, they are off to the next one. If I'd done one thing like that, I'd be talking about it forever.

"You did it, Matt! You did it!" I say as I climb back in. Blackie pushes his nose up against the metal grille. I hold up my hand for him. "How does it feel? Does it ever get old?"

"No, never. It's a huge, huge rush, to be able to do what Blackie and I did tonight. Maybe you're my lucky charm."

■

Later, when I share with Matt my notes on his and Blackie's successful capture, I figure he'll be pleased. I think I've gotten it right, just the way I wrote it—the way the suspect's car threw sparks as it raced ahead of us and the other police cruisers on its rims, the pedestrians and cars that we barely managed to avoid hitting as we sped past.

"It didn't actually happen like you wrote it," Matt says bluntly. I stare at him, stung.

"It may have felt to you like the other vehicles were cutting us off. That's tunnel vision. Your vision narrows to just what's directly in front of you. But to me, because of my training, I look around and can see a wide field of vision, so the cars didn't just appear out of nowhere, like they did to you."

I'm shocked. But what's even more shocking is the way my memory filled in the gaps. I thought I'd seen sparks from the suspect's car as he sped ahead of us just before the crash, but Matt said he was minutes ahead of us, that he hadn't even been in our sights during the pursuit. What had I actually seen, then, besides the other patrol cars? How could my memory have been so unreliable? I was there to observe, for God's sake. And I got it wrong.

Matt, being the decent guy he is, senses my distress.

"It happens," he says. "It's actually pretty common. There's even a term for it, what adrenaline dumps do to memory recall. We just have to train, and with experience and training we are able to overcome that tendency."

How much training would I have to do to be able to trust my senses at high speeds? I ride to emergency calls a number of times with different police dog handlers, but I never move past a state of overwhelming fear to that ideal state of heightened awareness. On top of that, I no longer entirely trust what I think I've seen when we are going fast. I make a point of asking the cops I ride with to share their accounts of what happened in high-speed situations. The gaps are fascinating. Some are small and unimportant, but in others, I miss entire events, miss helicopters flying directly overhead, miss the getaway car blowing past in the dark. In the heat (and fear) of the moment, I literally can't see what's in front of me. Humbling doesn't begin to cover it. My situational awareness, limited at best, goes out the window when things start moving fast.

I already knew why they were cops and I wasn't, but as a writer, I rely on my senses. Much of my job involves translating sensory experience to words. Now I know that at certain speeds and in certain intense situations, I'll be translating my own sensory myths.

What I can do, however imperfectly, is tell what I experience. If you were in my shoes, if you were me, sick to your stomach, clutching the truck door and praying, this is how it would appear. If you are, say, a mom of three who likes to walk in the woods and write poetry, and if you are, say, out in a truck riding shotgun with a dog whining eagerly by your right ear as you haul ass to catch a thief, this is what it feels like.

Every successful capture, like the one I witnessed with Blackie and Matt, is an amazing, dramatic story that will never be told. Nobody knows what happened except for a handful of cops and one criminal. Nobody knows what was prevented from happening, either. Families sleep in their suburban houses, briefly stirring at the sound of sirens. They wake to an ordinary day, with no knowledge of what happened on their street in the darkest hours. But I've had a glimpse. I have followed the dogs, and entered a world in which all my senses tell me I don't belong.

Matt tells me later how those eleven minutes actually played out. "At 23:55 the subject crashed and fled the vehicle. I started tracking at midnight. After we entered the trees, we came to a fence, where Blackie indicated track loss. Blackie immediately tried to jump the fence. I picked him up over the fence, and he's immediately looking for the track again, but I still had to get over. We went through some townhouses, went through two other yards and then came to another fence, where Blackie indicated at the gate. The gate was about five and a half feet tall. I usually lift my dog over to protect him, but he volunteered, he jumped the gate and started tracking between two houses. We came to a roadway, where I lost the track. We made one quick circle, and he relocated and tracked across the road to an open lawn. There was a cedar hedge that separated two yards, and around this point, Blackie's head went up. He ran up a walkway. There was a guy standing there, all illuminated, a guy waving his arms. It was a homeowner, and Blackie indicated on him, then lost the track. I thought, *You gotta be kidding, to be so close and lose the track?* At that point, you have to calm yourself and go back to your last known location. We went back to the road. I slowed Blackie down a bit there. He went down a little hill, and over another fence. I heard a crackling sound, and I stopped to listen. I saw a figure pop up and run. As the dog jumped the fence, the figure was running across the yard. I thought I saw something shimmer in his hands. He's known to carry knives in his waistband. My immediate thought was, 'he's got a knife.'

"I yelled, 'Police! Stop!'

"He said, 'I don't have anything!'

"I shouted, 'Get on your stomach!' He did, and I held Blackie back while the other officers moved in to arrest him."

In this situation, everything worked like it was supposed to. Nobody got bitten, nobody got hurt. I don't know what this suspect's criminal history was, but I have learned that if known criminals have been subdued by police dogs in the past, they are generally extremely motivated to avoid repeating the experience.

And if I was Matt's lucky charm for that capture, I felt as lucky as any person in the world, to be out with him and Blackie. Even though my eyes and ears played little tricks on me at high speeds, nothing could take away the essential truth: that I was riding faster than I'd ever ridden, and that I was right on hand when Blackie successfully tracked a criminal and brought him down.

■

I'm with Matt and another police dog handler named Scott in Tim Hortons one evening. We're getting stared at big time. The dogs are in the truck, big Blackie and Scott's good dog, Argo, waiting as we fuel up for the long night ahead. As I sit with the men in blue, it's clear the stares we're getting are not exactly friendly. Maybe it's because I'm there, and people don't know how to read me? The Police Dog Services members don't usually have a poet hanging with them at Tim Hortons, and for sure nobody could mistake me for a cop. But some of the looks are openly hostile. I ask Scott and Matt about it.

"Happens all the time. Happens so much, I'm kind of jaded," says Scott. His leg is jiggling, with pent-up energy, or maybe frustration. "It's so easy to become suspicious. People say hi, but they are recording me, taking photos. We're constantly being recorded now."

Matt and Scott are on edge. It's been a hard week. In Moncton, New Brunswick, Constable Dave Ross has just been shot and killed, along with two other RCMP officers. Two other officers survived with severe injuries. Dave left behind his pregnant wife, Rachel, their little son, and his police dog, Danny. His murder has affected every police dog handler, but especially those who knew him or trained with him. Scott was one of these men. Now he's trying to get a ticket back for Dave Ross's funeral.

"I have to go," Scott tells me. "It's respect. It's a sign of respect." Matt and Scott see themselves in Dave Ross. It could have been either of them. Dave went out for a routine call, a call of shots fired. He left the BBQ on and the garage door open, because he was only going to be a few minutes, because the calls of shots fired almost always amount to nothing, because he believed that he'd be coming home.

"I've always hated that term 'routine call,'" Matt had told me earlier on our shift. Matt's eyes were red-rimmed, like he hadn't slept. He brought up Dave's murder right away. "No calls are routine. You never know what's going to happen. Some members get complacent, and I'm not saying that's what happened in this case, not at all. But there's no such thing as a routine call."

We circle back to Dave Ross.

"You know, if there's something the officer did wrong, you can learn from it," says Matt. "But in this case, he didn't stand a chance. He didn't do anything wrong. The guy just happened to be hiding, and shot him through the window. Nothing that he did could have changed that outcome."

Scott checks again—he's just gotten a text from another handler who bought a ticket for $1,050, the best price he's seen yet—and they're letting his dog fly to Moncton free.

"I gotta be there," says Scott. "This is killing me."

Matt works to always be prepared, but he and Scott both know that there are going to be events for which you can't plan. As Scott says, "If your number is up, then your number is up. Like those four cops killed in Seattle in the coffee shop. That killer died. Scott is referring to the targeted attack and murder of four officers in a café in Lakewood, Washington. After a massive two-day manhunt, the gunman, Maurice Clemmons, was killed. In contrast, the killer of the four RCMP officers in Moncton, Justin Bourque, was taken into custody unharmed.

I look around at the people in the café, wondering if they see the cops like I did all the years of my life until this year. I saw cops as white men in uniforms who liked guns and liked to have power over people. How did I absorb this belief? Where did it even come from? It was a kind of prejudice I carried, one I didn't ever examine or even name.

Now I see these guys as Matt and Scott.

■

Some time later, I share this realization with Matt as I'm looking through my notes. I want him to know that I've changed from our time together, that I used to see cops as hard and power-hungry men, but now I see them as individuals. It doesn't go down at all like I think it will.

"I'm surprised to hear you say that you ever thought about cops like that," he says, and I can tell he's more than surprised; he's angry.

Then it's my turn to be surprised: Aren't most people suspicious of cops? Or is it just my circle of left-of-center writers and artists and hippie poet friends? But before I can defend myself, Matt continues.

"I understand if you've had a bad experience with the police. I guess I understand social influences, family influences. But at the same time, you should be open to everything, you should not judge something without knowing anything about it. That's just ignorant. The only time I feel prejudice against me is as a police officer. If I go to a party, half the time I won't tell them what I do. I say, 'Oh, I just work for the government.' Again, it depends on the crowd I'm with. I'm proud of what I do. I love my job, and I don't want to be judged before people get to know me, but it happens all the time. People act differently and judge me."

"Look," I tell Matt. "I'm being honest with you. A lot of people automatically distrust the police. They aren't even aware of it."

"I appreciate your honesty," says Matt. "It's like this. We're put in a position of authority. When some of us betray that authority when we're supposed to be doing good, it taints the public's perception of us. I get that. But it's no different than any occupation or anyone else out there."

"Okay," I say.

"If I stop someone, they'll immediately give me hostility."

"Really?"

"*Immediately.* Sometimes I call them on it. I say, 'What's with the hostility?' They'll say, 'I hate the police.' I say, 'Well, okay, step back for a second. I treat everyone with respect. You're saying every officer is corrupt and mean. Have I been like that with you today?' They say no. And I'll say, 'Well, why are you lumping me in with them?'

"They'll say, 'Well, most of them are like that,' but I'll challenge that too. 'Well, how do you know? Have you met all of them? Do you know that they are corrupt?' I remember one guy, I was driving home one day, along this rural road in Chilliwack. I see this guy standing on another fellow's property. He's peering through the hedges, look-ing at someone's house. I get suspicious. When he sees me driving up, he immediately starts walking, so I go and check on him. He doesn't want to provide ID. He's got his back up immediately. He gives me a story and finally provides ID, and he's got a criminal record. I ask what he's doing here. He says the police have harassed him. By the end of our conversation, I can tell he's a smoker. I don't smoke my-self, but I keep a pack of cigarettes in the back of the vehicle. I gave him a couple of cigarettes. He was floored that I would give him ciga-rettes. I said, 'Why wouldn't I?'

"Listen," says Matt. "I'm not an a-hole. I'm not a mean guy, I'm not a bad guy. But he immediately judges me. I could have judged him right off the bat, treated him with disrespect, but why would I? He's a member of the human race. Even after he's disrespected me, I still didn't disrespect him."

There it is, that Zen-like awareness that some of the cops I ride with have. They just let the small stuff go, and to them anything that's not lethal is probably small stuff. Having dealt with so many difficult and dangerous members of the human race, they know how to pri-oritize. Matt knows something I have yet to learn about human na-ture. I think I'm open-minded, but most of my life I've kept company with people who think and believe pretty much exactly what I do. Cops keep company with people from every realm, every class and religion and ethnicity. But they generally interact with people at the worst times of their lives.

"People love to complain about the police until they need the police. And then they are the first to call," says Matt.

"So when did you know you wanted to be a cop?" I ask, trying to change gears.

"I knew from the time I was a kid that I wanted to be a cop. I started working towards it after high school."

"Why?"

"I always wanted to make a difference. And I can't sit still, I can't be indoors, in a cubicle all day long. I'm not saying your job is like that, but I could never do a job like that."

In truth, my job *is* like that. Surrounded by words, sheltered from the worst of people and from the worst of the weather, I sit in a room with my imagination and try to create something out of nothing, try desperately to find the words that will allow me to connect with strangers. Matt isn't saying it because he's polite, but we both know the truth.

"What do you like best about what you do?"

"Working with my dog. It's definitely the most rewarding part. Now that I'm doing the dog thing, I couldn't imagine doing anything else."

Blackie shifts in the back, whines once, twice. I'm getting nauseated, scribbling notes in the dark as we drive to an out-of-control house party. Corny music on the radio is playing:

> *My eyes are the only thing*
> *I don't wanna take off you.*

As we turn into the cul-de-sac, the solid thumping bass of the party drowns Matt's music out. The whole house throbs. I can feel it in the truck. The garage door is open, and a steady stream of bodies moves up the stairs into the house. Matt steps out, leaving me and Blackie in the truck. Blackie whines again, and I know just how he feels, being left behind.

"Hey, Blackie," I say. "Hey. He'll be right back. We'll wait here, okay?"

Is it safe, one cop against however many drunken, loud people? What will I do if he doesn't come back? Could I drive this thing if I had to? The same anxious thoughts buzz in my head.

Luckily, in a few minutes the music shuts off, and Matt comes back, smiling. "They were actually reasonable about it," he tells me. "That doesn't mean we won't be back here in an hour, though, if they get it going again."

When we have a quiet stretch on the road, I ask about how Matt prepares for whatever might be coming.

"You know what they say, hindsight is twenty-twenty," says Matt. "There's always something to learn after the fact. But when you're in the situation, you don't have all the time in the world. If you're in a tactical mindset all the time, you're always thinking ahead of possible scenarios or outcomes."

"How would you define a tactical mindset?"

"An alert awareness as to your surroundings. Right now we're at Starbucks." (This is a concession to the poet, who wanted a latte). "If I'm coming to the front of this building, I'm thinking, 'There's windows in this building.' I'm scanning the windows before I go in front of them. I'm scanning the rest of the parking lot. What it boils down to: at the end of the day, I want to go home. If I have to be hypervigilant, if that's what it takes to survive, then that's what I'm going to do. We're all like that. Whenever we go for coffee, whoever gets there first gets the good seats."

"You mean the seats where you can see best what's coming?"

Matt nods. "It's just being aware."

"When do you let down your guard?"

"When I'm not in uniform, I let down my guard a lot more. But it's so ingrained in me. Even if I'm in civilian attire, I'm scanning the room to see who's in the room. I just got back from Vegas. On the plane I walk down the aisle, scan the seats. Obviously you blend in more in civilian attire, but you don't know what anybody's intention is. Officers have been killed just because of opportunity and chance. Those officers killed in that coffee shop in Washington State? The

Constable Darrell Moores and Cade. *Courtesy of Action Photography*

Constable Nathalie Cuvele and her brother grew up with police dogs. *Courtesy of the Cuvele family*

Constable Nathalie Cuvele training young Eryx at the airport, Nanaimo, B.C. *Courtesy of the author*

Senior Police Dog Trainer Tom Smith with Tag. *Courtesy of Tom and Roxanne Smith*

Cst. Robert Shanks, Cst. Jason Zaplachinski, Rachel Rose, Cst. Doug Cushon, and Cst. (now Cpl.) Jeff Wall. *Courtesy of Senior Police Dog Trainer Eric Stebenne*

Sue and John Charles with Dea. *Courtesy of the Charles family*

Constable Roger
Rempel, Cade's new
handler, with Cade.
*Courtesy of RCMP-
GRC*

Iowa City K9 Officer Brandon Faulkcon with Rakker. *Courtesy of Brandon Faulkcon*

Deputy Jason Moses with Espo. *Courtesy of the author*

Sheriff Gene Davis training Gunner.
*Courtesy of the author*

Constable Matt Noel with
Blackie. *Courtesy of the author*

Corporal Claudio Maurizio
and Chucky. *Courtesy of Claudio*
*Maurizio*

Corporal Michelle Onysko training in
Squamish, B.C. *Courtesy of the author*

Constable Emma Truelove under a
pile of puppies. *Courtesy of the author*

Constable Sara Ginn with Harper.
*Courtesy of Sara Ginn*

Brigadier Bertrand Bonnamy and Djimanthie. *Courtesy of Bertrand Bonnamy*

Sergeant Ray Wong and Hunter. *Courtesy of Derek Cain Photography*

Sergeant Ray Wong, Constable Al Arsenault, and Bear. *Courtesy of Sergeant Toby Hinton*

Rachel Rose with Dandy. *Courtesy of Benjamin Fieschi-Rose*

fellow who killed them hated police. He had a gun and walked in and killed them. It was nothing against them personally. You let down your guard even for a second and that's when something can happen."

I let down my guard all the time. I stare at Matt. I don't know how he lives like that. How does anyone?

"Then there's suicide by cop. A lot of them want to go that way. They want to make you do it."

I knew that. I'd heard that expression; we all hear about it. But hearing something and really thinking about it deeply are two different matters. Suicide by cop? In the past I'd thought only of the victim, driven to despair. Now I think also of the officer. A cop has to make that decision to fire, or to hold fire. If you hold fire, someone could be killed. If you fire, you become a person who has taken another life. No matter if it's justified, or self-defense, no matter if you are cleared of all charges and offered therapy—in the space of a single breath, when someone forces your hand, your life changes.

It's half a year before I ride with Blackie and Matt again. I don't know it at the time, but it will also be my last ride with them as a team. The night before, I can't sleep. Every time I head out, I know I will likely be shaken up. I know I will confront, however briefly, the possibility of death. Still, I keep coming back. I know it is good medicine for what ails me. Also, doing something actually dangerous seems to be resetting my anxiety threshold. It works like a vaccination. Generalized anxiety isn't bleeding into the rest of my life as often. It's such a relief to let some of it go.

This time we're on our own. It's just me, pulling into a nearly dark parking lot beside a chain-link fence, and Matt and Blackie waiting for me in Matt's truck. Our first break of the night to let Blackie run, I toss the Kong, and he runs to bring it back. He wants to play tug-of-war with me, and I hold the rope, bracing myself. But Blackie's so strong. He's at the upper limit for a K9, at a hundred pounds, and I'm no match for him. The rope burns through my palms. I let Blackie win, and turn away, rubbing my hands on my coat.

"Hey, Matt, do you ever read poetry?" I ask, when we're all back in the truck. He's taken my advice on other books, including buying and reading Laurence Gonzales's *Deep Survival*. But poetry's risky. He gives me a look. Matt will be the first cop I inflict poetry on, but not the last.

"No," he says flatly.

"Can I share a poem?"

"Uh, okay."

The poem I choose is Brian Turner's "Here, Bullet." In Matt's truck I play Brian Turner reading his work at a literary event. In silence we listen to Turner say these lines:

> *Here is that adrenaline rush you crave,*
> *that inexorable flight, that insane puncture*
> *into heat and blood . . .*

"That was actually pretty good," says Matt. He sounds surprised. "I actually liked that."

I grin in the dark. Turner was an infantry team leader in Iraq, so I thought there might be a connection. I want Matt to see the power of poetry, of words. I want him to be changed, even a little bit, by our time on the road. I've been changed so much by my time with the dogs. I want him to leave my company a little bit different than when we first met.

■

One thing that's changed for me is my awareness of when police officers kill civilians—or are killed by them. Justin Bourque, who targeted and murdered the police officers in Moncton, was sentenced to seventy-five years in prison without parole. His statement of apology after the sentencing was one of the most chilling I've ever heard. Bourque said, "I'm not a bad guy. I'm just a cop killer . . . I always think that I had a pretty good moral compass."[2] Later he said, "I want the families to know your husband is dead, your son is dead, your brother is dead, your friend is dead—it does mean something to me."[3]

To stalk and kill police officers because of their uniform is a kind of terrorism that leads to the eternal vigilance Matt describes. Assaults or murders based on factors like wearing a badge, or sexual orientation, or skin color, or gender, or religious garb, are attacks meant to terrorize. The statement Bourque made is not a statement of remorse.

When I call Matt to see when I can take another ride with him and Blackie, he doesn't get back to me for a while. This isn't unusual—all the dog handlers are busy guys. But after I've contacted him three times and still heard nothing, I start to worry. Did I say something wrong? Was I too honest? When he finally reaches me, he drops some news that I never would have expected: he's transitioned out of the Police Dog Services, and is working as a general duty officer in the Lower Mainland. Worst of all, Blackie is no longer with him.

"What happened?" I ask.

"To be honest with you, it was a bit of an up and down transition. It came about unexpectedly. If you had asked me when you were riding around with me, I would have told you I would be doing this for the next twenty years. But I took a different road."

"But where's Blackie?"

"Blackie's down in Texas. It's a little hard in that regard, since I raised that dog since he was six months old, and figured he'd be with me till the day he died, but part of life is letting go and moving on. For Blackie, it was a bit of a different situation. He was recently sold to a security firm. He's actually working with a security individual in the States, who used to be a police dog handler."

There's a brief silence while I absorb what Matt's telling me. Blackie's in Texas, and no, I don't get to say good-bye, and no, I won't see him again. The whole time I've been riding with the dogs, I've pushed away the thought that one day I'll have to stop. One day, the book will be finished, and I'll have no reason, no excuse to be out in the truck with these magnificent canines and their handlers. But every time I've had that thought, I tell myself I've still got time, plenty of time. I've stretched the weeks into years. I never imagined the end of the ride.

"What was it like when you said good-bye?" I ask. I know the question might be a hard one for Matt. I ask it anyway. I have to know.

"I said to my fiancée to come with me. I chose not to take Blackie to the airport myself; it would be that much harder on both of us. For him to be sitting in his travel crate, he knows something's up. We took him in the police truck, met with the other handler, let him out a few minutes, threw the ball around for him. Then I grabbed Blackie, petted him, gave him a bit of a chat, allowed my fiancée to say her good-byes, and got him into the other guy's truck."

"What did you say to Blackie?"

"I don't remember the exact words. I told him he's a good dog, I'm gonna miss him, it's probably the hardest thing I've ever had to do to let him go, but he's gonna be happy, with someone who would care for him and take care of him properly just like I did, and give him a good quality of life. I told him that probably the hardest thing I'll ever have to do is walk away from him today, but I have to, and he'll be okay. You almost treat him like he's your child at that point. You share your most intimate secrets. You get such a tight bond between the two of you, it's just hard to see him go. I thought I might see him one last time before he left, but I didn't have that opportunity. I just wanted to tell him I appreciate the fact he's been in my life all these years, I'll think about him every day, and he'll be all right without me."

Somewhere in Texas is a working dog named Blackie who isn't actually black; his coat is dark brown, the tips of each hair flecked with gold. Born in Innisfail, Alberta, raised by Matt since he was six months old, Blackie's trained and caught bad guys all over British Columbia. He's used to tracking through rain and snow, brush and boggy pasture. And now he's in Texas, working security. This is where this magnificent big dog with the gold-tipped coat will spend his final years.

I hope Blackie has a good life in Texas, with people who appreciate his incredible ability, his fearless heart and his friendly nature. I hope Blackie bonds with someone there who cherishes him and treats him right. I hope his bed is soft and I hope that when he gets old he's with someone who takes him in by the fire, like Matt would have. I hope he got someone who deserved him.

Blackie's story wasn't supposed to end this way. Then again, this is real life, not fiction. In real life, no matter what kind of tactical mindset you cultivate, you can't always anticipate what the ending will be.

It is surprising how often the dogs go through transitions, being passed from one handler to another, moving countries, changing hands. Yakk stays in the same unit, and gets plenty of opportunities to see Deputy Piccinini, even though his daily life has changed radically. Cade doesn't know it, but he'll be back with Darrell and his family in a few more years, and he's got another good handler to work with in the meantime. But Blackie? Texas is a big unknown. The fact that his new owner used to be a police dog handler is good news, as it means he likes dogs and has been professionally trained to meet their needs. But Blackie, like all dogs, lives at the whim of destiny and the decisions made by those who own him. He has no control over his fate. No animal that lives in proximity with humans controls their own destiny. He can be the best dog in the world, but he can't change that fact.

■

It took me a long time to connect with Corporal Claudio Maurizio and his two police dogs, Chucky and Racer. Corporal Maurizio is just not interested in taking me out. But Maurizio has just been commended for bravery, and he and his dog Racer recently won an award, and I'm very curious about him. I call him and e-mail him every few weeks, hoping he'll let me tag along.

Nothing works. I've talked with him a few times while I've been out with other teams, and he's always friendly enough, but Maurizio doesn't ever answer my e-mails or calls. He's a natural leader, always in the center of things, always making people laugh, offering dog training advice and funny stories freely to those around him. But he doesn't call me back.

It's not as if Maurizio doesn't know who I am. The first time I track with Darrell Moores and Cade in Squamish, I meet both Maurizio and his buddy Constable Jeremy Anderson, who happen to be two of the half dozen teams out training that day. They are complete opposites. Claudio Maurizio is wiry and cheerful, with dark Mediterranean eyes. He is disarmingly friendly, and likes both to laugh and make his buddies laugh. Jeremy Anderson, a compact, chiseled, ice-eyed man, is less of a joker. He wants to talk to me even less than Claudio does. There's a force about them both, as though they were handed out extra charisma at birth. They are turbo-charged.

The next time I meet Claudio, he's running a group training session at an abandoned school in Langley, a city an hour or so east of

Vancouver. I drive out at Darrell's invitation, and of course I get lost trying to find the school. I have to pull over to wipe away tears of frustration. When I finally find my way there, training has just begun.

At first the dogs warm up with a search scenario where they have to find a quarry barricaded in a classroom. I follow behind the dogs as they hunt through the empty classrooms, dimly lit in the dusty, filtered sunlight. Dog after dog makes a beeline to the cupboard or closet where the quarry is wedged. Each dog attacks and drags the quarry out, yelling and fighting. Next the teams do the big challenge that Claudio has set up for them.

With a quiet confidence, Claudio teaches all the dogs to dive into a twelve-foot drop in total darkness under the school. The dogs are deeply scared; the fact that their eyes are set farther apart on their heads than humans' eyes means they have less depth perception than we do. They can't accurately judge how far down the floor is; they have to trust their dads to make this leap of faith into blackness. It goes against every instinct they have. For all they know, they could be leaping to their deaths. So brave they are, these incredible animals, motivated only by loyalty to their dads. I'm struck by Claudio's upbeat patience as he works the dog teams. Some dogs jump in after two minutes, and some take fifteen minutes, but Claudio instructs their handlers with confident encouragement. The dogs embody the struggle between loyalty and fear so completely as they take on this mission: paws scrabbling for purchase, back legs trembling, as one after the other they leap into the abyss, where a bad guy is waiting, taunting them. Dad is right behind them, ready with heaps of praise and encouragement.

This scenario gives me a good picture of the kind of trainer Claudio is. He never loses his cool or becomes impatient with either the dogs or their handlers. But if there is an active shooter in a school and they get into a storage area like this, this is exactly where the dog teams will need to go.

Trust is at the heart of the relationship between police dogs and their handlers, and I see this played out as each team goes in. Those few who try to use force fail every time. There's only one dog who can't do it. His tail tucks between his legs, and his reaction is pure fear. Claudio coaches the team to get a bit closer and then has "Dad" lift his dog down, so that it ends in a win. Impatient men with incredible restlessness and drive themselves have to become patient, so their dogs can succeed. Standing next to the pit as each dog jumps in, my heart lifts, witnessing this bond of trust between handler and dog.

■

Another day out with Darrell Moores and the team at the Burnaby detachment, I get to sniff a whole briefcase full of drugs that the dogs are using for searching. Claudio and Chucky are there as well, and I manage to ask Claudio a few questions. They've set up three drug hides in the lunch room of the RCMP, and then brought the dogs in to sniff them out. In the middle of all this, a solid, middle-aged woman of unflappable calm comes in, spreads out her lunch, and begins to eat. Never mind that huge dogs are lunging around the room, leaping up on her table, knocking over furniture in their eagerness to find the crack and the ecstasy. This lady eats her pasta salad calmly, without looking up or engaging anyone in conversation. It is impressive. This is her lunch break, and by God she is going to eat!

I watch Claudio bring Chucky in, watch Chucky search the shelves and find the drugs. Claudio isn't one to idolize his new dog, Chucky.

"Chucky's not very smart," says Claudio. "He'll get his paws on the counter and then his head on the counter, and then he falls down—he's kind of stupid."

Chucky in the cold. (Claudio Maurizio)

"We love you anyway," I tell Chucky, who swings his big head around in my direction. "You have to work harder with him, I guess."

"You just have to be more patient," says Claudio.

I know Claudio Maurizio is the man other handlers turn to for help with their dogs. I know he's the one who wins medals for courage. I want to know more. Finally, out of desperation, I ask Darrell Moores to put in a good word to Claudio for me. The next day, I send

another e-mail requesting a meeting. Claudio writes back immediately asking me when would be convenient. I'm over the moon.

Always, the day leading up to a ride-along, I have a lot of extra
energy coursing around in my system. I dread that three-in-the-
morning fatigue when I can hardly string three words together and
I'm still trying to interview someone. I dread what I know will be
moments of profound terror.

Odds are I'll be just fine, but I still tell my kids how much I love
them, holding them a few seconds too long, so that they squirm away
in annoyance. I know that any of the cops I ride with will do their
utmost to keep me from harm. The tricky thing is, their job involves
putting themselves in harm's way whenever the need arises. The other
tricky thing is, what I, and most people, would consider dangerous,
for them is routine, and for them is sometimes the best part of the job.
It is always with trepidation that I drive to meet a cop for a ride-
along, and my night with Claudio is no exception.

We meet in Surrey, which is Claudio's stomping ground. I hop in
the truck and see he's got Chucky on board, with Racer in the back
as well, just for the ride. The two dogs ride quietly. It's early in the
evening when we meet up with Constable Jeremy Anderson for a
coffee at Tim Hortons.

"What do you like about being a police dog handler?" I ask, trying to make small talk.

Jeremy appraises me with those icy blue eyes and confidently
quotes Hemingway: "There is no hunting like the hunting of man,
and those who have hunted armed men long enough and liked it,
never care for anything else thereafter."[5]

I'm trying to find a polite reply, but I don't have one. It's so far out
of my experience that I can't find common ground. What have I
hunted? Frogs, fish, tadpoles, toads, grasshoppers, garter snakes. I
stalked them and captured as many as I could, though I let them go

after. I was a good hunter as a girl, but I didn't want to eat or kill what I caught—I wanted to look at them up close, and then release them. A vast chasm seems to separate my hunting instinct from someone like Jeremy Anderson, or Hemingway.

I sometimes went with my father when he hunted deer. I remember the blood-thrill of running to find the freshly shot animal. I poked its glassy eye. I recall one deer that had a larva in its nostril, something creamy that squirmed out of its now-useless host. I hated that the deer were killed, though I did not cry, and later I ate them. Was the pounding in my heart, the curiosity that made me run to look up close at death, the same drive that Jeremy Anderson has when pursuing a criminal?

Buried deep in me, and in you, resides a hunter. Somewhere generations past, we killed what we ate. We beat small creatures against rocks until they shrieked and died. Now we buy boneless chicken breasts in little packages. Like most of the public, I fear those whose hunting instincts remain sharp and true. I fear those who speak of the pleasure in hunting men. They have stayed true to a side of human nature many wish to erase.

We drink our coffees and the men eat their sandwiches. "So what are you afraid of?" I ask them, and Jeremy replies with another quote.

"Do you know Marcus Luttrell? He's a Navy SEAL. He says, 'Fear is a force that sharpens your senses. Being afraid is a state of paralysis in which you can't do anything.' I have known fear, but it just tells me to pay attention.

"It's more that I've seen things the public doesn't see. I don't have that trust. I don't trust a person until they've had the chance to prove themselves to me on three separate occasions," says Jeremy.

"Wow," says Claudio. "I don't know if I'd take it that far. But I guess we're all like that. We've all seen too much."

Jeremy continues. "Let me put it this way. You go to a supermarket, you get your cart. You might pass a few people going in to the store. No big deal; you might not even notice them. When I go into a supermarket, I am evaluating everything. 'Okay, that truck door opened, is that man armed? Where is he now? Okay, that lady just stepped off a curb. There's a Nissan Pathfinder behind me, turning left, approaching."

"Oh my God, that sounds absolutely exhausting," I interject. "To have to move through the world that way, evaluating everything all the time!"

"That's why a lot of us are friends with other cops," says Claudio. "We understand what it's like. A lot of people don't. Jeremy and I go hunting together every year, just us out in the wilderness. It's not easy for the public to understand. Everything that makes us good cops makes us bad in friendships and romantic relationships."

Claudio takes me by a warehouse where he has recently made a successful capture, a total of nine people taken into custody. "Some came out right away, but two of them tried to get away. I did a patrol with Chucky one hour later, and there, in the middle of the stolen property, Chucky found a guy between the boxes, just hiding out, biding his time, hoping. But we got him."

Claudio cut his teeth on the homicide team, then the Indo-Canadian gang warfare task force. "You have to know who's who in the zoo," he says. But he won serious recognition for his proactive approach to solving crimes in the break-and-enter section.

"It's like this. Break-and-enters almost always involve a stolen car. So I just took it back further, and saw what was going on with the stolen cars. Audi and Volkswagens were getting stolen. I was the first one to do the math. The cars were almost always dumped in this one area. I knew it was not going to be in front of their house, but I knew it wouldn't be far either. So I did a graph, and figured out the guy was in this one area, and then I spent about four hours just watching this gray Audi.

"These days you can't chase cars anymore like that—too many people get hurt—but we didn't have that back then, so I chased the guy down, and wedged him in to a cul-de-sac. When he couldn't go any further he rolled down his window, and that's when I pepper sprayed him. He got a couple of months in jail, and guess what? While he was gone, there were no stolen Audis or Volkswagens."

"Why did he steal only those kind of cars?"

"That's pretty common. Most thieves have one type of car they know how to steal. Only the pros can do any type of car.

"At that point, we were getting about fifteen hundred car thefts a year in Richmond. That's nothing. Did you know, in the mid-2000s, Surrey was the auto theft capital of the world?"

"No. I had no idea."

"I just started plotting the thefts, and thought, 'How can I be more efficient?' The answer was, disable the car, watch it, grab the guy. So this time I put what we call a rat trap under the Audi's wheel, so he'd get a flat tire, when the rat trap punctures the tire. I wanted him to pull over and get out to look at the car, and that's what he did. That's when I pursued him, and when I got him, he just looked at me and said, 'You again?'"

"How old was he?"

"Maybe twenty, twenty-two years old. So in one year, there was a forty percent reduction in auto theft, and I loved it. I was already working with a dog handler, A.J., at that time. I knew I wanted to be a dog handler. I started quarrying in 2001, and was accepted into the program in 2006. I knew a lot about cars, and that helped me out. My dad owned a business fixing cars, and I started helping him when I was five years old. I can tell any car from two hundred meters away. I make new recruits learn that. It's a challenge at first, but they need to learn."

"I know nothing about cars," I tell him. "I'm sure it helps a lot to know all that."

"I always want to get better. There's so much we all could do better. We have a problem with timing. So many guys, they'll follow the dispatch to where the guy was last seen, even if that was ten minutes ago. And you know what? That's the *last place on earth* the suspect is going to be. That's the only place you shouldn't go. You have to override your instinct, and use your mind. I think about the terrain, where the guy would come out. I map things out. Bad guys fleeing, they always turn right . . ."

"What? Why? Why do bad guys always turn right?" I wasn't even sure I'd heard him right.

"I don't know. They just never want to stop and make a left turn."

I file this away as one of those fascinating facts that feels like a game-changer but actually has no impact on my life, and never will.

"The best cops," says Claudio, "can think like a bad guy. The best cops are the ones who ran from the cops when they were little brat teenagers, drinking in the park. It's not book smarts, it's instinct."

I ask Claudio if he played sports growing up. I already know the answer, though. All the cops I've met either hunted or played sports, or both, so I'm not surprised when he says, "Soccer. I was on three soccer teams, I played all the time." I should have guessed it. Like many Italian kids in Canada, soccer was his sport. Claudio speaks a dialect of Italian from the northeast part of Italy, called Romansch, a dialect that emerged hundreds of years ago, sort of a mix of French, Italian, and Spanish.

Sometime in that long quiet night, Claudio says this to me: "You know, dog guys are kind of high-strung. We're perfectionists, and in some ways this is a bad job for our personality type. We are in a job where a good rate of success is ten percent. I hate failure. That's why I can't sleep at night. It keeps me up, thinking, 'What did I do, how could I have done better, how did he get away?'"

We've been driving in circles. Imagine taking your car from Boston to New York and back again all in the same night, with a few stops to run through industrial parks. That's what every ride-along is like. These trucks cover some serious ground, eating mile after mile of road. I shift my legs, trying to get comfortable, as I consider Claudio's concept of failure.

"You can only do your best with the information you have," I tell him.

"I only sleep three, four hours a night. But when my block of shifts is done, I crash for six hours. That tells me it's stress. My fiancée even made me try yoga, but it didn't help."

All this time, Chucky and Racer are quiet in the back. Some dogs are barkers, but not these two. Racer's small and quick and pretty much retired at nine, but he stays with Claudio whenever possible. "He's just worked so hard, he wore out his shoulder. He still comes along for the ride."

Chucky sticks his muzzle through the partly open barrier between his kennel and our seats. He looks more like a brown bear than any other dog I've seen. He has the same wide head and deep-set bear eyes, though his shaggy body is lean and lithe. He's big for a dog, ninety-eight pounds, but he's skinny, and won't overeat, even when he gets extra rations. Chucky was nearly failed out as a potential police dog. His first quarry wasn't treating him as he should have been, and he'd developed some serious issues.

"What's Chucky's personality like now?"

"He's a one-person dog. He's getting better, getting more social, but his whole life revolves around me. Me and my fiancée walk him every day. At first, he wanted to do bad harm to her. I am slowly getting him used to her—now she can let him out or feed him."

"Was she afraid of him?" I ask, thinking of the phrase Claudio used, "do bad harm to her."

"No, she's pretty good. One day, we were out walking Chucky, and she says to me as a joke, 'What do you think he'd do if I fall down?'

" 'Nothing,' I said.

" 'No,' she says, 'He would come help me. He loves me more than you.'

"So she falls down in the woods. Chucky doesn't do anything. He just keeps on going. A few minutes later I fall down, and he comes running right up, like 'Dad! Dad! Dad! Are you okay?'

"A few months pass. 'What do you think he'd do if he looked back and I'd disappeared?' she asks.

" 'Nothing,' I tell her. She hides behind a tree. I call Chucky. Again, he runs right past her. But then I hide. Right away he comes and finds me. I'm his world and I always will be. My old dog, Racer, could care less about me. Chucky's completely the opposite. We have a very strong bond, the two of us. He's calmer, much more chill now. Racer was a wired wing nut."

Claudio took a chance on Chucky. "He had a lot of confidence issues. But he had the ability, and I saw it in him. He was taken away from his quarry, who in my opinion did nothing with him. We had a lot of work to do to make him comfortable in his own skin. I'll empower him to make mistakes, but I'll be the one to correct him now."

Claudio is a sunny kind of guy. It's fun hanging out with him. He always has a smile and a joke, and ever since he's decided that he'll talk to me, he tells me exactly what he thinks. I feel good in his company. There are only a couple of times in that long night where that good cheer is gone. Once it's when we are discussing the Independent Investigations Office of BC, and once it's when I ask how being a police officer has changed him.

"The IIO investigators? Half of them have never done police work. They don't know what it's like. They are civilians, journalists, whatever."

Claudio's been through an IIO investigation, as is often the case in Canada when a suspect is seriously injured. During the course of the investigation, although there is no mandatory removal from active duty, he was legally advised to be off the streets.

"It's a bit disheartening. An investigation shouldn't be based strictly on the injuries. I have no problem with an independent body investigating every time there is a death during a police operation. The dead can't defend themselves. They can't open a complaint or investigation. If I had a family member who died during a police situation, I'd want an independent investigation. But if there was not a death, it's not necessary. Everyone can make their own complaint, and people do it all the time, whether it's justified or not. We already have those safeguards in place. Now, this independent body comes in, and you are guilty until proven innocent—it's hard. When someone receives a bite, they are more than willing to make a complaint if they feel it isn't justified. In the meantime, I can't do my job for however many weeks or months until the IIO concludes. That's a stress. To be investigated for doing your job by people who don't know what it's like, that's not right.

"I know I did my job, I did everything right, and that's why I'm always cleared. But they tell me to get a criminal lawyer, and I'm thinking, why do I have a criminal lawyer? I'm a perfectionist. I don't want mistakes. That's why I have such terrible sleep."

Claudio and Racer were awarded 2011 Officer in Charge Awards for how they responded to a homicide scene. He's an officer who works every scene over in his head, always trying to do better.

Claudio is a good storyteller. As the night wears on, he tells me about a knife-wielding suicidal man with mental health issues. I could see the man as Claudio describes him, high on an unknown drug cocktail, wild with pain. Claudio finds him; it isn't hard. He explains that criminals and suspects run to parks or schools. They like open spaces. So that's where this guy was. The two of them did a little dance around Claudio's car, the man clutching his knife, threatening Claudio with it. A less experienced or less confident cop might have resorted to force at that point, but Claudio depended on his instincts, and on his quick feet. The man ran away. When backup arrived, they found the guy up on a wall. He still held the knife that he had used to slash at his own throat and both wrists. He was bleeding, but very much alive.

"It's like this," says Claudio. "He was up on the wall, singing at the top of his lungs, 'I'VE GOT THE WHOLE WORLD IN MY HANDS!' One of the ERT guys finally jumped up and pulled him off the wall, shooting him three times with bean bags, but the guy felt nothing. And then Racer jumped up and hammered the guy in the arm, but he didn't respond."

"How is that even possible?"

"Drugs can block the pain. Only drugs. I've been bitten a number of times, and let me tell you, the pain is so intense that it drives all other thoughts out of your head. It puts a lot of people in shock. But when I saw he wasn't reacting to Racer, and he still had the knife, I knew we had to subdue him. I kicked him to knock the wind out of him. I heard the wind go out, WHOOSH, but even then he didn't react like a normal person. Anyway, we got him, saved his life, even though he kind of wanted us to kill him. Suicide by cop. They want us to finish the job."

Claudio's first marriage fell apart. Over the time I get to know him, he remarries, and they welcome a baby son. He has learned that he needs to do things differently this time around.

"I don't get upset over small things. When you've been in life-or-death situations, the small things don't matter, and honestly, they are almost all small things. But this can be a problem for everyone else who is not a cop. So when my wife asks, 'Which dress do you like better, the red or the blue one?' I could care less. Basically, if it's not a matter of life or death, it's not important to me at all. But it's important *to her*. I've learned the hard way."

This is not the only lesson Claudio has learned the hard way. He's a guarded man, having learned to watch his back. What he has seen, the weight of the worst he's had to witness, has changed him, put a barrier between him and the public.

Another time, I am scheduled to meet up with Claudio for a group training session. Claudio sends me a text to tell me he'll be meeting up with me, but late, and that I should just go to the group training in New Westminster. The other guys are already there. Claudio tells me to go to the casino and text them, so they can let me in to the ICBC lot where all the wrecked cars are kept—that's where they'll be training the dogs in extraction techniques: how to get a suspect out of a car without getting killed.

I drive carefully to New West and immediately get lost. I can't find the casino, and that usual self-hatred sinks in as I look at my map and try to make it conform with the reality of the streets I'm driving through. The street I'm on abruptly changes names, then changes back again. I circle in my car, blinking back tears, wondering why being lost always makes me feel crushed by self-loathing. Then I see that I've driven past the entrance to the casino twice! I pull in, park, and text Claudio. I decide to use the washroom in the casino, because I know this may be my last chance for hours. It's remarkably busy for ten thirty in the morning, its dark cavernous space a contrast to the May sunshine beating down outside. Three men in suits stand at the door, and I ask if I can use the washroom. A man with broken blood vessels covering the end of his bulbous nose looks me up and down and points wordlessly toward the neon restroom sign in the back.

I'm relieved to get out of that place. I head back to my car, and in a short time, I see them approaching, kicking up dust, those big dark trucks, each with an elite canine in the back. There are four or five of them circling around, and as they park I approach slowly, looking for a familiar face, but recognizing no one. I go up to two guys, setting their dogs off: the truck shakes with fierce barking as I extend my hand and introduce myself, explain that I'm waiting for Claudio. I meet Leo Rojas. Leo is originally from Costa Rica, and his dog, Fury, is a young female. Although she has only been matched and working with Rojas for a few months, Fury shows great promise. "Listen, I have the best dog in the world," Rojas tells me. "All the guys say that, but in my case it's true." I smile. Nothing better than how these guys love their dogs.

The training session is a lesson in extraction. The dogs work to get suspects out of cars in as many different scenarios as possible: dragging the quarry out of the front seat, across the passenger seat, out of the back seat. Each handler releases his dog and each dog approaches the problem of extracting the human from the car a little differently. Some are revved up, barking and biting. Others are quietly efficient, wasting no energy at barking and being scary—they go in silently and drag the quarry out fast and hard, paying no mind to the padded man thrashing and yelling, fighting them all the way. It's hard work for the dogs, but they meet the challenge with energy and focus.

As the teams talk strategy during a training break, I walk among the rows of damaged cars. The wrecks take my breath away. Some are shining twisted pieces of metal, and some are shells. I walk past a Lamborghini that is so badly charred that only the engraving on the hub cap tells me that this husk was once a gleaming $200,000 car. I walk among rows of cars with shattered windshields, refracting the sun in rainbow spider webs from their green knots. I look at a minivan where the metal has been melted, twisted like a Hokusai painting of waves, frozen in time. I am walking in a graveyard of cars, and of people, too; so many of these cars held fatalities. There is a little girl's bike in the back of one car; the car is contorted, a burned-out shell, and the bike is corkscrewed, too, its white tires bent, its pink streamers still attached to the handlebars. I pass one SUV and in the back, crushed with a spear of metal through it, I see a baby's car seat. Here is where we end, where so many of us end, though we think we will last forever.

I drive away carefully, both hands on the wheel, the shattered cars burned into my memory.

After following Claudio and his dogs through the years, and comparing them to other K9 teams, I realize how tough his dogs are. Neither dog is interested in me. They are nothing like the dogs I meet in the UK or in rural Washington. These dogs don't trust people and are not interested in me or anyone else but Claudio. "Has Chucky had any bad experiences with humans?"

"Chucky has only had someone try to choke him at the end of one track. He also had a guy manage to escape his grasp using momentum, which caused Chucky to drop off a steep cliff. Thankfully I had him on the long line. Racer, however, has been beaten on the head with a backpack full of tools, choked several times, and in one instance early in his career was *bit in the face* while he was biting and holding a suspect's forearm. I can say without a doubt that until Racer was bit in the face he thought tracking bad guys was just a fun game. After that incident you could plainly see that he was all business and was much more intense at the end of tracks."

Like their handler, these dogs have seen the worst of humanity. They don't let down their guard even for a minute, unless they are alone with Claudio.

The last time I am out with Claudio, Chucky, and Racer, it's a sunny, mellow day. I am soon to leave for a few months in Iowa, but

I am sure I'll keep hanging out with this team when I return. I have so much more to learn. We are out in Richmond, at a place Claudio likes to take his dogs to swim. Racer is over ten years old now, and Chucky is four and a half.

"How do they get along these days?"

"I can't let them play together. A, I don't want Chucky to play with dogs. Dogs are not an animal to play with. Racer used to be dog social, but then he got attacked by dogs so many times, so he's now dog aggressive. When I let them out together, which I've tried twice, I have to let them out muzzled. At home, they'll run by each other's runs and play. I suspect if I let them out on a walk, they wouldn't fight."

I ask how Chucky is around other dogs.

"Chucky's very social," says Claudio. "He has no dog aggression yet. He had a pit bull run up to us. I grabbed Chucky. The pit bull tried to grab his throat. We gave the bull a boot and got out of there."

"That's so scary!"

"My philosophy about pit bulls? Some believe their aggression is a learned behavior. But I've seen so many hunting dogs that are pets. They all freeze and lift that one leg. Why do they freeze and point? It's innate, just like a pit bull was bred to kill other dogs. You never know when that natural instinct will kick in."

Later, I do a little research on pit bulls. Originally a cross between terriers and bulldogs, some sources say these dogs were originally bred to fight other dogs; others say their first purpose was to grab and hold the faces of bears, bulls, and hogs, and then were used to fight other dogs and to kill rats. Even though dog fighting is illegal in much of the world today, pit bulls are still a popular choice for this brutal sport. The ASPCA statement on pit bulls does not support breed-specific bans, and emphasizes that, while some breeds may have a genetic predisposition toward aggression, much depends on socialization.[4]

"Why do you think they are so popular as pets these days?"

"You have two people who like pit bulls: those who like them because of that killer instinct, or do-gooders who want to fix them and save them. I don't know why they don't just adopt greyhounds instead."

"How old was Chucky when he first came to you?"

"I guess he was just barely over a year old."

The dogs head into the water for a swim. Chucky goes first, galumphing like a skinny brown bear. He tries to leap his way to the toy so he doesn't have to swim through the place where the Fraser River meets the open sea, but at the last minute the bank drops off and he has no choice but to swim it. Chucky swims out, retrieves the throw, and shakes copious amounts of water all over us. It's a hot day; I don't mind. Racer comes out next, shooting toward the water like a gold streak of lightning.

Despite his cheerful bravery, Claudio Maurizio has one fear—not that he lets it stop him. "I'm afraid of heights. Terrified of heights. Do you know what a Cormorant helicopter looks like?"

I shake my head no. "It's kind of like a Black Hawk, with big doors open in the back. With Racer we were doing a day where everyone was going to go up in the copter with the dogs, to familiarize the dogs. Each guy goes up with his dog and the back is completely open. I am literally against the opposite wall, my back to the wall as we go up, as far away from the edge as I can get. This military guy is sitting at the back with his legs dangling out over the edge hundreds of feet in the air. So Racer crawls up and lays down beside him, looking out through the open doors, way up in the air. The military guy, he's petting Racer. I wish I had a picture."

A few months after my return from Iowa, I reach out to Claudio, hoping to go out on a ride-along and catch up on things. I find out that Claudio's been promoted to corporal and been transferred to Yellowknife, the capital city of the Northwest Territories. A former mining town, built on the shores of Great Slave Lake, Yellowknife is one of the best places on earth to see the aurora borealis, the northern lights.

For me it's a shock, having no idea when I'll see Claudio or his dogs again. I know I probably won't meet old Racer again in this world. I write to Claudio to tell him the book's coming out, and I get the best note back. It says everything about the kind of cop Claudio is, and the way he lives life as one big adventure:

*Wow. Rachel. That is great news. CONGRATULATIONS. Jeremy forwarded the email to me today. I am up here in Yellowknife, NT. What an adventure so far. The work is slow at times for my and Chucky's personalities. And is it ever COLD! But some neat things have happened for sure.*

*How weird is it walking out onto a frozen lake for the first time ever. EERIE. Then try to drive out on it. Not something I have ever done in the Lower Mainland.*

*One Saturday afternoon my phone rings around 430pm, and 2 hours later I am on a 9 person chartered aircraft with three other police officers. We fly into a little community where the pilot turns on the runway lights with a remote control as we approach. Once we landed we ride in the back of a pick up that we commandeered. Chucky ends up catching our bad guy. And then we hop back on the plane, which waited for us, around 1 am. Bad guy is sitting across from me, and in front of Chucky's crate. And while we are flying back to Yellowknife I look out the window, and there are the Northern Lights bright as can be up in the sky!!! So cool.*

*Claudio*

# 5

## Chrisa—
## The Dog No One Wanted

Chrisa is an outlier. A large, solidly built black-and-tan German shepherd, she is one of the few female police dogs in the RCMP. Even a few females is a step up from the number of female working dogs just a few years ago: zero. Female dogs were considered a liability. Word was, females just weren't tough enough to come through in a crisis situation. Recently, however, breeders and trainers in Innisfail realized that such a blanket policy excluded those female dogs that had the right characteristics and temperament to be an ideal police dog. Now they test each pup as an individual. The fact remains, however, that few female pups make the cut.

Constable Jamie Dopson, Chrisa's handler, is a bulky, solid man with a ruddy complexion. He is a former rugby player for Canada. Constable Dopson exudes confidence. He is one of the few handlers who just doesn't care if his police dog is male or female; all he asks for is a solid working dog.

"At one point, Chrisa was one of only five female dogs working in Canada," says Constable Dopson. "I think now we have four in the Lower Mainland alone. There's been a shift in regards to thinking about female dogs. There was a time they thought the aggression in a female dog wouldn't be up to the standard. But now they seem to have found a nice mix in the breeding process, where they are getting really good results."

"So how did they come up with the evidence to start using female dogs?"

"They didn't really. They used them at one point in time. Then—this was a number of years ago, at least ten years ago—during training, a couple of females just turned and ran."

That, of course, would put their handlers at serious risk when they most needed defense. "At that point their blanket policy was changed to pull all the females. Now it's let's look at each dog individually. For the longest time the females were just brood, just for breeding, not really giving them the chance. Then they started putting them out in the field, and they seem to have worked out."

The first time I met Chrisa, it was during a group training with nearly a dozen police dog teams. We were in the huge lot where totaled cars are stored at ICBC. Chrisa was extracting quarry out of the interior of busted cars. She jumped in through a door or open window and pulled the suspects out with her jaws as they yelled and fought and held on to the door handle, resisting her every step of the way. At that time I was struck by Chrisa's focused efficiency. She didn't get revved up even a little bit—she went right into the car, attacked on command, and got the job done.

Today she's equally quiet. I step into Dopson's Chevy Tahoe to silence. Chrisa's not a barker. She moves closer and inspects me through the grille, and then proceeds to ignore me for the rest of the shift.

"When did you first get Chrisa?" I ask him.

"I got her when she was fifteen months old. She started late because she was a female. Not a lot of handlers wanted her. She was basically two years old at the point we started working. She was kinda looked over."

"Why?"

"Sometimes there's a stigma: big male guys with a female dog. I was new. I took anyone I could get! She's my first dog. I didn't know any different, so I was all for it. I wouldn't change the decision for anything."

Constable Dopson turns the truck around.

"We'll head over to the church. But first I'm taking her swimming," he says. "Too hot for her otherwise." The truck *is* hot. It's a borrowed truck, with no air conditioning. She needs to cool off. Chrisa's scheduled to do a demonstration to the Immaculate Conception parish and school for the community's mid-May celebration. We head to a swimming hole that is Chrisa's favorite place to paddle, a pond in Fort Langley near an old fish hatchery. Chrisa leaps out of the truck without even glancing at me. I watch her launch herself into the water, swimming out to get the red ball Constable Dopson lobs into the pond.

"Watch out!" warns Jamie, just before Chrisa bounds up the bank and shakes herself all over me. I don't mind. It's another hot day.

Constable Dopson throws the ball again and again. Chrisa dives in each time and brings it back. At one point the ball gets away from her and she can't get traction in the water. She bites and bites, but the ball drifts away. She's determined, though. She bites ten times, twelve times, snapping and swimming before her jaws finally gain purchase and take the ball captive.

In the time we spend together, I grow to appreciate her personality, though I don't think she likes me much. Chrisa, you see, has a bias against females herself—females of the human variety.

It's not that she's aggressive. It's more like I'm just in her way. Like she is shunning me. No eye contact, no bringing the ball back to me instead of Dad. I'm just landscape to Chrisa.

Finally, when we are all cooled down, Constable Dopson opens the truck and Chrisa leaps in. We hit the road to Immaculate Conception. Chrisa's an older dog, though I never would have guessed it if Jamie hadn't told me. She's got just over a year of service left. "Chrisa's turning six in August," says Constable Dopson. "She has the same birthday as my oldest daughter."

I mention to Jamie that I've ridden with Jason Moses and Espo in Washington State. Deputy Moses has already told me he trained with Constable Dopson.

"I remember him! " says Dopson with a smile. "It's very different, the way offices are run in the States. He literally has to have everything donated. 'You get all that? My boss won't give me any money for it,' he said. I came back with a way better appreciation for what we do get."

"I know! I had no idea," I say. "Some of the sheriffs I met in the U.S., their dogs were donated privately. So many of the units operate on a shoestring, with almost all private donations. If you'd asked me before, I would have guessed exactly the opposite. I would have thought the USA was all about law and order, that the government there would provide a lot of the funding to the police, way more than Canada."

Chrisa is completely silent in the back during our ride. I hardly know she's there.

"Tell me about Chrisa," I say.

"Chrisa's a quiet dog. She doesn't like other dogs much. With other police dogs she's perfectly fine, but when she sees a civilian dog, she goes a little squirrely. She's got really high drive. She's really independent. Compared to a male dog, her need for affection is minimal at best."

"Really? I would have thought the opposite."

"Oh, it's so different. Male dogs are dopey with Dad. Not Chrisa. She'll come for a pet or two, but that's it. She just wants to work. She's not about sitting around and getting petted for an hour. She's always on the go."

Dispatch cuts in as we're talking, some other channel, someone else's problem, but I find it hard not to listen on all the police interactions playing out across the Lower Mainland. "The female was yelling. A hostile male was waiting at the front entrance to get in," says the disembodied female voice.

"I grew up around German shepherds," says Dopson. "My grandfather used to breed and raise them. I was constantly around the dogs. That's when I fell in love with shepherds. It was dogs all day long. Probably when I was about ten to eleven years old, I started thinking, 'I need a job where I can play with dogs all day.' When the time came, I wrote every city police exam between Calgary and here, because I had two young kids and I didn't want to go to Depot. I failed them all—by one mark. I passed the RCMP with high scores. I don't know if that's good or bad. But the good thing about RCMP, once you're in the police dog unit, you can stay. I guess we can call it fate."

"Before you became a police dog handler, what did you do?"

"I was general duty. I had a little stint in Sex Crimes, a little stint in the Investigational Support Team. I did some time with IST. They investigate bigger crimes but crimes that are too small for major crime. I always went back to general duty. My first eight months I saw twelve dead bodies. I had nightmares, sure. Things overflow. The pot has to settle down. I wouldn't change what I do for the world. You couldn't pay me to do another job. You could pay me more to do this one, though! Please write your local politician."

I laugh along with Dopson.

"I trained five cadets in my time. I'm training a quarry right now. I always liked being the pointy end of the stick."

"You went to Depot?" That's the twenty-four-week basic training course required of all police cadets.

"*Everybody* has to go to Depot. Then you are allowed to start the quarrying program. It's usually six months to a year after Depot before you can take the puppy imprinting course. After you pass that you can become a quarry and start raising pups. I raised four dogs before I got in."

"How many of them became police dogs?"

"None of them. My first one medicalled out. He had irritable bowel syndrome. He was a great dog, but way too nice. He would have never made a police dog. My next, Brooke, she was a female. She was really good, but she was sixty pounds soaking wet. She just wouldn't grow. She's now at Kicking Horse Resort in Golden, working as a registered avalanche search-and-rescue dog. My next dog, Chum, just never panned out at all. Chrisa was my last one."

"Who raised her for those first fifteen months?"

"Someone on Vancouver Island; I'm not sure who. I would have loved to have her from the beginning. She had a few little quirks that I would have addressed."

"Like what?"

"If you spray the hose at her, she tries to attack the hose, the water. Someone may have used the hose to discipline her."

I ask him what his secrets to K9 training are.

"My philosophy is, dogs are black and white. They like to know when they are doing well and when they are not doing well. If you keep doing corrections, keep repeating a certain correction throughout the entire obedience session, if you don't teach them and you are constantly nagging them, that's a problem. They want one command. Keep it black and white. It's worked for me so far, and they feel more confident in themselves."

"So how long after you started raising pups until you were accepted to go to Innisfail?"

"I was lucky. It only took me seven years. Seven years and seven thousand volunteer hours of my own time. It took my original supervisor twelve years."

"Wow. So Chrisa's your first police dog?"

"Yes. We usually retire them at seven; she's always been very healthy, which is so fabulous. Only thing her teeth aren't so great; she used to chew her chain-link kennel to try to get out."

"Will you keep her when you get a new dog?"

"Yes, I'll keep her. If I was to give her up, my wife would give me up! Most of us will try to keep their dog. We have a house dog at home, a border collie, they get along well. We have enough dog hair everywhere!"

Dispatch breaks through again: *The male then pushed the female.* We are now driving on the highway through the farms and rolling hills of Langley. Like the rest of the province, Vancouver's red-hot real estate market has caused a boom that has swept even to the far reaches of this outer suburb. The whole region has experienced astronomical growth.

"Just a few years ago," says Constable Dopson, "this was a two-lane road."

Now we drive through recent developments of sprawling houses, row after row. The farms move out farther east; Vancouverites cash out and live in Langley, instant millionaires.

"Is your wife RCMP as well?"

"No. She was a homemaker for eighteen years. She just went back to work. I prefer to have her at home, but she wanted to get out a bit. Now our kids are older. They don't need her much anymore."

"So you're a rugby player?"

"I played seven-a-side rugby for Canada, played all through high school. I played club rugby, and then represented the Fraser Valley. Next it was BC. Then I represented Canada at the Japan

Sevens tournament. In 1996 I spent a year training in New Zealand. I traveled all over the world."

"Very cool," I say, nodding as though I have any idea what seven-a-side rugby is.

"Yeah, it was good. Got my travel bug out."

We pull into the parking lot of a big Catholic school. Crowds of people wander from one event to the next. Chrisa growls, deep and low in her throat. Children squeal. Mothers pass out hot dogs, and fathers lean down and offer their children balloons.

Two general duty officers, a man and a woman, guide the Tahoe into the parking lot. We look for a shady spot, but there isn't one. The crowd approaches, curious but wary.

"That's the dog in there," says a dad to his little son. "Can you hear him?" No one walking past imagines that this police dog is a female.

Constable Dopson waits for the crowd to gather, and the magic show in the barn to wrap up. He talks to the crowd, telling them to maintain a safe distance, not to pet Chrisa, and to keep their own dogs in the car. Then he shows off Chrisa's obedience skills for the crowd, how well she walks with him, intent on following his every step, whether it's forward, backward, or to the side. The kids clap when she stays at heel with him.

Dopson then puts on the bite suit.

"Have you ever seen a helicopter dog?" he asks the kids sitting in the front row, just before he commands Chrisa to attack. As she clamps down on his arm, he swings her around. The crowd claps. After he loads her safely back into the truck, he kneels down in front of the kids to pass out trading cards and temporary tattoos. Dopson runs out of the cards and loot long before he runs out of eager kids, but finally we hop back in the truck and take off. He wipes his face.

"It's a hot day to be wearing a bite suit," I say.

Chrisa during a public demo with Constable Jamie Dopson. (Rachel Rose)

"That was only for a few minutes. The record for us is a quarry who lost ten pounds in a day sweating it out in a bite suit."

"You and Chrisa were a hit! The kids loved the tattoos."

"Yeah, Joel's been really good about it, our new boss. He's spent a ton on cards and pins."

"Each positive contact with the police, I'm sure it pays for itself."

"Tenfold in the end."

"What was that last trick you taught Chrisa?"

"Walking between the legs? It's nothing that was taught to us in training. I thought, if I'm in the bushes and I'm hurt and can't cuff the perpetrator, she can guard him. What's better than having her walk between his legs? If he wants to spin and hit me, she's gonna take his leg off."

Constable Dopson is leafing through the calls that have come in on his computer. He shares one with me. "A six-year-old ran off from mum. She's freaking out. He ran off because he didn't get his way. One of the dog guys, Shawn Nigel, tracked him and found him, brought him back. The kid's probably thinking, 'I got to ride in a police truck! This worked out pretty good!'"

"Dear God," I say, picturing it. It's incredibly easy for me to imagine this scenario, as it is for most parents.

"In March of this year," Dopson continues, "we found an eighty-one-year-old woman. She took off from her nursing home. They called us in to track her; she'd been missing for twenty-four hours. She was last seen at two o'clock in the afternoon the day before. She just left her nursing home to go for a walk. She had diabetes, Alzheimer's. She was frail, and she went out in only a pair of pants, a T-shirt, a little light sweater. There's lots of paved walking trails, but I guess she decided to take what I call a goat trail. There's a bit of muddy area, and she seemed to fall down. She hit her hand and one side of her body. She just lay there curled next to a log. She couldn't move anymore."

"My God. Walk me through what happened."

"It wasn't a track. Those paths are walked by hundreds of people daily. They figured she'd gone off the track somewhere. There were groomed trails along the edge of the path. If she'd fallen there, you would have seen her. I thought to myself, she's got to be a little deeper in the bush somehow. I went off. We tried to use the wind to our advantage. The wind was coming from the east, so I went far west into the bush and then went back east towards where the main trails would connect."

"Chrisa was on a long line?"

"Yup. She doesn't usually pull when we're out. Then her head came up and she started to pull quite hard as we crested the hill. I saw the woman laying there. I didn't go very close. I didn't think she was alive when I first found her. I didn't want Chrisa to be too interested, or maybe bite. I don't think she'd bite her—she seems to be able to differentiate good guys and bad guys. Even so, I held her back. The other member went up and found the lady, found she was still breathing. When we got her on the stretcher, she said, 'The night was a little cold.' One of the members said, 'Why didn't you scream for help?' She said, 'I didn't want to bother anyone.'

"The lady's family was waiting in a room for the results. It was nice to go back to that room and say, 'We found her.' She was okay, but she needed to go to the hospital for a bit."

"What did they say?"

"A couple tears, a couple handshakes, and a thank you. I didn't stick around for very long. I got the *thank you* and I was out the door."

"That must have felt great!"

Dopson smiles and nods.

"Was there a time you were out with Chrisa where you feared for your life, feared you weren't going to make it out?"

"My first ever capture with Chrisa was on International Women's Day of all days. It was 2013. We were called to an armed robbery in Coquitlam. A fellow had a gun. He robbed somebody at a bank. We got there and tracked him through the area for about a kilometer and a half. We located him in a backyard of a house, hiding in a laurel bush on top of a short retaining wall. We went through a gap in the wall. As we went through it, Chrisa stopped tracking. She stopped dead in her tracks. I'm basically at her butt, I'm looking at her, watching her. She turns and she looks to her left. He's hiding right there in the bushes."

"How far away?"

"Inches. I gave her the command. She got him by the leg."

"Did you feel confident she'd bite?"

"No. I mean, you never know. You always hear stories that the first bite is the worst. You never want your first bite to be one you actually want or need. When I gave the command, I was yelling so loud. She bit him on the right thigh and held on. I grabbed hold of him, and proceeded to drag him out of the bush and put him into cuffs. I was dragging him out and punching him. He was trying to shake her off, but that wasn't going so well. He wasn't fighting me.

"He had been charged and convicted of seven armed robberies previously. He had a total of fourteen charges stayed. So he had twenty-one total of just armed robbery charges, with seven convictions. He was released only two weeks prior to this event taking place. It turned out the gun was a pellet gun, but I didn't know that at the time. That's probably the one I'd been the most frightened. I really wanted to go home and kiss the wife and kids after that one."

"So then you knew she was going to come through for you."

"Yeah. After that my confidence was built. If I really needed her to bite, she was going to do it.

"Boy, I got a lot of calls that first year. I'm only three years in, and I still wake up my wife every time I catch somebody. Chrisa gets a Timbit after every time she catches someone."

Timbits are the little donut holes in Tim Hortons donuts. You can buy them by the dozen and pop them in your mouth. "Does she like those?"

"She does. And I do, too."

"Was your wife always a dog person?"

"Oh yes, but it's a lifestyle choice to do the dog services thing. You never sleep in late; it's like you are always putting your dog before your family. Chrisa's in love with my family. They all hang out, play around in the backyard, play tug-of-war."

I ask about Chrisa's reaction to human females, since she seemed so cold with me. What I want to know is how personally I should take her rejection.

"If a colleague comes up and leans on my truck, even if it's someone I work with all the time, if it's a male, she doesn't do anything, but if it's a female, she'll come out and try to bite them. Even with my wife—they're good now, they have a great relationship, but when I first brought her home, I was out walking with my wife and Chrisa. My wife and I were holding hands, and suddenly—wham! Chrisa flew between us, knocking our hands apart. Then she circled back and did it again, and again. Then she came up behind my wife and jumped on her. My wife had her hair up in a ponytail, and Chrisa grabbed the ponytail. She didn't bite, but she pulled—she pulled the ponytail until my wife had to step back and step away. I knew I had to discipline her, and I did. I made Chrisa learn to leave my wife alone."

Clearly, I shouldn't take Chrisa's behavior personally. I change the subject. "I went to Innisfail," I say. "Got to see the new puppies."

"Our breeding program is huge. I sure hope they never take it away. There are a couple of breeding lines they've created over the last few years that have just produced some phenomenal dogs."

Chrisa has proven herself to be one of those phenomenal dogs. "We're teaching these dogs to bite human beings to protect me, to protect themselves. You never know what's coming. You have to be prepared for anything. If you think you are done training your dog, you should quit."

"What are some of your and Chrisa's craziest encounters?"

"Once I was on a file, tracking. Buddy pulls out a party canister of bear spray. I got sprayed a little, chased him a bit, then went back for Chrisa to track him. A little Asian guy sitting on the bus stop as Chrisa and I went by just pointed and said, 'That way.' By then, I can smell the bear spray. We're flying. But now I'm sweating, the bear spray residue is going in my eyes. I can't see. I'm about to call off the track when we get close to him, he turns and fills her mouth with bear spray, then takes off running. He got me, too. It affected her. This was a bad dude. I jumped on the guy. I couldn't see at all. There was no real way to train for this. We got him, though, and were able to put him in custody.

"I wanted to train her for this kind of situation. We came up with using a fire extinguisher, with only a little $CO_2$ left in it. She reacted the same way. We worked her through getting something sprayed in her face."

"That sounds like a very difficult thing to get used to," I said.

"It was. It took some time, but she did it. Now I know she's got a fighting chance."

The whole time we are together, I don't think Chrisa's looked at me for more than a few seconds, that first time I stepped into her dad's truck. At the end of the shift, I ask Jamie if he'll take a photo of me and Chrisa together. "I think that could work," he says, but he doesn't sound so sure. Chrisa stays near me on command, and looks alertly at Dad, but her whole body, her whole demeanor, is saying loudly, 'Don't even think of touching me.' So I don't. Chrisa's a dog who has overcome the odds against her. She's a dog who has caught many suspects, a dog who has saved lives, but there's no sisterhood between us, any more than there was between me and Sasha. I'm not Dad, and she's just not interested.

# 6

## Police Dog Families— Women in Policing

I f Chrisa is an outlier, so are female police dog handlers. They are rare, they are tough, and some of them have paid a terribly steep price for serving their country and their community.

In October 2016, RCMP Commissioner Bob Paulson issued an apology and offered a settlement to all women sexually harassed at the RCMP since women first began serving in the force in 1974. Paulson's speech signified a cultural change at this venerable Canadian institution:

> *I stand humbly before you and solemnly offer our sincere apology. You came to the RCMP wanting to personally contribute to your community and we failed you. We hurt you. For that, I am truly sorry. You can now take some comfort in knowing that you have made a difference. Because of you, your courage and your refusal to be silenced, the RCMP will never be the same. I must also apologize to all Canadians. I know how disappointed you've been with the Force as you heard some of these very public and shameful examples of disgraceful conduct within our ranks.[1]*

Discrimination against female officers is an issue in many police forces. In K9 units, there are barriers to women both getting in and staying in. In the RCMP, the physical fitness tests for police dog handlers are so challenging that few women are able to pass them. (I know. I tried. At the end of watching a group certification test, I gave it my best shot. Carrying the eighty-pound sand bag that was supposed to be my dog just about killed me. The instructor kindly told me that I would have to have extraordinary physical strength at my height—five three—to be able to pass the test.)

Anyone who cares about issues of social and racial justice in law enforcement must care about gender discrimination, because having women in policing makes all of us safer. According to *The Washington Post*, studies over the last forty years have shown that female officers are better at defusing potentially violent situations before these encounters turn deadly.[2] And yet, according to FBI statistics, the average percentage of women police officers in all departments in the USA is 11.6 percent.[3] In the RCMP in Canada, it is about 21 percent of all officers.[4] Because of the extra demands of K9 policing, the number of female K9 cops is far lower than for general duty officers.

For now, women police dog handlers in Canada and the U.S. are outliers. In my time in Innisfail, I only saw two new female recruits. Women like Nathalie Cuvele are coming up strong, but other female police dog handlers have left the force after enduring years of discrimination and bullying. This is a loss not only for them, but for the institutions they leave.

Who are the women who do this challenging work, despite pressure from the public and the sometimes-hostile reception of certain of their fellow officers?

One of them is Police Dog Services Corporal Michelle Onysko. We meet for the first time in the lobby of the police detachment in

Squamish, a small city nestled in the mountains halfway between Vancouver and the world-famous Whistler ski resort. A six-foot-tall blonde with bright blue eyes, Corporal Onysko crosses the room in two strides, crushing my hand in the powerful handshake of a fearless woman.

"Welcome! Come on in!" she booms. I trot after her like a poodle in the wake of a greyhound. Onysko could be a model, except she's too strong and powerfully built for the runway. She could be a cowboy, but she's tougher than most wranglers. This one, folks, is not like the other girls.

I take a seat while she leans back and plants one muddy black boot and then the other up on her desk, consuming a salad in large, efficient bites. I glance around at her office, piled high with files, fleece coats, RCMP memos, and jokes pinned to the walls—the place is a comfortable mess, like a frat boy's dorm.

"Go ahead, Rose," Onysko says, with a dazzling smile. "Ask me anything you want."

"How did you know you wanted to be a cop?"

"I *always* wanted to be a cop. I never wanted to be anything else. Since I was a little kid, seven or eight, that was always my goal."

"Really?" I say. "Not too many little girls want to be police officers when they grow up."

"*Absolutely.* Nothing else interested me."

"Tell me about your childhood."

"Well, my dad was my hero. He was in the Navy. I was not an easy kid. If it weren't for my dad, helping me burn off energy, I would have been put on Ritalin for sure. My dad believed in me. He got me playing sports and kept me busy. I was always a fighter, though. I was *always* getting in fights as a kid."

Michelle Onysko is not the first cop to tell me they would have been put on ADHD medication if that had been an option when they were kids. Some kids just seem to be born with a different threshold of intensity. I have observed that a lot of them become cops.

"Why were you fighting all the time?"

"Well, I fought to defend my best friend, Lance. I was only seven, but I protected him. Later my father remarried. My stepsister was being bullied a lot. Our town was tough back then. I had a reputation that I could fight, but I knew I had to keep it in check if I was going to be a cop. But if they were beating my stepsister up, I was like, '*Awesome*, now I can fight!'" Michelle pounds her fist into her palm.

"How did you know *how* to fight?" I ask. I'm certain that the thought "*Awesome,* now I can fight!" never crossed *my* mind when I was in elementary school.

"I used to wrestle with my brother. It was always great, like *this is fun!* I never made my mom happy," says Michelle. "She put me in ballet. I got kicked out. She put me in figure skating. I got kicked out of that, too. I was adopted as a baby. My mother wanted a little ballerina, but she got me."

"What did your mother do?"

"She did a few different jobs. She was a housewife at first. Then when we were older she worked as a meat packer. Later she had a job in the law courts. Like I said, as a kid, I wouldn't listen to anyone. If I wanted to do something, I would. Nobody could stop me. I was spanked by my teachers. Oh, I was *constantly* misbehaving," she says, shaking her head at the memories. "I just never wanted to be a *girl*, you know? At school when we had to line up in two lines, boys on one side and girls on the other, I always lined up with the boys. I didn't want to be a girl! *No way, they were weak!* I wanted to fight."

"Did you want to be a boy the whole time you were growing up?"

"No. By grade six, I had accepted it. *I'm a girl. It is what it is.* It was around this time that the popular girls started stealing clothes and stuff, and I thought, *I can't do this, I want to be a cop.* That was the end of a lot of my friendships, and my popularity. They weren't doing the right thing, and I knew it. Only my dad believed in me. He always said, 'You can do whatever you want.' I wanted to make my dad proud."

"And is he proud?"

"Yes," she says, and suddenly her blue eyes flood with tears. "What are you doing to me?" she demands, pressing the bridge of her nose until the tears shut off.

"My dad died last year. I miss him so much. My family went through some tough times. With my parents, there was some serious drinking when I was a kid. There was some serious fighting too. Every time I heard the knock of the police at our door, I would always let out a breath, knowing I would be okay, that the fighting would stop and I could go to sleep. The police made me feel safe. That's probably when I first wanted to be a cop."

Corporal Michelle Onysko and Drago on a track in Squamish, BC. (Rachel Rose)

Abruptly, Michelle stands up. "Come meet my dogs," she says. I follow her out of the detachment, her heavy black boots taking one stride for every two of mine. In the parking lot, she lets her dogs out of the truck. Michelle has two dogs, like a lot of the senior police dog handlers. Her first dog, Red, is a grizzled old shepherd, getting long in the tooth and gray in the muzzle. He can't keep up with the intense physical requirements of a police dog. But Michelle won't part with him. Although she works well with her new dog, Drago, who will be two in September, it's her old partner, Red, whom she still trusts with her life. Drago's the big young upstart, gradually winning a place in Michelle's heart, but Red? Red is *family*.

Red and Drago tolerate each other, but barely. It's a difficult transition for Red to make, from alpha dog to the old geezer who gets to come along for the ride but doesn't get to do the real tracks or the real work of being a K9. When Michelle lets the two shepherds out of the truck to do their business, they romp across the winter fields, tearing through the tall dead grass, jumping up to paw each other's shoulders like brothers wrestling. There's play in the wrestling, but there's aggression, too. All of a sudden the growls are not playful at all. Drago and Red are fighting for real, teeth snapping as they lunge and bite.

"Red!" hollers Michelle. "Cut it out! Drago! Get back here!"

Her boys ignore her. She yells again, so loud that all three of us turn to stare at her. "CUT IT OUT!"

The dogs, chastened, lope to opposite ends of the field. The minute Michelle's back is turned, though, they wheel and come back at each other to tussle again. Then Drago bounds over and leaps on me, grabbing my coat and tugging it. Truth be told, I am not crazy about this game.

Michelle opens the back of her big Suburban for the dogs. Drago hops in easily, while Red jumps with deliberate care, like the old man he is. I climb up front beside Michelle and we drive away into the cold, bright sunshine of the Squamish winter.

"So, are your relationships much affected by your work?" I ask as we drive.

"My *relationships*?" She laughs. "Oh, yeah! You can't turn it off. I'm on call 24/7, and that's the way I want it to be. I want to be the one they can always call when they need a dog handler. Recently, I went on a date. He made me dinner. I got a call, and I had to leave his house in the middle of dinner. I apologized, but I was only gone an hour, so I came back and tried to pick things up where we left off. But then I got called out again. I knew this was it. It was over. You just go into cop mode. It's tough. I have to date someone who understands."

"I'm sure there are guys who would," I say. Michelle shoots me a look, like, *Are you kidding?* "When I started my career, I had to prove myself. I couldn't have a family at that time. I had a relationship for six years. I took the calls on New Year's Eve, on weekends, whenever they came up. I volunteered for everything. I had a lot to prove. Raising puppies also took a toll. When we were camping, I always wanted to bring the puppies, not kennel them up. But my husband at the time was like, 'When is it going to be just us?' Once while we were camping, I saw the pup had climbed on a camp table and was chewing up my husband's swim goggles. I knew just then he wanted to drive me to Hope and drop me off."

Michelle's first marriage ended. Her ambition and the pressure of the dogs and the job were just too much. Any guy she dates will have to understand that Corporal Onysko's a package deal. Her pack includes Red and Drago. They are family. She refers to herself as Mom when she speaks of her dogs, her boys.

"Hey, Michelle?" I ask. "What are you afraid of, doing this job?" I can think of a lot of things she might say in reply. But Michelle's not going to help me out.

"I can't think of anything. Nothing really scares me."

*"Nothing?"*

"Nope, not really."

It's not the answer I want, but it's the only one I'm going to get. Michelle's in a good mood, her strong hands easy on the wheel as we coast down the highway. "I had a lot of support, coming through. Even though I had to deal with a few assholes, I always had good people around me," says Michelle.

"What kind of assholes?" I ask.

"The *fuck*!" responds Michelle, slamming on the brakes and smashing the sirens and lights on overhead. I look up, startled. I barely have time to register that a white car is driving in our lane on the wrong side of the highway, directly toward us. We can't move over. The other lane is full of cars. My heart rate red lines. Drago's and Red's claws skitter for traction in the back of the truck as we brake. Michelle's truck and the car skid to a stop facing each other, only a few feet apart. Michelle jumps out to confront the driver. All around us, cars slow to a crawl, inching past on the shoulder under the pulse of red and blue lights.

The driver is an older woman with the puffy, confused expression of a lost little girl. She leans forward in her seat, both hands gripping the steering wheel like a life preserver. Her blouse has entirely fallen off one shoulder. Her hair, in a loose bun, slips down her neck. Everything is coming loose, from the skin on her cheeks to her trembling pink mouth.

"You were driving on the wrong side of the road!" Michelle says sternly.

"I was? I don't know what happened," she says to Michelle. "I'm sorry. I just got on the freeway over there. I'm so sorry."

"That's the *off-ramp*," says Michelle. She's clearly pissed off, so I'm surprised when she lets the woman go with a warning.

"God bless you, Officer. God bless you. God bless you for being here today."

"Don't worry about it. You just drive carefully," says Michelle. She stands in the middle of the freeway, stopping traffic entirely so the woman can turn around and get off the road.

Whatever God had to do with it, Michelle, with her quick reflexes and her siren, was on the right road at the right time to prevent what could have been a terrible accident.

■

A few weeks later, I'm back in Michelle's truck, heading out to meet the two young Mounties she's training. I'm making small talk when she interrupts me.

"You asked me earlier what I'm afraid of," says Michelle, "and I couldn't think of anything. Well, I thought of something. I'll tell you. It's getting my dog killed because of something I've done."

Her voice rises. "I could *not* live with myself! If I died, I won't know about it, obviously. I'd be dead. But if I got my dog killed, I don't know if I could handle it!"

These dogs are Michelle's whole life. Their fate is in her hands, and she takes that responsibility seriously.

Today is a training day for Michelle's two quarries, Paul and Kyle, and their young dogs. Paul and Kyle are both RCMP constables who hold the dream of doing what Michelle does. Paul has driven over from Whistler, and Kyle took the first ferry all the way from the Sunshine Coast. They come every week, on their day off, so they can work all day on their own time and their own dime. If they've done a night shift, they come anyway, without having slept.

Before we head to the mountains, we do some training with all the dogs in the residential streets of Squamish. Michelle is a good teacher, encouraging but exacting. The guys listen with attention and respect to everything she has to say. On the way over, she tells me, "I never chase them down. They want to learn from me, they need to seek me out." And they do. Week after week, her quarries come to learn from her.

Paul and Kyle take turns hiding in the brush. Even though Red thumps his big tail and whines hopefully at her, it's Drago who Michelle takes on the track. She's about to retake her PARE test with Drago, the fitness test every RCMP dog handler has to pass, every single year. Drago and Michelle both have to be in peak form. If any dog teams fail, they have a chance to be retested once. There are no third tries. The second strike means that you lose your dog and are kicked out of Police Dog Services. I never see this happen, though there must come a time when every dog handler has to call it quits. No matter how good a team is, the sheer physical demands make it impossible, at some point, to pass.

Red and Drago are very different dogs, personality-wise. As Michelle tells it, "Red is an old soul. He is very sensitive. His loyalty and his mere presence is calming at home. I feel grateful to have him as my first partner. The most annoying thing when we worked together was he NEVER stopped barking. I mean truck-shaking barking! I couldn't pull up beside anyone and have a chat, nor could I talk on the radio. Whenever I keyed the mic there's a beep, and that would set him off into a barking frenzy. The dispatchers found it amusing. I'd let go of the mic to wait for him to stop barking and dispatch would say, 'Go ahead Kilo 12.' Often the mic would get keyed by him stepping on my radio, and everyone on that channel would hear me having a one-sided conversation with him, telling him to shut up and stop barking for a minute."

Drago, the new member of the team, is an intense dog. Michelle says he's got very high drive. "Drago is always moving at 100 miles an hour. He's faster than Red, who was more methodical, which is good and bad. When I first got him, you couldn't touch him. Now he likes physical affection but only for a moment because he can't sit still for too long.

"The most annoying thing? When we are called out in the middle of the night, Drago is like a teenager. He doesn't want to get up and gets mad when I try to wake him. He growls and so on, and I sometimes have to drag him across the mud room floor to the door before he gets up and jumps in the truck snarling at me. It's kind of funny, but when time is of the essence and he's being stubborn . . . ugh! By the time we get on scene, he's got his A game on, thank goodness."

Drago is dog aggressive, which is a concern for Michelle. He will have to pass a few dogs on this track, including another German shepherd in a yard who is barking his head off. His owner swaggers over to demand that we stay off his property.

Michelle agrees politely, neutrally, defusing the situation, but when we walk out of earshot, she grins. "One day, there was this guy who got up in my face and told me, 'Hey, hey! My dog can beat up your dog!'

"'Maybe so,' I told him, 'but I wouldn't let anything happen to my dog and I've got a gun.'"

Drago runs the track well, ignoring the other German shepherd and the three small dogs that pop up like firecrackers, jumping and barking, teasing him from behind the fenced yard. Drago even ignores the cat that darts across his path. He tracks down and chomps on Kyle, then does the same to Paul. Michelle grabs Drago, roughhouses with him and praises him, shouting, "Good dog, Drago, atta dog!" Drago leaps on her, panting. Then, at her command, he jumps in the truck beside old Red, who growls.

We get into the police truck to go to a remote location. Michelle drives easily, her truck straddling the divide between lanes on the empty road. Paul and Kyle follow behind in another truck with their young dogs. We drive past Squamish, through a First Nations reserve in the basin of Paradise Valley, through the bottom of a massive geological bowl cut into the rock, ringed by snow-capped mountains. "There's Anderson Beach," Michelle says, pointing at a glint of water beyond the trees. "You should bring your kids up one day. It's beautiful. Just avoid the long weekends, or you'll see a lot of drinking. Around here is where *Saw Dogs* was shot."

*Saw Dogs* is a show about master chain-saw carvers. It's a man's man kind of show: "Eat. Sleep. Carve. It's what we do," says the trailer. Figures it would be filmed in Squamish, a rough logging town. Vancouver, with its glass towers, gluten-free dog bakeries, and yoga studios, seems like another planet.

We pass farmhouses and run-down trailer homes. A few dogs run after our truck, barking. We drive past a whole family walking along the side of the road, the young mother in a wind-whipped calico dress carrying a small child on her back. Their faces are devoid of expression. They could have stepped out of the last century. This valley seems so cut off from the rest of the world. At the beginning of the drive, I'm thinking, *It is paradise, this valley. We could live here!* but after I pass the family, I think, *Maybe not.*

We pull up alongside an empty yellow field, and Michelle kills the engine. "There's the monastery," she tells me, pointing up the hill to a modern building, with tall glass windows made to capture the light. "Queen of Peace. I know most of the sisters pretty well by now, Sister Bernadette and Sister Mary Adam and all the others. We have a deal. I help them with their crazy dog Grace, and they pray for me."

Sun illuminates Michelle's face as she talks. We are bathed in golden light. Four bald eagles keen their high, warbling cries, circling the rugged cliffs while Paul and Kyle set the track.

We run the young dogs on several tracks. It's hard to keep up, but I trot behind, scrambling to cover as much ground as the rest of them do.

A half hour later, a nun walks the path down from the monastery, accompanied by a black, shaggy dog that I once might have thought looked aggressive, before I'd spent so much time around protection dogs. Now I look at the dog's plumy tail, waving like a feather duster, and I hear her trumpeting bark as a call of welcome. She rushes up to us and sticks her big head in my hand, demanding a scratch.

Sister Mary Joseph smiles beatifically at us both. I've never talked to a nun before. Mary Joseph is so young, so pure of face and serene. I can't see even a wisp of her hair beneath her wimple, but her eyes are dark and her skin is translucent. She is from somewhere in Europe, and has only been here for a few months. She looks so un-self-conscious in her joy at seeing Michelle, as she holds Michelle's hand in her own. Michelle, who towers over the little nun, beams down at her. We follow Sister Mary Joseph into the monastery to meet the monastery Mother, Sister Claire. The nuns here are both busy and creative: they have carved the massive wooden benches themselves, painted the faintly Byzantine murals on the walls, and farmed the honey that they sell. When I see the massive carvings I think they should film an episode of *Saw Dogs* here at the nunnery. "Eat. Saw. Pray. It's what we do."

Inside the chapel, the Mother whispers to Michelle that they've been having problems with a local gang harassing them. They've been coming onto the monastery, tearing around the property in the middle of the night.

"What? Why didn't you call me?"

"I didn't want to make any trouble," says the Mother.

"You have to call me. *Call me!* If you don't let me know what's happening, how can I protect you?"

Sister Claire drops her eyes, but she promises to call the minute they show up again. Michelle promises to make more nighttime patrols of the monastery. Then Sister Claire puts two jars of dark amber honey in our hands and calls to Sister Mary Joseph, who runs lightly up the stairs to walk us out to our cars.

Sister Mary Joseph and Michelle talk about dogs, while the monastery dog lounges on the road, slapping her plumed tail on the ground when anyone says her name. Finally, Sister Mary Joseph has to go back. "I'm on kitchen duty today, and last week, I burned the bread. This week I must be more careful!"

As we say good-bye, little Sister Mary Joseph gives me the lightest embrace, her soft cheek against my own like the brush of a butterfly's wing. Here we stand, three women who don't, or can't, fit in. We couldn't have less in common, but we have this in common. Michelle has refused motherhood, I've refused men, and Sister Mary Joseph, though she wears a wedding ring, has refused the kind of husband who leaves his dirty underwear on the floor.

"I always feel good after visiting the Sisters," says Michelle as we drive back. "I figure they'll put a good word in for me. I'm not religious, but with the work I do, with the things I have to see, it can't hurt, you know?"

"Definitely can't hurt," I say. "So, Michelle, did you always like dogs?"

Michelle grins and nods. "Always. I got my first dog, Jake, when I moved out on my own. My mom basically threw me out when I was fifteen. She thought I was messing around with someone, but I wasn't. Nothing I could say convinced her. My mom allowed me one trip home to get my stuff, and that was it. She always thought the worst of me. So my dad took me in, he and my stepmom. He was living with two stepkids in a single-wide trailer, and they took me in. My stepmom said, 'We'll be like the Brady Bunch.' I was so grateful to them. I was a lot of trouble, though. I was fighting all the time, getting black eyes, not coming home at night, going to parties and getting drunk."

Michelle peels a banana and makes it disappear in two bites.

"My dad tried to watch out for me. But eventually I was too much for them. I moved out on my own. This was when I got my first dog, Jake. I had Jake from a puppy. I took him everywhere with me. We had a huge bond. I felt, 'Nobody cares about me,' but I had Jake. From that point on, I always had dogs in my life."

"I get it," I say. "I totally get it."

Michelle was accepted to be a sheriff, which she did for a few years before she put in an application for the RCMP. She was accepted there, too. But before she could call herself a Mountie, she had to go through Depot, the paramilitary training that all new recruits must pass.

"What do you remember about Depot? Was it rough?"

"I didn't think Depot was that hard. We had to work together to get things done. I followed the shit and shine method. That's where you get in *shit*, so they notice you, and then you *shine*."

I laugh. Trouble has always been Michelle Onysko's middle name. She could have been one of those girls at high school who wore biker gloves with the fingers cut off, those girls who smoked outside the school, and if they didn't like you, they'd find a way to butt their cigarette out on your arm and make it look like your fault. Like you were stupid enough to walk into a burning cigarette. *Those girls.* The miracle was that Michelle had channeled that tremendous energy, that fierceness, into becoming a cop.

"I still remember the first time I got shot at. I was thinking, 'This is fun! This is exciting!'"

"For real?" I say.

"I loved it. There was one bad time in the RCMP where I was about to quit. Definitely there was some ostracism there. I was being left out because I was female, sure. I wasn't invited along with the team for coffee. They avoided talking to me because I was the woman. I made it through. You learn really fast who you can trust and who you can't. Through it all, I had my dog. Red was my guy. I trust my dogs more than anything."

"You must have seen a lot."

"Oh yeah. Other officers used to think I was cold when we went through training. I have seen some terrible sights. There was only one time I lost it. One time. I knew the mother, see. I'd been out there on domestic calls. I saw that he was controlling her, controlling her access to her son. He was bullying her."

"Like how?"

"The stuff that stands out for me? She split up with him but—as I saw for myself—he *could not take no* for an answer. Once I went there because he was trying to force her to sign an agreement, he was physically trying to force her to sign this custody agreement. She phoned the police. I happened to be the one on. I went there, and when I arrived, his attitude changed. She spoke in broken English. She was an immigrant, and she wanted to wait and review the agreement that she'd just seen when he pulled it out. I looked at the agreement. I looked at him. I said, 'You can't force her to sign this, you need to back off!' She was under duress to sign it. So he took the kid and left. He was going ballistic. She was trying to calm the child down, saying, 'It's okay, you'll go have a fun time with Daddy, it's all right.' She was trying to keep calm, do what's best for the kid. She always did that. In my experience with her, she always put the child's needs first.

"She was a lovely lady. I would go there and handle things, try to help her out. She really was grateful to me. Like after I saw him try to force her to sign the agreement, she rode her bike down. She didn't have a car; she had limited money, but she had flowers in her front basket, the kid in the back. She brought me flowers to thank me. She didn't have to do that but that's the type of personality she was.

"Things never got easier for her, but she kept trying. She's making a life for herself, single, and living one block from a school, a good public school where she wanted her son to go to kindergarten. But no, the father evidently wanted the kid to go to private school. So now she has to get up in the morning, take the kid by bus to the city. The kid was in school for half a day, but the mom never could have made it home, so she had to wait around there, bus all the way back, and that was her day. The court ordered that that would happen. The mom asked if there was anything I could do. I told her that if the court ordered it, there's nothing we could do. And that was the truth. The law is about what's legal or illegal, not what's right or wrong. I think she was wronged the whole way through.

"It was shortly after that. The call came in. I was first on scene. I came in, and the mom was laying on the floor naked. She had taken a bunch of drugs and she was really foggy. I said, 'Where's your son?' She said, 'In the living room.' The child was laying down on a pillow. He looked like an angel, I'm sorry to say it. There was a note on his chest that the mom had written, something about how the courts had screwed her over. I checked the child. The child was gone.

"I said to the mom, 'What happened?' She told me that she suffocated him with a pillow."

"What was going through your mind right then?" I asked.

"It was more of a business set of mind. The little boy is gone. I have to move on. I have to prioritize. I can see it in my head right now, exactly how he's laying on that pillow. But I thought, 'The mom needs help, I don't want her to die. Let's move on.' I was not emotional at the time. Not until afterwards does it hit you. I said, 'Okay, what did you take?' She said she took a bunch of pills. By this time the ambulance had showed up, but we were losing her. I said, 'Where are the pills, where are the pills?' She wouldn't answer. She was slipping under. They were working on her. She was almost dead. I went to the garbage and I found the pills.

"I didn't go with her to the hospital. Someone else did. I had to hold the scene. It was now a murder scene. We had to leave and get a warrant to start seizing evidence. I got relieved. I now had to go and sit with the detectives and tell them what happened. There's no time to be sad at the moment. Then later on, it's bad. Even now I still get pissed. From what I saw, he just wanted to win. Well, he won. 'Congratulations, you won! You won, and you lost everything.'"

"That's so hard," I say.

"I knew the mother well. I'd seen what she'd gone through. And there on the stand I was testifying under oath. They asked me a question about the murder, and I turned and looked at her. She looked right back at me, and I burst into tears, and so did she. We were both sobbing. It's a terrible thing I did, breaking down like that while testifying. She was sentenced to life in prison because of me."

"Are you sorry you lost it up there?" I ask.

"No, because she did it, she did kill her child, so she deserved to do the time. I just think no one was protecting her. Including the court. She didn't see any way out. I don't think she expected to live. But when I met her eyes, I couldn't hold back. I just lost it."

And as she's telling me, as she's remembering, Michelle's eyes fill with tears, and a single sob breaks through. She squeezes her eyes shut, pinches the lids with a finger, and pushes the tears away. My own eyes flash flood with tears.

"That's the only time. The only time I've lost it on the stand. It was just knowing them the way I did, over the years, it just broke me."

A child lies suffocated on a pillow, looking like an angel, as his mother, who is also his murderer, drifts off on a haze of pills. This tough cop who wanted to be a boy when she was little, who got into every fight she could, the cop who thought, "This is fun!" when she first got shot at—this cop takes the witness stand and breaks down.

The only thing Corporal Michelle Onysko's afraid of? Causing the death of her dogs, the two beings who matter to her more than anything. Red and Drago are the kind of family that never throw you out, never degrade you or do you harm, the kind of family that loves with no conditions—unlike the human families Michelle has known.

■

When I meet Police Constable Sara Ginn in London for a ride-along, it's a revelation. Ginn belongs to the first police K9 unit I've ever seen that is staffed by a majority of female dog handlers, and led by a female sergeant, Clare Masterson. Clearly, this K9 unit in London is doing things differently than we are in Canada and the U.S. Sergeant Masterson is awaiting her first police dog, and she's thrilled.

In the unit office, I chat with Masterson and then with Constable Emma Truelove. She works as Constable Ginn's van partner much of the time. Interestingly, both the female K9 officers I get to know are married to men who work as K9 officers in other units. Officer Truelove's father was also a police officer. And Prince, Emma Truelove's dog, lives with his brother, Tanian, who is also a police dog. It's all just one big happy family at the Metropolitan police dog unit. I wonder if having this male support offers some protection to these female K9 cops in dealing with whatever issues arise on the job.

Constable Sara Ginn has two dogs: Sampson, her shepherd, and a little brown and white English spaniel named Harper. At eleven months, Harper is, as Sara says, "A little cracker. I have four boys at home and she rules the roost. My husband's in the dog section as well, so there's his working shepherd and his working spaniel, and mine, and his retired dog, who is fourteen and still going strong. It's a bit crazy sometimes!" Sara and her husband, David, live in a house full of dogs. They have their son, Zach, who is eight, along with dogs Rhum (David's retired dog), Wilson (David's current dog), Sydney (still a puppy at eighteen months, and soon to be David's drug/firearm/cash dog, also an English spaniel), and their other spaniel puppy, Harper. I can only imagine mealtimes at their house.

Constable Ginn and Sampson won their unit's base trials last year. This is a team to watch. Sampson, a handsome brown shepherd with golden paws and gold marks on his face, is a friendly upbeat dog. He's focused on Ginn but doesn't give off aggressive attitude. We pause for a photo. Sara Ginn and Sampson smile at each other like newlyweds, while I'm the third wheel smiling at the camera. The bond between this dog and handler is palpable. As Ginn says, "I spend more time with him than I do my husband. He comes home with me and he comes to work with me, and he doesn't answer back—it's a perfect relationship!"

Sampson is not a Trojan dog like his brother Boysie. (The Trojan K9s are trained as highly specialized antiterrorist dogs.) But Sampson is a cadaver dog. He and Ginn are trained to identify and rescue deceased victims through scent detection of blood and flesh. It's definitely not work for the faint of heart.

As Ginn remembers, "The year before it was my birthday. I was out on the cadaver training. My friends asked, 'How was your birthday?' I told them, 'Well, I spent the day digging a grave and burying a pig.'"

"Fresh or rotten?" I blurt.

"Rotten. We buy it fresh from the butcher and then we just use parts of the pig throughout the course. It gets worse as we go along."

"Is it very bad?"

"It's horrible! The smell was very strong, the smell of rotting meat. You have to make sure you have gloves on—the last thing you want is to get it on your fingers and get a bad stomach."

"I'm sure you don't want Sampson to get into it either!" I say.

"Absolutely not."

"Do you smell that?" asks Ginn, waving a hand in front of her face.

I breathe in. There's a smell in Constable Ginn's car. It's not foul, like rotting meat; it's pungent, lemony, and almost pleasant.

"That's Bite Back spray. We use it if we deal with a dangerous dog. One of the canisters compressed and went off yesterday. That's the smell."

"How do you deal with dangerous dog calls?"

Constable Ginn lists the arsenal: "We have Bite Back spray, electric shields, dog poles, a fire extinguisher. You get the occasional dog that might be a bit ballsy, a bit more in your face, and we have to deal with them, too. But nine times out of ten they back off. Pit bulls are an illegal breed here. I love the pit bull terriers, I think they are a beautiful breed to look at, a beautiful looking dog, but they're not allowed as pets."

*They are in my country*, I think. Again, it's that startling shift in perspective, that a country so similar to mine can study the safety evidence and come to such a different conclusion about which dog breeds are fit for pets and which are not. Later, Constable Ginn clarifies that while pit bulls are a banned breed in the UK, and it is against the law to own them, some are still kept, with certain provisions, including that they are insured, tattooed and chipped, and must not be bred. I look up the UK laws, and they include possible seizure of the dog if it appears to be a banned breed and it is on public property. Up to six months in prison can result for the owner, as well as the possibility of the dog being destroyed, though owners have the opportunity to prove their dog is not a danger to the public (in which case they can receive a Certificate of Exemption, valid for the rest of the dog's life.)

As the training continues, Constable Ginn teaches me about the art of decomposition, about trusting your dog to tell you when something appears to be blood and isn't, about how to read blood for clues, how to track it to its source. There are so many variables, including whether the victim has been exposed to water or not.

"Sampson's also trained in water recovery," Ginn tells me. "I think there are only five dogs trained in water recovery." (I learn later from Constable Ginn that some victim-recovery spaniels are also being trained in water searching, which will give the K9 unit more tactical options.) Constable Ginn shows me a photo of her training with Sampson on the cadaver-search course. Sampson, looking dashing in his yellow doggy life preserver, is just about to leap off the boat.

At the unit headquarters, I watch Ginn paint a sample of human blood high on a small corner of a brick wall. She dabs a bit more

Constable Sara Ginn in the boat. (Staff, Metropolitan Police Dog Section)

under a tire. Sampson tracks the blood, finds it, and alerts on it. The wall is easy; the tire proves more challenging for him. This critical work can make the difference between closure for the victim's family, and the agony of permanent uncertainty.

"He did his victim-recovery course a year ago in April. We get called to scenes of blood in the street, a pool of blood, or blood drops, and we are asked if we can pick up the trail. We get a lot of those calls. Our first blood trail was probably one of the best ones that we did. Basically a guy had collapsed in a petrol garage. He'd been stabbed or slashed, and there was blood leading from the petrol garage down the road. Then basically the blood ran out. Sampson had just come off his course. I put him on the blood trail to start. He was picking up another blood drop, another blood drop; he probably went at least half a mile until he got to an address where it was clear that a disturbance had taken place. Later it was established as the scene where it had happened. You get nervous, 'Oh gosh, I hope this works now.' There are lots of distractions for the dogs, boxes of kebabs, chicken bones, it's very different than in training."

Sampson found his way to the scene of the crime. He used a tool that no human and no machine is capable of replicating: his super-nose. Super is no exaggeration; the average dog is far superior to the average human in sensory ability, possessing an olfactory device that is between ten thousand and one hundred thousand times more acute than our own. According to James Walker, former director of the Sensory Research Institute at Florida State University, "If you make the analogy to vision, what you and I can see at a third of a mile, a dog could see at more than 3000 miles and still see as well."[5]

"Sampson switches off when he gets home," says Constable Ginn. He switches on again the minute she suits up. "When he sees the blue uniform go on, he drives me *potty*! He makes this whining noise and starts spinning around the second he hears the jangle of my belt going on. When he starts doing that, I have to get him in the car so I can get ready. He *loves* going to work; he *loves* getting into the police car."

"Is Harper working yet?" I ask.

"No, not at this age. We don't allow puppies out. When she's trained we'll let her out. At the end, she'll be trained in firearms, drugs, and cash. Fingers crossed she'll make it! She's such a little high drive thing, she's wonderful. I've had shepherds for ten years, I've been in the dogs for ten years now, nearly eleven. I joined in 2005."

"So Harper's your first spaniel?"

"Yes."

We are driving down a narrow one-lane road about as big as a North American sidewalk when two cars pass each other at alarming speed just ahead of us. I swallow hard, holding on to the door.

"So, did you and your husband go into K9 training at the same time?"

"No, David joined in 2001 and I didn't join until 2005. I just loved what he did, and I thought, 'I really fancy that as well.' He's been really lucky with his dogs.

"It's so hard when you put everything into a dog and they don't make it. The first one I had, a bitch, she did everything indoors, but if you took her out, she just wanted to chase squirrels. Then I had Jake, he was lovely, but he injured his back. He had to be retired early. After that I had Eddie; he was a gift dog. He got through the basic course with me, worked through about two months, then I was pregnant, and he got allocated to another handler. Then I got Arnie, he was a Belgian Malinois crossed with a shepherd, but his wildlife chasing was an issue, unfortunately. Then I got Sampson."

"Were you a general duty officer before?"

"Yes, I started in 1999. I worked in Brixton until 2005, where I was lucky enough to get dogs on my first application."

"In Canada it's really hard to get into the dogs section."

"Same here, we can get one hundred to one hundred and twenty applicants for six spaces. We don't always get in the first time."

A few minutes later, we pull into the puppy breeding and training facility, the second one I've ever visited, besides Innisfail. "Welcome to the dog school," says Constable Ginn with a flourish, "where all our training happens, where miracles are made!"

I follow Constable Ginn and Constable Truelove and their sergeant, Clare Masterson, into the puppy barn, where, with no prompting, we each sit down and cuddle the pups, who climb all over us,

Clare Masterson, with her new puppy and her niece. (Helen Verschoor)

biting our pants and tugging our shoelaces with their needle-sharp teeth. Protocol is different than in Innisfail, far more relaxed, and I make the most of it.

Sergeant Masterson is especially happy because, in a few short weeks, one of these fuzzy pups will be hers. Constable Emma True-love breathes deeply, inhaling the fuzzy head of the puppy snuggled in her arms. "As good as a baby," she says.

Constable Ginn and Sampson are called away to do a blood search, exactly the kind of operation where Sampson's elite training is essential. I very much want to go with them, but my daughter is waiting at her aunt's for me to pick her up, and if I go, we could be on call for hours and hours. I elect to hang out with Constable Truelove. She plans to give Prince, who smells a little ripe, a good bath.

In the puppy pen, the pups tug and climb on us. Then one puppy defecates on the cement. All the others crowd around, nudging and then lapping it up. They bumble over to me after, two of them, with crumbs of yellow puppy shit clinging to their whiskers, blinking their blue-gray eyes. I make a hasty decision to stand up.

Prince hops up in the special steel sink for washing the police dogs. He doesn't look thrilled, but he tolerates it. I am glad that Constable Truelove passed me an apron, because when Prince is done being hosed down, he shakes off, showering us both with a torrential spray.

After the bath is done, Constable Truelove runs Prince through his paces on the training equipment outside.

Truelove believes dogs need jobs. "Pet owners of dogs miss out on so much, because they could be having fun with their dogs and train-ing them. I feel sorry for a normal domestic dog, really, I just don't think they're enlightened in their world."

Prince loves to work, and responds with zest to Emma's commands to jump, climb ramps, and crawl through tunnels, and even leap through a "window."

"I absolutely love this," confides Constable Truelove on our drive back to London. "My dad was in the police. He went into the river police. They worked up and down the Thames, fishing out the bodies. From about six years old, that's all I wanted to do, was be a dog handler with the police. It shows it works: if you get a dream in your head, you can do it."

"Have you found it difficult to be a female dog handler?"

"No. I think it's a male-orientated job, but if you're aware of that, then you can deal with it. I think you're tested. I also don't think that everyone can be a dog handler. That's why they test you. I'm not saying I'm the best handler in the world, but I can do the job. I had a sergeant—he was the first person to say 'I thought I could do this job, but now I know I can't.' There's a lot of pressure on you from inspectors, chief inspectors, but you are kind of an expert in the field. It's quite a nice position to be in."

"How long have you been in policing?"

"Thirteen years. I worked in London for a publishing company for seven years. I wanted to go straight into policing, but my dad said I was too young."

"A publishing company—that will be perfect when you want to write your memoir!"

Constable Truelove laughs. "I heard you write poetry. My sister wrote one on my wedding."

It's not difficult to imagine Constable Truelove's marriage, and how close-knit her family is, having a husband and also a father who understand exactly what she does and what challenges she faces, having children who have grown up with Prince and Tanian from day one. It's a sweet picture I imagine, and when Constable Truelove shares some photos with me, they are a confirmation of exactly that sweetness. The one I like most is of her baby son, resting in complete trust and total relaxation on Prince's shoulder. I used to rest like that on the shoulder of my father's German shepherd mix, Jackson, when I was small. I never felt as secure as I did then.

■

Constable Truelove has worked hard to get where she is, but her love for what she does is palpable, even with all the challenges it brings. One challenge is the lack of support for retired police dogs. Like most officers, Constable Truelove wants to keep her K9 companions when they retire. As she tells me, "From the day the dog gets retired to you, we don't get one penny's help. It could be retired at three years. They rely on your good will." There seems to be a lot of that reliance in police dog work. The RCMP relies on volunteer labor to raise and train their puppies, and the London K9 unit relies on the bond between handler and dog to ensure the handler pays for all the dog's needs after retirement. Policy makers know that police dog handlers love their dogs, and would do anything for them, so they avoid the expense of caring for retired dogs, even though they may have significant medical needs after years of public service.

We are nearing London. Luckily for me, Constable Truelove keeps talking. "Nights are better for us, by nature of the work. At night people don't even know we've been in their gardens. We always say the cover of darkness is our friend."

I nod. I've heard this before, from almost every K9 cop everywhere. No matter how tired they get from the shift work, they prefer the solitude and freedom of working when everyone but the bad guys are asleep.

"Once, I was searching some back gardens with Sara. We climbed over a big fence, which was the only way to get out of the garden. Sara went first. Then we had to lift Prince out. Prince thought she was assaulting me and bit her."

It seems to be an unwritten rule that every K9 cop receives a few real bites from a dog.

Constable Truelove drops me off at the tube station. I wave good-bye to her and to her handsome Prince, promising to keep in touch. When I get off the tube, I pick up my daughter from her aunt's and stop in a London market to get us something for dinner. All the way home, I can't stop talking to her about Sampson and Prince and the police dog pups. When I make it back to my friend's empty flat that night, there are teeth marks in my shoes and I smell like puppies. I couldn't be happier.

■

I meet Sergeant Robert Suggitt and his dark and handsome police shepherd, Boysie, outside London's Morden tube station. The whole tube ride, I had worried I wouldn't be able to find them in the crowds of London, but Sergeant Suggitt's Ford Mondeo stands out, with its big neon green stripes and blue letters on the side that read: DOG SECTION. Sergeant Suggitt is a large man in a small car; blond and muscular, he fills the space. Boysie stares at me from his kennel in the back, black ears pricked forward, but he doesn't bark as I climb in. Boysie is one of the elite Trojan force, K9s trained to support Britain's counterterrorism units. In all of London, there are only fourteen dogs with Boysie's level of expertise. Boysie and the other Trojan dogs have a challenging role in the fight against terrorism. Boysie has to be able to turn his aggression off or on according to what-ever the situation demands, and must remain at all times equally competent at tracking and attacking. He is trained to enter a possible terrorist stronghold silently and efficiently, delivering important tac-tical information to the team of humans who depend on him, only attacking on command.

Boysie and his four brothers came to the Metropolitan Police Dog Support Unit when they were ten months old. These brothers are unusually talented, driven dogs, and I'm lucky enough to ride with two of them: Boysie and Sampson, Constable Sara Ginn's K9.

"It would have been nice to get Boysie earlier," says Suggitt, as we head to the unit. "We give our dogs to our handlers at eight weeks old." These supremely talented K9 brothers were raised in Cornwall, and came to London when they were about ten months old. "There they give them to puppy walkers. The people who had him, they hadn't let him off the lead for six months." This strategy has the distinct disadvantage of delaying the bonding and training period between police dog and handler. It is a testament to the skill of both Boysie and Sergeant Suggitt that they've managed to make up for that lost time.

The Metropolitan K9 section takes a different approach to policing than those units I've visited in the U.S. and Canada. None of the police dog handlers I meet carries a gun. It's odd to look at their belts and see no holsters.

"What is it like to not be armed?" I ask as we prepare to track through the lush green ring of countryside surrounding London, with Boysie and Hardy, Constable Ben Hendley's young and enthusiastic new dog.

Sergeant Suggitt says, "I think that if they did a poll if police officers want to be armed, over ninety percent would say no. I've never met one who *did* want to be armed."

I'm thinking of what a contrast this is to the U.S., where both citizens and cops seem locked in an arms race, and police forces are acquiring more military gear every year as a defensive strategy. He must see the pensive expression on my face, for Sergeant Suggitt says gently, "They need to be armed there, don't they, whilst the gun laws are what they are?"

I don't know how to answer. I don't know how to grapple with the violence that grips North America. It makes me sick, which is part of the reason I'm here. I want to see a different way of policing.

"They're very hard on people there, aren't they?" asks Suggitt. I nod, for it's the truth. We are all harder on each other in North America.

"Are you required to wear body cameras?" I ask.

"No. We're getting them soon, which I'm all for. I'm like, 'Bring them on!' It will take some time to do. It's twenty-eight or thirty thousand officers; that's a lot of cameras, isn't it?"

I have dressed inappropriately. I had assumed this ride-along would be through the busy streets of London. I didn't know we'd be out in rural countryside, so I'm wearing city clothes: thin dress pants, nice shoes, and a light wool sweater.

As I run after Suggitt and Boysie through stinging nettles nearly as tall as my face, I know I am following a dog of incredible drive. Boysie is on a mission, nose down to the scent, black body shooting out over the tall grass like a cannon. At the edge of the field, they turn abruptly and start downhill. "Can you still see me?" calls Constable Hendley from up ahead.

"I can *hear* you," I say, trotting as fast as I can. I scramble around some trees and find Hendley waiting for me. We make the turn downhill together. Moving quickly, I am just behind Suggitt and Boysie when Boysie finds the hide. Suggitt claps him on the shoulder and shouts his praise, wrestling with Boysie a little. On the way back to the cruiser, Boysie trots through the field proudly, tail waving like a victory flag.

Next I am invited to experience firsthand London's unique "bark and hold" method of apprehension, where criminals are stopped in their tracks by a dog savagely, furiously barking—but a dog so carefully trained that it will only sink its teeth into them if they run away or attack.

As I crouch in the nettles and brambles behind Hendley, I'm looking for that hit of adrenaline, terror mixed with odd excitement that I've experienced a few times now. Suggitt shouts "Police!" and demands that we give ourselves up. Boysie speeds through the trees, sliding to a stop just in front of us, where he barks furiously. Hendley throws him the Kong and Suggitt swings Boysie around and tells him what a hero he is.

Perhaps if I hadn't been bitten a few times already, I'd be more afraid than I am, but knowing that if I hold still, Boysie won't attack, I stay calm. Constable Hendley is beside or in front of me the whole time. My heart beats a little faster, but there is no danger that I'll need Depends.

I'm glad I got to experience the "bark and hold." This unique approach saves countless suspects from being bitten or mauled by police dogs. Of course, it can only work when a suspect doesn't have a gun; otherwise, they'd just shoot Boysie.

It is hard for an outsider like myself to tease apart why a Londoner is at far less risk of being shot than someone living in, say, Chicago. According to *USA Today*, the gun homicide rate in Wales and England is one in a million. The U.S., having six times the population, has 160 times the homicides.[6] Perhaps it is simply that one country has made owning guns illegal and the other has made it a cornerstone of its national identity.

But if the general public in London is far less likely to shoot or be shot by a police officer, the terrorist threat remains real and omnipresent, though the individual risk is still low. I ask Suggitt how they are managing.

"We've definitely got a problem. We've been luckier than most in terms of terrorist attacks because we're an island. For such attacks, we need three things: ammunition, explosives, and the people who are willing to use them." Suggitt pauses thoughtfully. "Poor old France gets hit so much. You just drive in from anywhere in Europe and you're in." These words prove to be eerily prophetic.

After chasing and catching me, Boysie has turned off the K9 rage and is ready to play. As he romps for a few minutes, I ask, "What do you think is Boysie's best quality?"

"His ability to switch on and off. He can be the most beautiful, nice, well-balanced dog. When I need it, he will switch and back me up to the hilt. I have absolutely every confidence he will deal with anything that comes his way. Which could be to his detriment, but he will *not* back down."

Boysie has only been a Trojan dog for about a year. Trojan dogs like him are there to work with the firearms team, the exceptionally skilled sharpshooter team. As Suggitt says, "We're not talking about shoplifting; this would be a high-level criminal. I'm there to support the firearms team. Ultimately, everything is down to them, and I'll just tell them what my limitations are. I'm just a tactical option for them. They don't have to use me, but nine times out of ten they will use me."

"Why might they decide not to?"

"It can be stupid things that can stop them from deploying us; for example, cats in the house. If a cat stands up to Boysie, he'd probably rip him up, as most police dogs will. If they're fairly convinced the bloke's in there, the cat might just have to take his chances."

Suggitt and Hendley work young Hardy, training him to both bark and hold and also to bark and bite a rubber ring, praising him hugely at every success. Hardy was brought in from Portugal, and is showing great promise as a new police dog, (unlike Hendley's first dog, who had to be retired after only eighteen months).

I get back in with Suggitt, and, behind us, Hendley loads Hardy and follows us down the winding country road. As we drive, I consider what it must be like to not be armed. Even though it's statistically less dangerous all around, these officers don't have that option at their disposal. I wonder if that makes them less fearful or more, but it's a tough question to answer, unless an officer has policed in both countries. "How do you deal with fear in the work you do?" I ask Suggitt.

"I'm not a big one for overthinking," says Suggitt. "I thoroughly enjoy the adrenaline. As soon as I get an arms call, it's exciting, it's absolutely wonderful. I never give it a second thought. Although I think something could happen, I think it won't happen to me. I just enjoy the calls and try to do the best job I can. Toni, my wife, always asks me if I'm worried about Boysie. Don't get me wrong: as devastated as I'd be if he were to be shot, that's his job, and he'd probably save someone's life."

"Does Boysie live in a kennel?" I ask. The trip back to London is long; we are clogged in traffic, which gives me time to ask a million questions.

"Yes, he has a kennel in the back garden. Basically when I first got him, he was so manic, he had to be there. Now when I'm in the house, he's allowed in the house. He's clean, he's chilled out with the kids, and he doesn't make a mess, so why wouldn't you let him in the house with you? He's part of the family." There's pride in Suggitt's voice. He continues:

"Here's a story to show the intelligence of a dog. It was a three-year-old girl that had gone missing. They thought she'd gone out the front door of the house. 'Have you searched the house?' I asked. Yes, of course they had searched the house. I said, 'I just want to make sure she's not hiding somewhere you've missed.' I get them all out of the house. Once they leave I see Boysie's gone underneath the dining room table. His tail's wagging. I look under the tablecloth. She's fallen asleep under there where no one could see her. Obviously we've never trained on children. It just amazed me that he realized she was a small child. He just gave her a kiss and wagged his tail."

Boysie is a dog of such intelligence and skill that he can differentiate between a terrorist and a little girl who, like Sleeping Beauty, just needs a kiss to wake up.

■

My ride-along with Constable Turner the next day is the first time I get to see the Metropolitan's English springer spaniels in action. Constable Turner picks me up outside Morden Station, and we go straight off to Camden for a drug search. Russell Turner has two dogs: a big German shepherd named Arthur, and a lovely little English spaniel named Amber. He's had Amber since she was an eight-week-old puppy, but of course no one knew then that Amber would become a champion. Although she only started police dog work in November, in four months she has claimed so many results that she won the Manning Trophy for best search dog of the year in 2016, an award given by the Metropolitan Police. Constable Turner himself is an athlete, and looks the part, toned and alert with short blond hair and blue eyes. He plays rugby on an all-police team that recently traveled to New York City to play against the NYPD—and won.

In London, defensive searches for guns or explosives are nearly all done by English springers. I have not seen these terrific little dogs recruited as K9s in Canada or much in the U.S., though one springer, Mindy, was a very successful police dog with the Maine State Police.[7] These feisty little dogs are tireless, and are able to get down low or be lifted up high to search shelves in places a shepherd couldn't manage.

As Turner says of spaniels versus shepherds, "Totally different kettle of fish they are. Spaniels just want to be loved. I've had two shepherds before that. Unfortunately a lot of shepherds are dominant dogs, dog fighters. I can't go to dog parks or anything. With the springers I can go to a pub lunch. I can take her walking. It's just a breath of fresh air, really. It's lovely."

It was Amber's job to secure Winfield House before Obama's visit to celebrate the Queen's ninetieth birthday in 2016.

"It was fantastic," says Turner. "I got to walk around the most amazing house, as well as the gardens. We were up to Windsor Castle later. We did the Queen's terrace area and all the state rooms. At home we don't let Amber in the house. At Windsor House, she goes into the state rooms, she goes into the Queen's private room. She's not allowed in my house, but she's perfectly able to go into the Queen's quarters and clear them."

Turner continues, "There was a job at central London. It was probably the best job I've had with Amber. We were working with the City of London Police. We've got this guy we've been watching for some time. They arrest him. He's arrogant, very confident. 'Here's the keys for my house, go search my house,' he says. I open up the cupboard, there's boxes and boxes of trainers (athletic shoes). Amber gets up on a box, I pull it out, open it up, it's just full of cocaine. I think it came to a street value of thirty thousand pounds. I'd love to be in an interview with him. We don't get to interview people. But he went guilty, he admitted." I agree that it would be hard to deny a shoe box full of cocaine.

"What's the hardest thing for you doing the job you do?"

"I've got two young kids. The hardest thing for me is shift work, late nights coming home to two kiddies, when a three- and five-year-old are getting up. That's pretty difficult. It's brutal, really hard. The hardest thing I've found with kids anyway is fatigue, but the shift work doesn't help." Shift work is brutal on anyone, but it is a special kind of hell for policing parents, who have to sleep, or not, around the needs and noises of their children.

"My wife does shift work as well, not night duty, but early days."

From Constable Turner I hear again that keeping pit bulls is illegal in London, although breeding and buying them continues under the radar. One breed, the Staffordshire bull terrier, has become a status symbol in London gang culture.

"Us handlers go to the dangerous dogs calls. It's very much a gang culture to have a big rough Staffie, which in my opinion is a big lovable dog. If one of these dogs has bitten a human, even if the bite's very minimal, the magistrates will put some rules or regulations on it. Once it's bitten someone once, you can't be seen to put it out on the street."

Both PC Sara Ginn and Turner have mentioned the legal restraints on pit bull ownership in London. I have a mistrust of pit bulls, stemming from the fact that my son witnessed a female pit bull tear apart a miniature pinscher and eviscerate it. A girl and her mother were walking their two miniature pinschers on our street, both leashed, when a pit bull ran across the street and attacked. The pit bull was also leashed and was muzzled, but the muzzle was loose, and did not prevent the dog from ripping into one of the two pinschers. I rushed out just after the owner of the pit bull had fled the scene, dragging her dog with her. The girl whose dog had been torn apart was distraught, holding her surviving dog to her chest, as her mother fled to the nearest animal hospital with her fatally wounded little dog in her arms. I petted the daughter's other little pinscher, Mary, who was trembling violently, and waited with them both for her mother to return from the vet, where the dying Yuri was put down.[8]

After the mother returned and they drove away, I walked home slowly, feeling sick to my stomach. That was the week our dog Dandy stopped being friendly to other dogs. Before that time, she'd want to play with any dog she met. After that day, sensing the change in me, she'd leap aggressively at any dog that came by, barking wildly. This is a ridiculous (and potentially lethal) habit for a Maltipoo. From that day on, I've picked her up when I see any large dogs coming our way, particularly pit bulls.

London has once again chosen a different path from Vancouver, my city, or most American cities, legislating public safety and the greater good over the personal choice to have potentially lethal dogs. Many people I know who would absolutely support gun control would fiercely protest legislation against pit bulls, and yet there is evidence for both in terms of public health and safety.

Constable Turner drives me, Arthur, and Amber through the clogged streets of London to search a house for drugs. The detectives are waiting, but nothing can help us speed up the snarl of traffic that is London. As we crawl along, I point out two mounted police officers, each riding a massive dark horse. I get my camera ready: I've always been horse crazy. And then the best thing happens.

"Is that my wife?" asks Turner. "It is!" He rolls down the window and calls out, "Hello!" I hop out and snap a quick photo of Liz, his wife, on horseback with her police partner. *What a cool marriage*, I think to myself. As well as being a mounted police officer, Liz is a champion in dressage.

Husband and wife say a hurried good-bye. Traffic is moving along at about the pace of a walking police horse, and finally we reach our destination. We enter a run-down apartment where a mother lives with her grown son, a convicted drug dealer. The living room is stuffed with garbage bags full of clothes and cushions; searching here will not be easy.

"We'll have to ask you to step into the other room while we search," says one of the officers to the mother, a tired-looking white woman.

"Oh, go on, then," she says, with a sigh, flapping a hand at us, and wanders into the kitchen. Amber is already tugging at her leash, desperate to begin.

German shepherds are competent and capable searchers, and I've seen many successful finds. But Amber is like the Energizer Bunny. While Amber leaps onto sofas and shelves, squirms under beds and into boxes and bundles (the walls are stacked nearly to the ceiling with bags and boxes of stuff), her nose is alive, taking in audible whooshes of scent as she works room after room. I've never seen anything like it. Without being lifted up, she identifies a stash on a high shelf, alerting Turner with a clear, unmistakably fixed gaze. As Turner rewards her, Amber does a happy dance. It's true, what Turner says: a spaniel like Amber is a completely different kettle of fish.

■

The United Kingdom as a whole has a lower number of minority police officers than the U.S., a total of 5.5 percent, with the Metropolitan Police in London having the largest representation of minorities of any force, at almost 12 percent. Interestingly in terms of gender and violence, the UK has achieved more gender equity than either Canada or the U.S., with 44.5 percent female officers.[9] Although London is one of the most ethnically diverse cities in the world, its police force does not reflect that diversity. Yet despite not having representative diversity, neither London nor the rest of the United Kingdom are plagued by the kind of violence and distrust as the U.S. British cops kill the same number of people in a year that American cops kill in a day. Those few British cops who are licensed to carry firearms are extensively trained, and are not allowed to open fire except under extreme circumstances. The emphasis, as Sir Peter Fahy of the Manchester Police explains, is on preservation of life. "There's a huge emphasis on human rights . . . I constantly remind our officers that their best weapon is their mouths. Your first consideration is, 'Can you talk this through? Can you buy yourself time?'"[10]

I did not have any intention of becoming obsessed with police training tactics when I set out to learn about police dogs, but it happened anyway. It wasn't possible to spend time in the company of police officers and not be challenged to think how things could be done better. And I believe that the U.S. police departments would be better served by following some of the more stringent training protocols in the UK. I don't believe it is possible for officers in the U.S. to patrol without guns, but I believe changing officer training techniques would preserve citizens' lives in the U.S. even without stricter gun control (which I also advocate as a public safety measure). In the UK, training to become a firearms officer is rigorous and difficult.

I have spent some time pondering what it must be like to be an African American police officer at this point in U.S. history, when many members of the African American community are fighting back against police brutality, and everyone has been touched, even vicariously, by the simmering tensions playing out around them. According to *The Wall Street Journal*, African Americans make up just 12 percent of all local police officers in the U.S., while the population is 13.2 percent.[11]

But those statistics surprised me, not because they are bad, but because they are pretty good. Of course, they could be better. Hispanics actually have less representation, being on average 17 percent of the U.S. population, and being represented by approximately 10 percent of police officers working.[12] But it is clear that the violence that plagues the streets of America will not be remedied by hiring more minority cops alone, at least not if they are men.

*The Wall Street Journal* quotes FBI statistics which show fifty-eight thousand African American police officers working in America in 2013.[13] Each of them has his or her own story about what it is like to navigate that fraught ground between wearing a badge and being a member of an oppressed minority. I have always found much to learn from people who navigate such complex identities, who are able to see both sides of an issue, because they belong to both. We need to listen to these people, to seek out their stories, the people who both experience discrimination and have made a career out of defending and protecting citizens from harm. And it is time American police forces (and the American public) listen to and learn from forces in other countries who are doing the same job, but doing it better—with fewer lives lost, with more funding, more support, and more training for their police officers, and with a greater respect both for human rights and the rights of officers to work in a safe environment. Clearly, more research needs to be conducted on how female police officers defuse violent situations without lives being lost. Clearly, the U.S. and Canada too have much to learn that would benefit the public from police units in the United Kingdom.

My experience with the police dog teams was positive in every country I visited. Whether it was California or Vancouver Island, the officers I met were people I genuinely liked. But in London, the police officers I met were happier than anywhere else. There wasn't the same kind of armor that I saw with officers like Faulkcon and Darrell Moores and Michelle Onysko. When I saw Sara Ginn and Emma Truelove with the puppies, they were just joyful in what they did, genuinely delighted at their good fortune. They loved their jobs and were proud of being K9 cops, as were all the other officers I met. The difference was, the London K9 officers didn't have that added layer of stress and conflict with the public that I saw in forces in other countries. Both the male and female K9 officers in London were more open and less guarded, and I thought to myself how lucky they were to be policing a country where they don't have to think about killing people or being shot and killed while making a routine traffic stop or domestic violence intervention. They don't carry that added burden, a burden that can shift in a handful of seconds to a deep trauma. The social contract is distinct in London: it's built on faith, not force, and that makes all the difference.

# 7

## Grave Threats

They say Paris is a city of contrasts, and I affirm that this is true. In the evening, I dine at my in-laws' elegant apartment with family friends who discuss just who in their circle is selling their château, and who else is on the market looking for a new castle (but just a small one) to buy. The next morning, I will take the metro and a commuter train to the outer suburbs of Paris, where I will spend the day watching antiterrorist SWAT teams run through their drills in the bowels of the city, and be attacked by dogs wearing steel-reinforced muzzles, dogs who have learned to torpedo through the air to body-punch instead of bite.

I don't know it yet, but I am soon to be *renversée*, bowled over. Literally.

I have been lost in London, lost in the wilds of British Columbia, and lost on the back roads of Washington State. I resign myself to getting thoroughly lost crossing Paris from Neuilly to the huge police facility just past the very edge of Paris on the other side of the city, in the 12th arrondissement. I follow the directions Commandant Sylvain Heritier has sent: first a metro, then a suburban train, and the grand finale—a twenty-minute walk through light rain. The yellow mud of Paris sticks to my shoes as I make the long trek through the woods, following my map, but not trusting it. It becomes my own personal treasure hunt: I pass the national headquarters for the police, follow the path for twenty minutes along a road, past the most famous hippodrome (racetrack) in Paris. Then I traverse a parking lot and find myself standing outside a high blue gate, where I've been instructed to ring the bell and wait to be let in.

Commandant Sylvain Heritier welcomes me into his office, a small portable trailer with a desk, a cluttered couch, and an espresso machine. He's a solid, olive-skinned man with a shaved head, a big nose, and deep-set, dark intelligent eyes. The police dog unit is a curious mix of ancient and modern, with the stone wall that frames one end of the unit one of the original defensive walls of Paris, and the prefab trailers, obviously, quite new. Portables are used here, Heritier explains, because when the city of Paris was being built, the dirt was moved to this very ground, which remains unstable.

Sylvain Heritier doesn't come from a police family, and never set out to be one of only two commanders in all of France for the Brigade Cynophile, the French K9 Brigade. He had planned to make a career in law. But when policing beckoned, Commandant Heritier never looked back. As we talk, the commandant mentions an early childhood event that marked him: when he was ten, he and his family were robbed.

"It was a violent theft," he tells me. "Doors were broken, things were thrown all over the place. But when the police came, they really reassured me. I was deeply impressed."

"So your first contact with the police was positive," I say.

"*Oui. Très positif.*"

Likewise, Commandant Heritier's love of dogs springs from boyhood. When he became commander of the police dog unit, he was not a police dog handler, and was under no obligation to take the three months of training required of all French police dog handlers. He did it anyway.

"I had a prejudice that it was easy to be a dog handler—you just go ahead, just attack! Those three months showed me that what I thought would be easiest was the most difficult. It was more difficult than my law studies. I had to learn how to work with a dog, how to understand dogs, how to talk to them. It was very precise work. For three months we thought only about our dogs. For three months, we dreamed of dogs."

Because Commandant Heritier not only is the commander of the force but also understands how police dog teams actually work out on the streets, he has a deep appreciation for the members of his unit. He has generously set up a week of training for me in all sorts of situations, with various Brigade members. It is to be, as he says, my own apprenticeship into police work with dogs in Paris. In preparation, I am sent an official program with useful facts about the Brigade and a schedule for my week's adventures. (The fact sheet notes, helpfully, that these eighty dogs produce thirteen tons of "croquettes" per year—that's a lot of caca!)

We are soon joined by Brigadier Bertrand Bonnamy, who comes to show off his little female Malinois, Djimanthie. Bonnamy is a friendly man, easy to talk to, even with my hesitant French. He's married to a cop who works as an inspector in Paris. They have two young kids. Djimanthie, age seven, is a dog that got a second chance.

When she was eight months old, Djimanthie was rescued from the SPA, the *Société de Protection des Animaux* (the French equivalent of the SPCA), where she was on death row, soon to be injected for the long sleep. "She was so little," recalls Bertrand, "and so fierce!" Bertrand knows nothing about her owners, but thinks it very likely she was abused. She would cower when he would raise his hand, and her aggression flared unpredictably at first. But he was an experienced and patient police dog handler, and he saw remarkable potential in this tough little Malinois. A skinny, short-haired, reddish dog with a permanent grin, Djimanthie has a fighting spirit. As Bonnamy tells me, Djimanthie has a place waiting for her at his house when she retires. "This little sweetheart is part of my life and part of my family," says Bonnamy.

Djimanthie, and many of the other dogs of the Brigade, are garbage dogs. Thrown away by owners who no longer want them, or who find them too aggressive, these dogs are rescued and rehabilitated by the Brigade. Indeed, the Brigade Cynophile is the only police unit I know of where most of the police dogs are former rescues. The rescue and rehabilitation of these amazing animals is, obviously, a great accomplishment. At the same time, it shows how cash-starved the Brigade program is; most countries either buy their dogs from specialized breeders, or raise their own in controlled breeding facilities, where they can ensure the quality of the process and the results at every step. Even without the resources many other countries have, the Brigade is full of success stories of survivor dogs like Djimanthie.

Djimanthie's first task will be to search for drugs. Brigadier Bertrand opens one of the heavy black cases in which all the drug samples are stored, and asks me to choose a couple. The Brigade has a veritable smorgasbord of drugs and a roll of real euros (carefully cut in half) for training purposes. The cases also contain injectable antidotes for dogs that have ingested any drugs while working, as certain substances can prove fatal to a canine within fifteen minutes. Djimanthie is trained to alert on a number of drugs, as well as on cash. Bonnamy invites me to select the drugs, but I can't seem to make up my mind. Finally, we decide on crack cocaine and the roll of euros. Bonnamy handles all the drugs and bills with tweezers so as to avoid contamination. When both finds have been hidden, Djimanthie is brought in to search. She's hot to trot, straining against the harness in her eagerness to get to work and find the hides. This is a dog that wants nothing more than to prove herself.

Within a few minutes of being released to search, she has found the crack, which she identifies by going nuts, scraping and biting at the cupboard in which it has been hidden. There's no mistaking her signal. There's also no mistaking the bond between Djimanthie and Bertrand Bonnamy. Whenever she looks up at her handler, this dog grins. It's as if she knows just who saved her, and wants to be sure he feels the love. Djimanthie got a reprieve. She's seven, so in a year or so, she'll be retired, and she'll spend the last years of her life at home with her handler. Djimanthie has cheated death to serve France.

■

The Cynophile unit is a hive buzzing with constant activity. The name of the unit in English, the Dog Lover Unit, sounds strange in translation, but I come to like it. After all, you can't be a K9 officer without being a dog lover. It is a fundamental fact that goes beyond training differences, beyond language or culture—every single K9 officer I meet is an unofficial member of the Dog Lover Unit. Officers jog outside with their dogs, dogs bark and whine from the kennels, people pop in and out of Commandant Heritier's office with questions and reports, and dog teams and aggressors train in the fenced-in yard beyond the trailers. I follow the commandant, taking it all in.

It is peculiar to North American eyes to see tough, grizzled French cops greet each other by kissing bonjour on each cheek. Not everyone does this, but some do; the rest shake hands. And everyone, without exception, says hello and shakes hands with everyone else, including me, every single time they pass. It takes a lot of time, but to do otherwise would be considered rude. We do a lot of hopping up, greeting, kissing, and sitting down again. Keeps the blood flowing.

On my second day of training, I meet Major David Berceau, Bertrand Bonnamy's boss. He's a hard-faced man with hooded blue eyes that he trains on me with a piercing intensity, but he answers every question I ask with a thoughtfulness and patience that soon puts me at ease.

"How did you become a police dog handler?" I ask.

"Me, I was always passionate about dogs," he says. "As part of the Brigade Cynophile I was able to combine my two great passions. But it's not that the police work made me interested in dogs. Working with dogs came first for me. I had a French Ring Sport dog before I ever became part of the Brigade."

Major Berceau explains about French Ring Sport. Related to the German sport of Schutzhund, it differs in a number of training aspects. The word Schutzhund in German means "protection dog" and this sport tests dogs to see if they are competent working, tracking, and protection dogs. While both Schutzhund and Ring demand demonstrations of obedience, in Ring competitions, for example, the

Major David Berceau (Courtesy of Major David Berceau)

dogs are worked without a leash or collar, and in protection work, they are allowed to bite anywhere on the body.

David Berceau worked very hard to get where he is now. He has trained police dog units all over the world, in Mexico, in Chad, and even in Iran.

"It was all interesting. Chad was fascinating. Mexico, too. Iran, I found challenging."

"I'm not going to Iran, as much as I'd find it fascinating. Not for this book," I tell the major.

"No, for you as a woman I would not recommend it. Even for me, it was difficult. I had concerns."

The major's first narcotics dog, Pacha, was awarded a hero's medal. The major tells me that Pacha was the first dog to be decorated from a Paris K9 unit, by the Société Centrale Canine, for acts of courage and devotion. After superstar Pacha, he had Gullit, and then a female dog, Guess, who specialized in explosives detection by laser.

With David Berceau I make a stupid French mistake. He's telling me the names of his dogs, and what they each specialized in, and I'm taking notes in an odd mélange of English and French that makes sense only to me, and even then, not all the time. The phrase in French for a drug detection dog is *un chien stupéfiant*, which is often shortened to *un chien stupe*. When he's talking about his dogs, I think he says, *"Mon chien, Stupe,"* and I write it down as his dog's name, which is, when you think about it, really funny. "My dog, Drug." What the major's actually saying is his dog is *"un chien stupe"* a drug-searching dog. It is a testament to his professionalism that when he catches my error, his mask never breaks—there's not even a glimpse of a smile from him as my face grows hot.

Major Berceau is the first to tell me, without any preamble, about the role the Brigade Cynophile had during the terrorist attacks at

Guillit hanging as he searches a bus. (Major David Berceau)

the Bataclan on November 13, 2015. In these coordinated attacks, 130 people were killed by terrorists armed with machine guns.

"We were called there immediately. We used our dogs to get the bodies out. We had to use dogs because there was still the risk of explosives, either in or on the bodies. There might have been explosive vests that were only partially detonated; there were other risks. It was a terrible thing. I saw pieces of flesh, dismembered body parts, and blood, so much blood. It affected us all. It affected the dogs as well as the police."

What do you say to such a revelation? I force myself to meet his eyes and listen quietly. I have no words in either language that will comfort.

"It was terrible," he says again. "But we had to do it. We had to be sure that the place was clear of explosives so no one else got hurt."

Since the Bataclan attacks, the unit has been working hard on what to do in the next event. No one pretends Bataclan was an isolated attack. Major Berceau walks me through what they will do in a future situation. First, they would use a remote-controlled car to disrupt the Internet and phone lines so the terrorists can't make phone calls. Then they send in a dog team. A special forces dog will go to a door silently, at the command of his handler, and indicate by looking at the door whether there are explosives behind the door or not. As Berceau says, "I don't want my dog hurt. But the alternative is that one of us goes to that door, and then the whole unit faces the explosives. There are choices to make. I think it's a good choice."

Our talk is informative, but not easy. But when we head to the training grounds near the racetracks, and I see Berceau with a SWAT team, preparing for a raid on a terrorist cell, my mouth goes dry. Who are these men who crouch forward, a dog unleashed, walking silently between their legs, into a room where they are likely to be blown up? Who are these men who wear life so lightly that the rest of us are free to post kitten photos on Facebook and complain about the high cost of raising kids these days?

What I mean is, after hearing Berceau's recollections, these exercises do not feel like exercises. They feel terribly real. Do you think altruism is putting a coin in the hands of a homeless man? Passing sandwiches to strangers at a food bank or shelter? Rehabilitating injured wildlife? Yes, I've done all that. But here I have seen another example of altruism. It doesn't look anything like I want it to look. Maybe it looks nothing like you imagined. Maybe it looks like what I see: a row of men with weapons drawn, running down an underground tunnel into the brutal jaws of jeopardy.

"How did the attacks change you?" I ask. "How did they change the way you work?"

"We are much more prepared now. Within the international context, we have to be prepared for the eventuality of the next attack. We have to be aware of the risks."

"And what about for you personally?"

"What I saw will stay in my head all my life," says Major Berceau. "To see what happened to those people, who went to listen to some music on a café terrace . . ."

His voice drops off. We sit in silence for a moment, a silence so deep it could be a prayer. There is nothing to be said.

■

Trainer Stéphane Goubet is a specialist in defense intervention. At present, his training duties prevent him from having a police dog of his own. But he knows the dogs of the Brigade well, having trained so many of them. These are dogs for whom the Brigade was their last chance. Staff at the SPA know what kind of dogs the police unit is looking for.

As Goubet says, "They always call us. They say, 'Look, we have a dog that's going to be put down. He has too much character to get the needle.' Sometimes it's a divorce: they have kids, they don't want the dogs anymore. So SPA will call us, 'We have a dog to give you.' We test it. Does it play well, is it aggressive? Then we decide where it goes."

"Are all the dogs rescues?"

"No. There's a budget for buying dogs, but it's small. We can spend twelve hundred euros maximum. We buy some dogs, but very few."

In the RCMP in Canada, a fully-trained, operational police dog sells for $10,000 or more. In contrast, the Brigade gets its dogs untrained, rescued from this holding tank where dogs go to be adopted— or to be killed. "We find great dogs," says Stéphane Goubet.

"What happens after the dogs are finished working? After they retire?"

"After they retire, it's usually their masters who keep them, but if not we have a waiting list of people who take them. We don't put them in families, but we always find a place. We have a long list of people waiting for our dogs. Also, some of the dogs go into film after. There's one person who takes some of them to be film stars."

With the right handler, these dogs would be great in action movies. They are smart, feisty, and willing to work. Their lives are a fraught story with a happy ending. The discarded dogs are rehabilitated. They get a second chance. They learn a job, and bond deeply with a handler. These dogs work hard for a number of years, and then, if nothing goes wrong, they are rewarded with a few years of hardwon rest and excellent care.

Most working dogs in the Brigade are kenneled on location at night. They are out working and training most of the day, but at night they sleep like soldiers in a barrack. It isn't a comfortable life, or an easy one, and I can't help wishing all these dogs got to go home with their handlers, as they do in the other countries I've visited. Yet, if dogs need a purpose, these dogs know theirs. They work with spirit and eagerness, and they take pride in their work. How do I know? It is in the vigor and zest with which they do their jobs, the pleased pride they exhibit when they are successful at their jobs, and the intensity of the bond they share with their handlers.

Are they fundamentally happy dogs? It is hard to answer that question. They are happy at work; that's undeniable, and they work a lot.

Dandy, our family dog, is a pet, not a working K9. But even so, she has three jobs: to tuck in and comfort the kids at night, to lick their ears when they are sad, and to bark when someone knocks on the door. Other than that, she spends the rest of her days snoozing, head on my slipper, or belly-up on the couch. Her walks are short, unless we get to go to the beach for a run or a ride in the kayak. Sometimes she heaves a deep sigh that sounds to my ears like boredom. She would probably be happier with a more purposeful, more stimulating life, even if it were less comfortable.

Around me, the new recruits are working together to bandage the hind leg of a dog named Rocky, who is not thrilled about the application of antibiotic cream to his wound. Two hold his head and talk to him while two care for his leg.

I find myself standing next to a brand new, young, and very friendly

Pierre Nachbar and Nicky, the rescue dog. (Pierre Nachbar)

human recruit, Pierre Nachbar. His rank is Gardien de la Paix, the English equivalent of a general duty police officer. Nachbar tells me with pride in his voice about his dog, Nicky. He promises to introduce us soon.

Later, another dog that has been running a fever is brought into the yard to have his temperature taken. The recruits work as a group, some at his head, soothing the dog, some at the hind end.

There is some good-natured ribbing. I don't catch all of it, but enough to get the gist. "He's not fighting this," someone says as the thermometer slips under the tail. "Look at him. Your dog likes it."

"Ha ha."

"Did the thermometer go in?" demands Goubet. The recruit nods.

"How far in?"

The recruit shows him, his fingers and thumb measuring the depth of the thermometer. "Watch out you don't get shit on you," someone calls.

"How long did you leave it in?" demands Goubet.

The temperature reads as normal. But Goubet is not satisfied, and the procedure is repeated. The dog seems nonplussed about the whole event, every once in a while turning to look over his shoulder at what the recruits are doing to his derrière.

As the recruits clean up and prepare their dogs for training, Goubet teaches me how defense dogs are trained by the Brigade.

"The dogs are muzzled here by law. We are only allowed to remove the muzzles in certain situations, when the suspect is armed. We see videos on YouTube of dogs in America biting people who are not armed, and we think, 'Wow. If we did that we would be in prison.'"

It's a unique approach, one I don't fully appreciate until I am standing on the grass being charged by an attack dog.

"Is it a problem, working with dogs who are muzzled?" I ask.

"It can be a problem in hot weather. It can be hazardous for the dogs to work. They can't cool themselves properly with the muzzles on."

That's not really what I mean. The question I want to ask is how a muzzled dog can possibly defend anyone. But I won't find out by asking. I'll find out by being on the receiving end of an attack.

Commandant Heritier introduces me to another member of the Brigade. He gives me only his initial, J., and instructs me not to photograph his face unmasked. J. is at too much risk. As a member of the BRI, the Brigade's SWAT. team, J. was called to duty on November 13. J. has a long, noble face, like a portrait of an ancient saint, with deep-set black eyes and a black beard splashed with silver on each side.

Rocky, the dog that was being bandaged earlier, is J.'s dog. He has had him since September 2014, inheriting him from a colleague who left.

We sit down and speak of hard things. This time I think I'm more prepared.

J. was in a SWAT column during the attacks. SWAT team members are not members of the Cynophile, though they work together closely. J. was one of two members who went in. The other isn't working now because he was injured, but he's also a member of the Paris Brigade Cynophile.

"Bataclan was not my first intervention with Rocky," says J. "We were also working together with the SWAT team during the Porte de Vincennes attacks at the Jewish market. We were part of the final assault and rescue of the hostages."

The Porte de Vincennes terrorist attacks on January 9, 2015, occurring in the wake of the Charlie Hebdo murders two days earlier, left four Jewish hostages dead. Individuals within the market, both

Jewish and Muslim, resisted heroically (even at the cost of their own lives), and a number of lives were spared because of their actions. J. and Rocky are part of a battle-seasoned antiterrorist intervention team.

"What was your feeling when you were going in there?" I ask.

"For Bataclan, it was a very particular feeling. I didn't know I was going into that place. It was so exceptional, so out of the ordinary. In the days after, it wasn't images that came, but really a feeling of strangeness in the head. As if, 'This is not possible.' Intellectually, it's bizarre. How could this have happened?"

"It must be so difficult for you, for your family too," I say.

"At the beginning," says J., "I didn't tell my family what I did. For my wife, there's an anguish. She knows what I do. We live directly in the line of danger. The risk is continual."

"After the 13 November attacks, was the training different?"

"Yes. Before, we weren't prepared to intervene in mass killings. We train differently now."

"How do you find the courage to do what you do?" I ask.

"To serve, to be of service . . . There have to be people who fight these things. We have to have people to do it." J. pauses. "That's a good question." He pauses again. "In fact, it's better not to think too much about it."

This is my cue to change the subject.

"Tell me about Rocky," I say.

J. smiles for the first time in our interview. His whole face is transformed, talking about his dog. "Rocky? We also call him Scrat, from the movie *Ice Age*, because Rocky is funny like this character. Do you know that movie?"

"Yes!"

"Rocky, he listens well, he works well, but he's a bit funny."

If Rocky, aka Scrat, has a funny side, it's one he shares only with

J. The dog I see is a fighter through and through. Often it's only their handlers who see the true personalities of their dogs; I see only the public face.

Commandant Heritier has a van waiting to drive us to a training area. Stéphane Goubet and I head out to where the new recruits have loaded their dogs into a van. We are going out to practice, so I can see up close how the dogs of the Brigade fight while muzzled—and when their muzzles come off.

I load up in the truck with the new recruits, sitting across from Pierre Nachbar. His little Malinois, Nicky, balances in a small wire cage perched on top of the cage of another dog. Nicky is a striking female with a golden coat and a dark face and paws. Nicky, like most of the dogs in the Paris Brigade Cynophile, was a dog on death row.

Nachbar tells me that Nicky has become a mascot to the new recruits, because she's such a gentle and obedient dog. Ironically, her owners had relinquished her to be put to sleep because they said she was vicious. She was mere days away from death when she was adopted by the Brigade, and then by Nachbar. They are a dynamic duo.

■

The next day in Paris, I meet with a family friend, David Desforges. Born and raised in Paris, David is curious about my days with the Brigade Cynophile. His sister, Bénédicte Desforges was a Parisian cop who wrote a bestselling memoir, *Police, Mon Amour—Chroniques d'un flic ordinaire* (*Police, My Love—Stories of an Ordinary Cop*) about her experiences. David takes me to Le Winston and buys me a grand crème, espresso with milk. "So," he says. "Why are you interested in police dogs anyway?"

David is not the first to ask me why I should be drawn to write about K9 cops. Everyone wants to know what a poet is doing riding around with these cops and their dangerous dogs. For me, it's not nearly as strange as it appears. Neither does it feel out of character. The best part of being a writer, for me (aside from making things out of words) is entering other worlds, connecting to those who are nothing like me and somehow finding common ground. Writing allows me to be an amateur anthropologist, and to experience things I would otherwise never see or do. I enjoy the challenge of being in places where I don't belong.

"Perhaps it is because of my sister," says David, "that I have this natural sympathy toward the police. Others, who are less sympathetic, feel that the occasional riot is necessary to let off steam, and usher in change. I've never agreed."

And then David says something about policing that remains one of the truest things I've ever heard. "When you are disordered inside, you crave order in the external world. That's how it is for me."

It was one of those *Aha!* moments. Is it not one of my truest reasons for writing, to make order out of chaos? I crave order in the external world. Terrorism, violence, sexual assault, shooting sprees, police brutality, rioting crowds after a soccer game, injustice in any form— all these tear at me. I don't care much what people think, but I find random destructive disorder intolerable. At the same time, I never crave order over justice, over individual human beings. Physical violation repels me. My first trip to New York City, in the bus terminal, I watched a mother repeatedly slam her young daughter into a seat, the girl's head smacking as it hit, again, again. I called a security guard, made him follow me, and then got away as fast as I could so I wouldn't have to watch. To hear. To know I would never know the end of the story.

I am disordered inside. I write to impose order, even if it's an imagined order. In this sense, I identify with these rough cops and their dogs. They want to make everything safe. They want to force everyone to follow the rules.

France is unique in both its idealism and in some of the challenges it faces in maintaining the peace. In its insistence on being a color-blind society, France doesn't gather general population racial statistics at all.[1]

It is also very difficult to find accurate statistics on citizens killed by police in France. A study quoted in *Le Monde* reported that almost one hundred citizens were killed by police forces between 2005 and 2015, though this included those who died in car crashes while being pursued. At the same time, between six and twelve policemen are killed in the line of duty every year.[2] For a population of 66.03 million, these numbers are impressively low, though of course every death is a tragedy.

It is evident, despite the beautiful political discourse and noble history, that France has numerous simmering racial tensions, and that racial minorities are frustrated by their lack of police protection and support. Over thirteen thousand demonstrators gathered in Paris recently to protest lack of protection of the Chinese community from police, after a series of racially motivated attacks. "If we don't even get a basic welcome in the police station, people start to wonder," said Wang Yunzhou.[3]

Other minority groups have their own complaints and concerns. France has adopted a radically secular approach that often is at odds with those who wish to publicly show their faith.[4] Although the National Institute for Demographic Studies in France announced that 20 percent of the police workforce was of foreign origin, these statistics do not differentiate between Europeans and visible minorities.[5] Although there is a push to employ more female police officers, the lack of statistics makes it hard to tease out how many barriers remain for women. They make up 27.3 percent of the national police force, but this does not separate how many of those positions are administrative, out of the line of fire. It is unclear how many women are on the front lines, dealing with the public.[6] And through all these simmering tensions, embodying the noble but imperfectly realized values of the state and charged to protect all its citizens, the Brigade Cynophile continues its dangerous work.

■

I spend most of the next day in the passages and tunnels under the Hippodrome, the most famous horse racing and showing arena in Paris. I am once again under the watch of brigadier and trainer Stéphane Goubet. J. and Rocky bring up the rear of the SWAT team, providing cover as they go through the tunnel. I have to keep reminding myself that this is only an exercise, that there are no actual terrorists lurking in the hidden passages or tunnels. It is terribly easy to imagine the training as real.

Whenever there is an antiterrorist training exercise, of course, the dogs are unmuzzled. They don't need a command to bite—as soon as the muzzle is removed, that's the command they need to attack as soon as a suspect appears—it's all systems go. These are dogs trained to cover ground in silence. There are no verbal commands given. J. holds a whistle in his hand, one that works at decibels only dogs can hear. He uses this whistle to tell Rocky when to enter a room and when to return. J. and Rocky work at the back of a column of cops, providing protection and coverage. Rocky walks between J.'s legs, matching step to step in a seamless pas de deux.

After the terrorist training is completed, the new recruits work their dogs in muzzle intervention and defense. It is a curious thing, to watch muzzled defense dogs in action. They use their bodies as weapons, their heads as battering rams, punching with their steel-reinforced muzzles. Inside the muzzles is soft protective padding, so the dogs' sensitive noses won't be hurt with the blow. The dogs, basically, have learned to box with their heads. A well-placed blow can

Underground tactical exercise with J., Rocky and the B.R.I. team. (Rachel Rose)

knock someone's wind out. Those few precious moments give the human members of the team enough time to regain control of the situation, make an arrest, and get the suspect into handcuffs. The other interesting thing about muzzled dog attacks is that they almost never have lasting effects on the suspects, unlike North American K9 techniques, which can leave deep puncture wounds and scars.

Down in the tunnels under the racetracks, dog after dog goes through the exercise, hurling through the air to hit the agitator. Each K9 head-butt to the chest produces a tremendous amount of force.

I am impressed, once again, by the human and K9 ingenuity. The police officers of the Brigade, constrained by law to using muzzled dogs, have taught their dogs to launch themselves like canine torpedoes. The dogs, constrained by their handlers, have taught themselves to hit the face rather than the chest. It's like brass knuckles stuck on the end of an eighty-pound fist.

Every time I see a dog root out a hidden agitator and bring him down, there is a rush I'm not proud of—the vicarious, primitive thrill of the hunt, the rush spectators must have felt in the gladiator ring.

"Do you want to try an attack?" Stéphane Goubet asks me unexpectedly.

"Yes. No!" I say. "I don't know. Can I watch some more and make up my mind?"

Goubet agrees. I watch all afternoon, attacks both muzzled and free-bite, but I can't make up my mind whether or not to try one myself. I had no intention of experiencing another dog attack. Even as an observer, I can see how powerful the blows are. I don't want to get hurt so far from home. Who am I kidding? I don't want to get hurt, period. Been there, done that.

I overhear Stéphane tell the commandant I may try an attack myself, which puts the pressure on. I also don't love that there are at least ten other people, half of them experienced K9 cops, and the other half tough new recruits, who will be watching me. And yet I know that nothing compares to firsthand experience. We near the end of the training session; only a couple of dogs are waiting to go through the exercise.

Goubet asks me again, "So, do you want to try?"

"I don't know!" I wail. "I do want to try, but I don't want to get hurt. I want the experience without the pain!"

"That I can't give you," he says.

"I just don't want to be injured," I say.

"It almost never causes permanent injury," says Commandant Heritier. "It's not like a baton strike. There's a shock, but I've never seen a fracture or a long-term injury."

Just what does the commandant mean by "a shock"?

The teams finish their last attack. The agitator is pouring sweat. He has been attacked again and again all day, without a break. Most teams I've seen in other countries switch agitators out during training exercises to give them a break, but not the Brigade. They just keep it coming, one attack after another, one dog and then the next. The dogs who like to punch to the face knock the agitator's helmet back, snapping his neck most unpleasantly.

It is not until Goubet asks me for a third time that I find myself saying, "Fine. I'll try it. I hope it won't hurt too much."

He flashes a smile my way, and leads me to the change room to put on the protective gear. I have never felt this much reluctance in my life.

"I really don't want to get hit in the face," I confess.

"The trick is to snap your neck back just as he hits. You just have to be relaxed," he says, giving me perhaps the least relaxing advice I have ever received.

I pull on the pants and the padded suit slowly. It's hard to get it on. I do not want to be here. What if I am so bruised I can't take my daughter out the next day? What if I get seriously hurt and I have to go to a French hospital? Why did I say yes, and why, frankly, am I even here? This will be the last time, I promise myself. The last time I say yes to a dog attack, ever.

Wordlessly, he hands me a jock strap. His jacket is so padded that he looks like a Michelin Man who has just stepped out of the shower. Sweat streams down his face and neck. I hold the fragrant thing in disbelief. But then I think of the dogs punching their aggressors and I step in, pulling the straps tight around my legs.

Finally I am ready. I walk past what feels like a gauntlet of cops, all standing around waiting for my attack. Stéphane Goubet is there, and walks with me to the middle of the grass. It's comforting knowing he'll be on hand.

The attack dog, Maxou, is brought out. He's a Tervuren Belgian shepherd, a reddish, long-haired dog. He snaps and snarls and barks through the muzzle, straining against the leash of his handler. Goubet stands behind me and agitates the dog to get him even more pissed off. He hits my chest a few times, reminding Maxou where to attack, and reminds me to keep my hands at my side. I stand my ground, prepared for the strike, yelling and waving my arms. I'm in the moment, fully committed to whatever comes next.

What comes next is Maxou. He hits me like a cannonball, square in the chest, and I fall down. The wind is knocked out of me as I hit the ground. As quickly as I can in my padded suit, I stagger to my feet, using Goubet's hand to pull myself up. This time, he keeps a hand on my back, in case this powerful dog sends me flying a second time. Maxou strikes my chest again. I put my arm out to defend myself. It's some kind of instinct.

"No arms! Get your arms out of the way!" yells Goubet. Maxou attacks for the third time, and this time I manage neither to fall over nor to get my arms in the way. It's a victory, and I'm laughing inside the helmet, so elated and relieved to have made it through! But Goubet isn't happy with Maxou's strike, and he sends him in for a fourth strike, directly at my chest.

This time, I can hear myself groan. But as soon as Maxou's pulled out of reach, I am once again grinning ear to ear. My chest and stomach are sore, but I feel it again: that rush of being alive, that rush after great fear. I've learned two things: that smart dogs can be taught anything, even how to punch, and that there is nothing better than being on the far side of an experience I dread.

On the third day of training, I talk with Commandant Heritier about why French dogs are muzzled in the first place.

"We can't work the way they do in the U.S. It's seen badly."

"Is it because of the Nazi era?" I've read how the Nazis used police dogs to terrorize Parisians.

"Yes, absolutely, it comes from the Nazis. It is a French trauma. We had the Nazis use the German shepherds against our population."

"Did they use them in Paris?"

"Yes. When they rounded up Jews, they used dogs for guarding the crowds. It takes us back to those periods. This is a very French problem, and it is only a problem in France. After the terrorist attacks in Belgium, there were Islamic neighborhoods that were evacuated with unmuzzled dogs. In Belgium, they can use dogs to maintain order; in France, it's forbidden. Belgium has assimilated this period differently. In France, we keep these traumas alive, particularly in Paris. This is my point of view only, Rachel."

"I understand."

"Once, while I was out for an antidrug mission in Paris, I was confronted by a lady. 'You are like the Nazis!' she said. I told her, 'He's a very nice dog, a Labrador, and he's only searching for drugs. He's Snoopy!' She was a young woman, under forty. She didn't know the war, but still in her imagination, the police dogs were associated with Nazis."

"Is the distrust a constant issue?"

"No, not at all! It's paradoxical. When we have a public display, the crowds are enormous. They love to come up after, to discuss things with us. But when we're in a tense moment or when we are working, it's: *'Vous faites comme les Nazis!'*

"We also have dogs trained to save people, to protect people, but the public mixes it all up. At one time I worked in the 13th arrondissement. There were two hundred thousand inhabitants, but it was always the same hundred and fifty people who committed all the crimes. The public doesn't understand how we use dogs, or who we are after. It's a very simplistic response, it's dangerous, to say '*These dogs are Nazis.*' We want the simplest response, the fastest. It's the Internet. The Internet has opened many doors for us, but people choose the easy response. The level of journalism now in France is solely to sell papers. It's the lowest level."

"Has anything changed after Bataclan?"

"Yes. There are many more signs of sympathy than defiance."

■

My time with the Paris police dog unit is a linguistic challenge. All of my interviews are in French, which I understand quite well, but not perfectly, and which I speak functionally, but not beautifully. I have never done interviews in a foreign language, and my plan is to type everything in French, ignoring the mistakes, and then to translate to English later. But my plan doesn't take into account my embarrassment at how badly I write French. I don't want them to see my dropped accents, my dozens of errors. When I include the accents, I get hopelessly behind in writing, so I just leave them off. If I don't know how to spell something in French, I write it in English.

The obvious questions are not difficult. But speaking from the heart in French is difficult. Despite Isabelle being from Paris, we hold our most important conversations in English. All of our fights are in English, and when we make up, it's in English, too. So when the officers of the Brigade share their stories of trauma with me, I struggle to respond. In the end, I am left without language, hoping that what is in my heart is carried through my eyes and somehow reaches those who have suffered. The dogs can do this; I hope I am equally capable.

Commandant Heritier has 120 police officers and 80 dogs working under him in the Brigade Cynophile. Defense dogs and dogs used for criminal intervention can have more than one master, but dogs used to sniff explosives and search for drugs have a single handler. Search dogs must have an incredibly close bond with their handlers. As Heritier says, "These are playful, sociable dogs. They have a great dependence on their handlers. Defense and intervention dogs have a much more independent character. They are dominant dogs, with a weaker relationship with their handlers. As soon as our defense dogs are out of the car, they are barking and making people afraid. That's our goal—to dissuade the public. We work with this goal, to not even have to use the dogs."

"What do you call the agitators in French?" I ask. "The guys who the dogs practice attacking?"

"This is another very French problem," says Heritier. "Officially they are called assistants. We have to soften the term for the public. But here at the Brigade, they are called attack men."

"Had you dealt with major events before the Bataclan attacks?"

"No, it was the first. Bataclan changed everything. We had two dogs from our unit who were part of the SWAT team. I had all the other dogs outside prepared and waiting. Once the terrorists were killed, were neutralized, we had to ensure that the bodies themselves were not rigged to explode, or that the terrorists' vests were not only partially detonated. We entered the club in convoys. My role was to take the teams into Bataclan, and to work with them on all the bodies. Before I took them in, I had to ask, 'This is going to be hard. Are you capable?' I told them what they would see. Not one man refused."

As we are speaking, the commandant's eyes grow wet and bright. "I don't know how to tell you what it was like. If you've ever imagined hell, it would be like that. When I understood the situation, I told the dog handlers, put boots on your dogs' feet, because there's so much broken glass and so much blood. It was strange, because the electricity was cut. It was dim, heavy—such a somber ambiance. There was nothing but the security lights. Actually, my brain began to search for a strategy so it wouldn't be so hard. I saw piles of bodies, one on top of the other. My mind said, 'It's okay. They're just sleeping.' I knew it wasn't true, but I had to work anyway. We were looking for grenades, explosives. The most appalling thing was they were people our age, our generation. We felt so alive. We knew there was no one left alive in the place but us. We felt this responsibility to do this work, to protect those who were going to be coming in after us—the other police officers, everyone."

The commandant pauses. I want to say something, but I don't know what to say. I look directly at him, hoping he can read the sorrow reflected in my eyes as I witness his account. He takes a breath and continues. " 'They're asleep,' I told myself. It was my strategy to function. Even though there were bodies that were badly injured, damaged . . ." his voice trails off. "We were there for an hour and a half. I felt like I was in a dream. They were all dead. All their phones were going off, in the darkness. The phones were lighting up and ringing. People had heard, families had heard. All those phones ringing in that half-darkness, and nobody was going to answer."

"Did you receive psychological support?"

"Yes, we had a reunion here after. Everyone was invited to speak. Police school doesn't prepare you for something like this. Death for us could be a car crash, two or three people killed, even a murder, but this was violence of a completely different scale, terrible violence. It's important to speak about this. We do have a psychologist on staff. She made appointments with anyone who needed it.

"After, I needed to see each victim, to see their history. I saw them in *Le Monde*. I needed to see them as individuals. After Bataclan, I needed to live bigger, to travel. It's strange, you know, we spoke about it after: when death comes, it's so definitive. When I was a young policeman, I had a nightmare. Now I think it was a dream premonition. In the nightmare, I had to go to the Gare d'Austerlitz. While I was there, I was walking among dozens and dozens of bodies. It was bizarre. For several days after that I couldn't sleep. It really marked me.

"I hope it makes us stronger in our organization, in our spirit, that we are prepared to be better than we were for Bataclan, that we have progressed. This is the lesson from Bataclan. We were strong, but we need to be even stronger, even better. We need to take those lessons to heart."

His eyes glisten throughout our conversation, but no tears fall.

"It was an experience that was unexpected in my career. We were the first generation of police to see such violence since the Second World War. The days that followed Charlie Hebdo and Bataclan, I listened to my radio with the greatest fear that there would be another attack. It was so unjust. The attack came from people who had such a simplistic view, people who couldn't live together, who wanted to impose their way of life on us. Our democracy is not perfect, but we have respect for the law. They wanted to attack it. We don't want their way of life, their laws. You know, I went to Syria in 2000. It was beautiful, this antique city of Palmyra. I saw the sunset there, this great orange sun. The place was full of beauty and it held the history of humanity. They destroyed it. There was an ancient theater there, I sat and wrote postcards there, it was such a beautiful moment, but they have destroyed it all, the Islamists. It's inhumane."

"It's a negation of humanity," I say.

"We have to fight against it. We modernize our techniques. We have to be aware of the new explosives, and adapt accordingly. There's a drug, Captagon. Terrorists use it before they commit crimes, so they don't feel any pain. We don't know if it's here yet, but if we find it, we know that the terrorists are here as well. That drug is used only by terrorists. We have to constantly modernize and adapt."

"It must be difficult for you to deal with these new threats," I say. Heritier nods grimly.

"They will reopen the Bataclan later this year," he says. "But I will never go back. I went once before all this happened. I listened to music. That night I laughed so much. But now I will never, never go back. It's good they will reopen. We can't turn every site into a memorial. But unless I am called there in the line of duty, I will never return."

The door of the portable trailer opens, and Gardien de la Paix Charly Gravier pokes his curly blond head around the door. The commandant invites Gravier in. "Charly is an explosives specialist. I'll let him talk to you for a while," he says.

"Oh, you get the boss's seat!" I say, as he takes the commandant's chair. "What's your dog's name?"

"My dog is J'ikki. He's two years old. He was donated to the police force by someone who didn't want him anymore. J'ikki was too much for him to handle. So he was taken to the Centre National, where they trained him, and then we worked for three months together to complete our explosives training."

"So this is completely different than the work you did before, the defense work?"

"Yes, it's all focused on explosives. We don't use the same criteria for the dogs. For explosives, they use dogs that are more sociable and playful. He's not muzzled, I'll show him to you in a minute."

"Was it Bataclan that changed how you work?"

"No, I wanted to change but the attacks made it clearer that I should change."

"Do you work with a SWAT team?"

"No, not at all, I work alone most of the time. When I work with a team, we secure the place before important people arrive. Like the president, the prime minister, cinema stars, VIPs, football stadiums.

We do it right before the person arrives, then the place is completely secured and closed down.

"During the November terrorist attacks, we just happened to be right nearby the restaurant. It was myself and three others, in the area just by chance. We got a radio call that there was an attack at Le Carillon and Le Petit Cambodge. Not even two minutes passed between the call and our arrival. We were only in the area by chance, but we heard the cries, the screams. We saw the bodies."

"I'm sorry. I'm sure it's hard to talk about."

"It's better now. We got out of the car. It was an absolute massacre. We weren't prepared for what we saw. With gun fights and ordinary crime, you see one or two people killed at a time, maximum. I did everything I could to save people. We put on latex gloves and we each went in different directions, because there were so many victims who needed our help. As soon as I went in, right at the entry, there was someone lying dead. His family was crying beside him. Right away I started chest compressions and CPR. The more I pushed on his chest to try to get his heart pumping, the more blood he lost because he had been so shot up. There was a doctor there who came over, he said, 'No, stop, it won't do anything. This person is dead.' I saw his friend who was crying. I said, 'I'm sorry.' I left him and went inside the restaurant.

"Someone else called me and said, 'I need help, I need help!' Again, I did CPR; again, a doctor came up and said, 'No, he's dead. It's better to go to someone else.' So I moved on to the next person crying out in pain. He had been shot in the leg and shot in other places too. I tried to stop the blood gushing out of his leg. His other gunshots were no longer bleeding. I tried to stop the bleeding. When I looked up there were five or six other injured people in front of me. One of them was in shock. He was rocking back and forth like a baby. It shocked me to see. The firefighter and I tried to talk to him, but he didn't hear anything we said. The firefighter took charge of the victim I was assisting, and I went to find other victims outside of the restaurant."

"Were there any victims who were not badly wounded?"

"No, I didn't see any small injuries, only people who had already been killed. I did everything in my power to help them, but it was really a feeling of powerlessness. *We had to try to help without the ability to help.* Even so, my team was able to stay strong and react to what the situation demanded."

"What did you do after the four of you left?"

"We came back to the base. We met with the commandant. We needed to talk to him, and we needed to talk to our colleagues. We spoke about what happened, what we saw and what we did. We had a beer and decompressed. We stayed at the base for a very long time. The commandant required each of us to write exactly what we did and what we saw during the attacks. It permitted us, at least to some extent, to leave it in the file."

Gravier keeps talking, unspooling the horror of the night. His blue eyes lock on mine. Suddenly I can't bear to hear any more, not one more word. I had not prepared, when I came to the Brigade, to witness such traumatic stories. I haven't slept well in a couple of nights. My mind replays the brutality, the shock, the horror: all that these hands I have shaken have had to bear. I think of the dogs, the happy dogs of the Dog Lover Unit, the dogs that are so eager to work, called this time into the nightclub. I think of their bewilderment at the scene, as they are sent to work in their protective boots, searching for explosives through blood and broken glass and bodies. Abruptly, I snap my computer shut.

"Can I meet J'ikki?" I ask. I spend the last minutes of the day out in the yard, with J'ikki frolicking around us both, posing for pictures and doing what dogs do—bringing us out of our heads and back to the present moment.

I go home that night to the elegant apartment of my in-laws in Neuilly. We eat rack of lamb from Normandy, new potatoes, and white asparagus, prepared by my mother-in-law, Michèle. Jerôme opens a bottle of the best French wine and pours with a flourish. My daughter pushes a silver cart to the table, loaded with everything we could want. The meat is lush with blood. Outside, the streets are filled with rain, pattering on the green leaves of the huge plane trees.

My last day with the Brigade is not at the unit headquarters. The commandant picks me up in Neuilly, outside the family apartments. As soon as I receive Commandant Heritier's call, I take the tiny elevator down and step out into the street, but I don't see a car. Heritier and Constable Marc Alexandre are in an unmarked car but are following a police escort, and it's only by their uniforms that I recognize them.

We drive along the dangerously swollen Seine; trees are half-submerged. The cops are in a hurry, and I truly regret having had anything to eat at lunch. The team in front of us has lights and sirens going, and we move quickly through the Paris traffic. Driving in Paris is already an unsettling experience. Going around the Arc de Triomphe, for example, is a game of chicken that leaves my stomach in my shoes. And driving with lights and sirens on these narrow streets, even though we are not going full out, is not fun times for me. Paris drivers are good, but aggressive. They pass each other with inches to spare. Two days before I watched a woman hit a pedestrian. "*Trouduc! Connard!* You could have killed me!" She brushed herself off and walked away, yelling over her shoulder at the driver, who said, with extreme Parisian politeness, "I beg your pardon, madame."

Today, Constable Alexandre drives us. He has an attack dog back at the unit. At one point, gripping the door, I feel as if I may be sick, and Alexandre turns to reassure me. "Don't worry." I smile greenly.

We whip past Parisians and tourists gathered along the flooded banks of the Seine to take pictures. We are heading to the hotel where some of the Euro soccer players will be staying. Before they can arrive and be settled, the Brigade Cynophile must secure the building. It is no small task: every single room and corridor must be checked, first by the dogs, and then by the explosives team. We are met by a number of dog teams and a French military unit. The Russian team bus is parked outside.

I am paired up with K9 Chief Brigadier Karine, (who prefers to keep her family name anonymous, for her protection), head of the explosives section, and her energetic Malinois, Isis. I am startled when I hear Isis's name.

"Did you say your dog's name is *Isis*?"

"*Oui*. Isis." She says it forcefully, then spells it for me so there can be no mistake, but doesn't elaborate further. I wonder if the dog has been named Isis as an act of defiance. Later I ask Karine about it, and she tells me that Isis was named by the owner who gave her up for adoption. (Before Isis became the acronym of a terrorist group, of course, it was the name of the Egyptian goddess of fertility.)

However her name was intended, Isis is one of the smartest, friendliest police dogs I meet in Paris, and Karine never loses her smile through the long hours of searching. Karine loves her job. As she says, "I go to work with a smile and the desire to be of service to my country." That desire was tested during the terrorist attacks, where Karine and her former dog, Bucky, were pressed into service to check the murder victims for explosives before their bodies could be released. "We had to go to make sure there was nothing left on the victims," she explains—no bombs that would detonate when paramedics or investigators were working. "No one was prepared for it," she says. "Even Bucky was surprised when I told him to search the victims. It was a very difficult job."

Isis has never known such difficult work. She's three years old, young and trusting and full of energy. Karine has had her only for eight months, since the previous September when they began training together. Like most of the dogs in the Brigade, Isis was given to the police by a man who didn't have time for her anymore. He just left her out in the garden all day. Now Isis lives with Karine, and, unlike the aggression dogs, she goes home with her trainer at the end of the working day. As soon as Isis is out of the car, she is ready to work, pulling on her harness in her eagerness to get going.

Isis is not trained for defense or aggression, and is never muzzled, as it would interfere with her job. She works only to find explosives. She works at a distance as well, so she can enter hostile environments in dangerous situations. Karine has trained her to be directed only by laser. Isis is able to detect silently. If she finds explosives, she makes no noise to alert terrorists or criminals that she's there. She touches nothing. Such a dog is an incalculable advantage.

Securing a huge hotel is a nearly impossible task, but K9 forces take on the nearly impossible all the time. The threats against the Euro Cup, and indeed against all of Europe, are real and imminent. Each police dog team gets one floor, which is dozens and dozens of rooms. My heart sinks a little as I see how much work is ahead of us. Isis is young and full of drive, which is a good thing, because the work is draining. Karine and Isis work each room exactly the same way. Every corner, from under the bed to the upper shelves in the closet, must be checked. Isis is tireless, jumping on her hind legs to check countertops one minute, crouching down to check a crawl space between rooms the next.

After the check, the hotel is supposed to be secured from all outsiders until the guests arrive. But one of the rooms is not made up, which means that someone will have to enter it, which means there's no point in doing a check to secure the space. Karine, with some irritation, talks to management, and they ask if the team could just come back later. "No," she says, "I can't stand around waiting until whenever you are ready; this should have been done." The message is clear; the room is made up immediately, and we return a few minutes later to search it.

A room or a wing of a hotel may be searched for explosives and cleared, but there are so many variables—an open window, a new staff member who hasn't completed a security clearance. It is an exercise in harm reduction, and no more. I notice that I am the only one not wearing antiexplosive gear, and quickly put that thought out of my head.

After only an hour of work, we've made it through perhaps a third of the rooms on the floor. Karine is interrupted by a phone call from the prefect of police. He wants to know if she's done yet.

"Not even close," she says curtly. It's clear she's not pleased. "They don't understand what we actually do," she says after she hangs up the phone and gets back to work.

It's hard not to delight in watching Isis work. She's a fabulous dog. In she goes, and whoosh, her nostrils flare like a racehorse's, taking in massive lungfuls of scent. Up on her hind legs, paws scrabbling on countertops, down on her belly, tail in the air, Isis is a whirling detection machine, moving so fast that most of my dozens of photos register as a blur with a tail. As soon as we have secured a room, the explosives unit from the French military moves in and checks it again with their machines. But no machine can do what Isis's nose can. Every half dozen rooms or so, Commandant Heritier hides some actual explosives for her and Karine to locate. Without this reward system, she would find the work less and less interesting. Every dog needs positive reinforcement; like all of us, Isis responds to success.

No matter where Commandant Heritier hides the explosives in a room, Isis tracks them down immediately. I watch carefully, thrilled at that moment when she silently drops to her haunches, staring intently at the place where the explosives are hidden. She enters a room where I've seen the commandant hide something and makes a beeline to wherever it is—high or low in the room doesn't matter. Isis makes it look so obvious that I almost wonder why I can't smell it myself.

Our floor of the hotel is secure. Isis has found no bombs, no explosives but the ones the commandant hid for her to find. I stand outside the hotel in the thin sunlight, shaking hands with dozens of people as we make the good-bye rounds: cops, hotel staff, military people. I stay close to the commandant, Karine, and Isis. It's the first day without rain since I arrived, and my last day with the Brigade and the commandant. I don't want to leave. The pure pleasure of seeing dogs and people working together, in a place beyond language, in a relationship built on play and trust, is intense. It is a game to the dogs, but their handlers know it is a serious game, one upon which thousands of lives depend.

One last kiss on each cheek with Karine and then with the dear commandant, a last pat on Isis's head, and I leave, making my way back to the apartments where my daughter waits for me to take her out to see the other Paris, the Paris of glamour and the Galeries Lafayette, perfume and pâtisseries, flower markets and priceless paintings.

I fly home on June 8. On June 12, a terrorist attacks a gay bar in Orlando, killing forty-nine people. On June 13, a terrorist stabs a Paris police officer and his wife to death in front of their three-year-old son, live streaming the murders on Facebook. When the news flashes on my Twitter feed, I feel sick. I check the names, knowing the K9 units will be involved and on high alert. I scan for names and familiar faces from the Brigade Cynophile, yet feel no sense of relief knowing that the couple who were killed were people I'd never met. Their little boy is now a traumatized orphan. My writer friend in Istanbul writes of the attack in her city a few weeks later, where forty-one people are killed. Next, a week later, another writer friend in the Middle East writes of ISIS's attempt to blow up a mosque in his city. He posts photos of incinerated cars, the fingers of a hand, and writes, "By the way, you can go to hell Isis. I'm going to sleep." On July 14, Bastille Day, a driver in Nice runs over crowds of families and friends watching fireworks together. Eighty-four people are killed. Every week brings new terror.

We are all connected, for better and for worse. How societies are policed tells us a great deal about their values. And how societies respond to threats does as well. In this sense, I think no police force has shown more courage than the Paris Brigade Cynophile. There will certainly be other attacks, and the Dog Lover Unit knows it. They see the risks clearly. The muzzles will come off their dogs for this fight. But only for this fight, because the Brigade also respects the values of France. Unlike American or Canadian laws, French (and British) laws prohibit the use of dogs to bite or attack unarmed citizens. *Liberté, Egalité, Fraternité*—the foundation of liberty, equality, and brotherhood, the heart of democratic idealism—is being sorely tested by these grave threats. At the Brigade, the dogs stand on guard, muzzled, but ready to fight.

Everything shifts when I know the police officers involved. Everything shifts when a hate-filled Islamist extremist enters a gay bar, or a mosque, or a police officer's home, or a crowd of families pushing their children in strollers. The ground is unstable under my feet. Because I know that there's no end in sight to the brutality, and I know that the police officers and police dogs I have come to know will be involved, and will lay down their lives. They are prepared to do so. In the meantime, they are isolated from those they protect, having at times a closer bond to their dogs than to any human. As Commandant Heritier tells me, what matters to his police officers is very clear: "Il y a Dieu et il y a leur chien, tout le reste n'est que diversion." (They have God and they have their dogs, all the rest is a distraction.")

It's just so hard not to lose heart. With America so gun-sick, so enthralled by an ideology that gives them permission to own weapons of war, with death-cult recruits slamming into the bodies of people in cafés in Bangladesh, in Iraq, in Paris, in Istanbul, everything is disordered.

The bar Le Carillon was run by an Algerian family, and Le Petit Cambodge was, of course, a Cambodian restaurant. The terrorists did not discriminate. They attack young people who want to laugh and drink and listen to music together. The disorder is profound. There is no cure, and I can feel it infecting my mind, this virus of terror. I shut off the social media and take my dog to the woods. I read to my kids. The only relief is to be in the company of all the good people and the good animals, to walk in the forest and be startled by eagles and a coyote, to love wholeheartedly and without reservation. You know: like a dog.

# 8

## Bonds from Beyond the Grave

The sad truth of police dog work is that both dogs and officers sometimes die in the line of duty. In my time on the road, I meet a few officers whose dogs had been killed on the job. The first is Doug Lewis. Several RCMP dog handlers have mentioned Doug Lewis, and I'm nervous about meeting this survivor face-to-face. My fears are put at ease when he answers the door with a tiny Maltese/Yorkie puppy nestled in his muscular arms. I knew Lewis was retired; I just didn't know he'd be so young and so fit. Tall and sun-bronzed, with dark hair, he and his wife, Christine, look like they have stepped out of the pages of a fitness magazine.

He holds the pup as I sit down, while two very affectionate cats and another dog trot out to greet me. One of the cats keeps jumping on my laptop as I take notes, her tail curling over my arm. Even though his house has the good company of cats and dogs, there are no more police dogs in Doug Lewis's life, and probably never will be again.

"So," I ask, "how did you get into policing?"

"By grade three, I wanted to be a police officer. My dad was in the marine section of the RCMP, but that didn't encourage me for police work. I found Dad's job very boring. I went out for many hours on Dad's boat. When I was thirteen, my mom took me aside and said,

'Dad doesn't want to take you on the boat, because you can't sit still like your brother.' It was true.

"The big influence on me as a kid was my older brother. He was a top athlete. He used to beat me up lots. It was, 'I'm going to make you tough.'

"One time my brother was beating me up. Mum had hit him so many times with a broomstick, so she got a frying pan and hit him between the shoulder blades to get his attention. Mum had to hit him twice."

I think about my sons, and try to picture anything remotely similar to this situation. My imagination fails me. But Lewis doesn't seem fazed by what he went through. It's obvious after five minutes of conversation that Doug Lewis and his brother were hell on wheels as boys. When they were young, they were called The Crazy Brothers. It's clear they both earned the name in those early years. "My brother choked me once on the ferry until I passed out. After a while, we had it out and he never challenged me since." It took joining the RCMP to channel that intense youthful drive.

"My brother joined the RCMP four years before I did. He got out of high school and right into the RCMP. I wasn't the greatest kid to be going in. I had a lot of traffic violations. I had a lead foot. I wasn't violent, just a teenage boy showing off. My dad was stationed on Salt Spring Island. Well, it was two days after I got my driver's license, I was doing donuts and hit a pole.

"Later I got involved in rollovers and other traffic violations. When I actually put my application to the RCMP, I was asked, 'And how do you explain this?'

"'Due to immaturity, sir.' I was rejected the first time, due to eyesight. I thought my world had come to an end. I tried exercising my eyes. I stopped wearing glasses to strengthen my eyes. I did that for two weeks. So it was one and a half years later, I was working at a lumber mill, pulling off green wood, I get this phone call, 'Are you still interested?'"

"So that's when you joined the RCMP?"

"Yes. You had to grow up—except you still got to drive fast. I put in eight years of service. I was pushing the idea of the antiterrorist team. At this point, Bill Sweeney was the assistant commissioner. He said, 'Doug, you want the antiterrorist team, you're in.'

"Then the dog man shows up a week later. I said, 'So you get to hunt people, drive your own wagon, the dog's your partner?' I said, 'Can I go to Peace River and train with you?' I spent four days at this dog man's house. I'll never forget the first bite. I was scared, but I was excited. I just couldn't get enough. I wish I would have known that before.

"I helped to raise five dogs. You pay for your own gas, you do twelve-hour shifts, then it's nighttime, you take the dog out for a walk quickly. Then you lay tracks and get bit."

"How did you find the strength to do what you had to do?"

"You don't feel invincible, because you know people get hurt, but you feel 'I'm not going to get hurt out of this, I'll come out of it okay.' When I first got into the RCMP, I only wanted to catch bad guys. I thought my dog, Reiker, was invincible. He was one hundred and seven pounds of solid German shepherd. We were catching people left, right, and center. Anybody with weapons, he'd take them down.

"As time got along, I realized, 'Dogs are like a bad date, they never leave you.' They are always there. With Reiker, he was handler-soft, he'd go on his belly if I yelled at him, but with everyone else he'd go bonkers. I remember people saying, 'My god, he's got a bite like an alligator.' Once on a training I saw a guy put on two arm guards. I said, 'What are you doing?'

"'I've heard about your dog's reputation,' he told me. Some of the quarries would scream because of the pressure of the bite."

Lewis keeps talking. The cat curls softly around my arm.

"Once we were out on a call and someone shouted to me, 'Doug, he ran down that alley!' So I go, I'm circling the dog, but he's not picking anything up. I soon realized that it was the next alley over. We go, I'm yelling at my dog, he's down on his belly, then I circled him again. I realized boom, he gave it to me. We got the guy. I realized my dog will give it to me if it's there. I don't need to yell. You can't force your dog. You have to make it fun. Make it bubbly."

*Make it bubbly.* That expression stays with me. The hardest work in the world, where lives are at stake, and to get your dog to do his best work, you have to make it all a big game.

People sought out Doug Lewis for training advice when they were raising dogs and working as quarries, hoping to be chosen as police dog handlers.

"I wanted to see a real commitment to dog services. You gotta be a go-getter."

Doug keeps the stories coming. "Once we were on a domestic violence call. It had nothing to do with dogs. Her husband had threatened her before he left, said he'd come back and kill her, then he drove away and she called us. My dog started walking around the house and all of a sudden I see the tail wagging. Then I hear this SCREAM! My dog's got the guy in the shoulder blade. Her husband had come back. He had a gun lined up to shoot the policeman that was coming up the walk. I had shivers going down my spine. The other cop said, 'That dog saved my life.'"

Lewis has seen more than anyone should of the worst of human nature.

"Once we were called about this nineteen-year-old raping a seventeen-year-old at knifepoint. The victim came running out of the bushes by the White Spot Restaurant. She was all torn up. My dog ran across to the other side of the road. The guy was hiding there, with his pants still half done up. We got him, and then we backtracked and found the weapon."

Now I'm the one with shivers going down my spine. It's not hard to picture the guy, crouching in the ditch with his pants undone, the girl crawling out of the bushes at White Spot after being raped. It's not hard to picture the knife held to her throat, then cast into the grass as the guy tried to escape. What if the dog hadn't been there, and the rapist had gotten away? And even though he was caught, what about the rest of her life, all the days that come after, with the memory of the knife against her throat?

I had heard what happened to Doug Lewis from other cops. When I ask him about it, though, he gets up and leaves the room. He comes back and hands me his official police statement. I read it carefully. It seems like such a nonevent: a suspect who fled without paying for gas, and refused to stop when the cops pursued him. Doug, who was off duty at the time, was buying dog food at Buckerfield's in Chilliwack. He arrived at the scene with his dog Chip, wearing nothing but jeans and a T-shirt, unarmed but ready to track. He had two uniformed members to back him up, both members of ERT, the Emergency Response Team.

Dog handlers move much faster than anyone else. This can be a problem for those who want to keep up, even if they are exceptionally fit ERT officers providing cover for a K9 team during a pursuit. The dog teams often move at a run, and seldom slower than a trot. Once the dog is on a scent, he is in full pursuit mode.

Twice the ERT members who were providing backup to Lewis yelled at him to slow down, which he did. But when he didn't hear from them again, he followed Chip through the brush at a rapid pace, assuming his backup team was right behind him.

When he found the suspect and told him to surrender, the man refused. Chip was sent in to subdue him, which he did, grabbing his left arm. This is where the statement gets hard to read. I quote it directly:

> *To my disbelief I saw the suspect come around with his right hand holding a knife. Without anything said or any hesitation the suspect stabbed "Chip" in the neck area. The suspect then pulled back to stab him again and I saw the blood squirt out of his neck. I then dropped the long line I was attached to "Chip" and started to charge the suspect so I could stop him from stabbing him again. The suspect saw me charge at him and he stopped stabbing at "Chip" and started running towards me. "Chip" then came off the suspect and came back to me and circled around me and charged at the suspect again. As "Chip" had circled around me he dragged the twenty foot leash behind him and ended up tying my legs together so I couldn't move out of the way of the suspect swinging the knife around. The suspect ended up knocking me down to the ground wailing the knife at my face and chest area. I tried several times to block the blows but he kept stabbing at me. At one point I felt the knife go into my chest and at the same time I felt "Chip" biting my upper right thigh area. I knew he was doing some damage to my face when I felt the blood going into my right eye. I did manage to grab the knife blade and held on tight to it as he was yelling at me "I'm not a killer, I'm not a killer." I responded to that comment that he wasn't showing me a good example of this.*

Just as children sometimes lash out at their parents, police dogs will sometimes bite or attack their handlers in times of extreme stress or pain. This is what Chip did after he'd been stabbed. The brutal fight continued. Doug Lewis wrote: "He kept on trying to punch me and was yelling at me 'go out, go out, let me put you out.'" But Doug kept fighting, and kept on yelling for Nigel, one of the cover officers from ERT. Finally, the suspect demanded Doug's money, his wallet, pager, and keys, and then ran off into the woods.

*I went over to "Chip" and saw that his eyes were glassed over and his tongue was hanging out the side of his mouth and I could barely see any blood coming out of his neck area. I then took my t-shirt off and tried to stop whatever bleeding there was left coming out and as I looked at his head he let out a gasp and there was nothing else there . . . I wiped the blood from my watch and it was 3:10 p.m.*

I put the sworn statement down and meet Doug's eyes. It's a heavy moment.

"What was going through your head at that point?"

"We learned that whenever you are in a situation, don't give up. As it was happening, I'm not thinking of quitting. I'm thinking, 'How do I subdue this guy? How do I get him to stop stabbing me?' Apparently Nigel could hear me, though I couldn't hear him. He was running through the brush, trying to find me, and he couldn't. He kept hearing me and wasn't able to help."

At this point, Doug Lewis knew he didn't have much time left before he bled to death from the wounds in his head and chest. But he made one last attempt to save his own life. He was able to slide down the brush until he made his way to a road. Several cars drove around Lewis, refusing to stop as he tried to wave them down, covered in blood. Finally a driver stopped and drove him to the hospital.

"My stabbing, I got nine knife wounds and my dog got killed. The guy who did it, he got ten months in the mental institution. Then the media called to tell me that he's being released less than ten months later. I was frustrated. I was mad. I was told he would at least do a few years, but ten months later he's released to his parents. This is proof we have a legal system, but we certainly don't have a justice system. I said this, and it went on the news. I was called in by the Superintendent of the RCMP district. He told me, 'You can't say that.'

"I put my hand out and said, 'Slap me, because that's all you're going to get.'" Nobody, no matter what their rank, can stop Doug Lewis from calling it as he sees it.

"After all this, the guy applied for a firearms certificate. His application was rejected. Everyone knew what he did to a police officer, and that he killed a police dog."

At times, as he tallies his losses, Lewis tries to joke, but I can tell that the pain is fresh. The price he paid was so high. To Doug Lewis, his dogs are his partners. It eats at him that he couldn't protect Chip.

Lewis lost Chip, lost his first marriage, and nearly lost his life, but he fought his way back from every loss. "They gave me all the time in the world to heal, but I couldn't sit still for very long. I located another dog, Zack, and in less than a month I was back in Innisfail at kennels training with him. As I was sitting in the bushes after laying a track for one of the other fellows, I looked down at my hands where the stitches had come out, and I asked myself, 'Should I be here?' It was a very strange feeling, but I shook it off and continued my training. I tried so hard not to think of Chip. He appeared every night in my dreams, and still does."

Lewis is still on that long path toward recovery, though he won't work as a police officer again. He talks openly of his experience and his mistakes, so that others can learn from his ordeal.

When I said good-bye, Doug was holding his tiny puppy, Nika, to his muscular chest, cuddling her as she snuggled against him. Nika closed her eyes, snoozing in the crook of his arm, completely secure in her world in a way that her owner never can be again.

■

Sergeant Ray Wong is the first cop I ride with from the Vancouver Police Department. He is also something of a legend among Canadian police dog handlers. Not only are he and his first dog, Bear, the overall title winners for the Canadian Police Canine Association national dog trials for 2007, he is also one of the first to successfully perform CPR on a K9 who had stopped breathing and gone into cardiac arrest. That dog was Bear. He almost didn't survive. But his dad, Sergeant Wong, saved his life.

When Sergeant Wong lets his new dog, Hunter, out of the truck to meet me, I brace myself, ready for whatever is coming. Only a few nights before, Cade got a bit too toothy and enthusiastic about me and my backpack. But all Hunter wants to do is come over, tail wagging, to say hi. Hunter is not a police dog with a lot to prove.

It's early evening at the Vancouver police kennels, and one of the dogs being boarded in the kennel for the night throws himself against the chain-link fence over and over, furiously challenging Hunter. Hunter heads over to show he's as alpha as any of them, and Sergeant Wong has to intervene. I get a tour of the detachment before we hit the road. Sergeant Wong shows me a few different guns, which would interest a lot of people, but don't interest me, and a calendar of the Vancouver Police Department dogs, which does. Sergeant Wong gives me a calendar to take home, full of happy dog teams in action, or posed next to their cars, looking dapper.

"How did you get into policing?" I ask as we drive off to begin the night shift.

"I always wanted to be a police officer, ever since I was a little kid. It always stuck in my mind, good versus evil. The whole idea of capturing a bad person always resonated with me. I geared my life for that, throughout school.

"I grew up on Vancouver Island. I was born and raised in Victoria. Got my degree in criminology with a minor in psych from Simon Fraser University, and then while I was in university I volunteered with the Coquitlam RCMP. They said, 'We're not hiring, go complete a diploma.' In my fourth year I applied to police departments in Vancouver, Victoria, and the RCMP. Vancouver was the first to give me a phone call. The RCMP called a few weeks later, but I'd already said yes to Vancouver.

"I never grew up with a police family. I'd never actually been in or around policing at all. Everything was fresh, new, exciting. When I went along with the K9 unit as part of my training, I thought, 'That is the best job.' I knew that it was going to be my calling from that point on."

Wong raised two dogs before he got Bear. "The first dog I raised failed on courage and the second failed his medical exam. My third dog, Bear, was perfect for us. At eleven months old, he got to be partnered with me. What's crazy with him is he had the same birthday as me, September 16."

What's also crazy is that in 2002 Bear was electrocuted while he was on the job. Ray was out with two other officers, Randy and Al. They had just finished searching a house that had been broken into and were walking back to Wong's patrol car.

"I remember walking down the sidewalk. The sidewalk was covered in snow, except for this one plate that was two feet by two feet. I thought, 'That's weird, maybe the salt melted it.' Bear's on his short leash with me. Suddenly he starts yelping, then he's starting to bite me. He's biting my leg, my arm, starting to urinate, then he just collapses and falls on his side with his tongue out and his eyes rolled back."

"Did he fall on that plate?"

"Yes. I didn't know what was going on. I tried to touch his head. I could feel this current going through his collar, but I still didn't know what the heck was going on. I said, 'Randy, feel that plate.' Randy got a shock and then I knew. I grabbed Bear by the collar and dragged him off the plate. Then Al did chest compressions and I started CPR. I was the one doing mouth to snout."

"Did you know how?"

"We were given a vet lecture way back when. But you know what? We were winging it. Al's partner drove up with a police car. We loaded Bear into the back of the police car. We'd been doing CPR on the street, it seemed like an eternity but in reality it was about three to five minutes. We continued the CPR in the backseat. We radioed ahead to dispatch and told them we were en route to the ER. The rest of the officers in the city started to lock down all the intersections so we could get through all the lights. I remember it was super frustrating because they had cable chains on their car, so the maximum we could do was eighty kilometers. By that point, we'd been doing CPR for eight to ten minutes. It was right around Main and Hastings— Bear took a deep breath and started waking up. He came back from the electrocution. When we made it to the clinic, he went straight to the ER. They were worried about one thing: pulmonary edema. If it wasn't for the fact that he was so young, such an active dog, he most likely would have died. Flowing through that city plate was two hundred and forty volts. The wires had become corroded and charged that plate. If you had stepped on it barefooted, you would have been electrocuted."

I had no idea that this was an issue. From that moment on, I have been careful not to let my dog walk over an electrical plate.

Sergeant Wong continues. "After this incident, I started researching. It's a real problem that people aren't aware of. If you Google 'Dogs that have been electrocuted,' it happens in a lot of cities as the infrastructure ages."

"How did you feel when Bear first started biting you?"

"I was dumbfounded. I did not know what was happening and why he was biting me. I thought he was having a seizure. He's never shown aggression to me. What happened was he's in pain, and thinks I'm the cause of that pain. He's just trying to get his frustrations out."

Bear reacted just like human kids do to their dads when they are frustrated or in pain—they lash out."

"What about when Bear collapsed?"

"I started getting emotional. He was dead. His tongue extended, hanging out the side. That saying about the eyes are the window to the soul, that's true—there was no life in 'em. I knew he was dead then. I was yelling into the radio for an ambulance. It was taking forever, I was frustrated we were waiting for an ambulance to show up. They normally don't show up to animal emergencies, they maybe didn't know it was a police dog and that they could do something for him."

"How do you do canine CPR?"

"It feels very awkward. We've now got dummy dogs to practice on doing CPR. Basically, it's grasping him by the snout, making sure his mouth is sealed. His airway was obviously through his nasal cavity—"

A light bulb goes on in my head. "Ah! I was trying to picture how you'd make a seal with their big mouths, those long tongues in the way. But it's through the nose!"

"Yeah, that's the only way you'd get a proper seal. All this time, Al was doing chest compressions. It was just hope for the best. We just kept on going."

"Bear recovered one hundred percent?"

"Yeah. He stayed in the ER for about two days. He was a very tough dog both before and after. Loved going after bad guys. I remember like three days later, all my dogs live in kennels outside, but because of what had happened, I allowed Bear to come in the house so I could keep him close. The remote control fell on him, and he jumped up, started yipping, 'Ai, Ai, Ai,' and looking around. In the back of my mind, I started wondering if Bear could do this job from now on. What's he going to be like in the next fight?"

"So what was he like?"

"I found out just a few weeks later. We were patrolling like we are now. We were called to Starbucks by Kits Beach, where a stolen car hit a police cruiser. Both the passenger and the driver bailed. The driver had a warrant out for his arrest. I was the second K9 unit to arrive. I got Bear out, hooked him onto his tracking line and cast him in the general direction. It was twelve or one in the morning. Bear's nose tipped down and off we went. We went past Kits Pool to the boat storage locker. Bear went to the chain-link fence, which was about eight feet high. His body language is telling me the suspect is inside the boat compound. I couldn't go through with Bear, so I was looking at how to get in. At one end of the fence, it went out into the ocean, purposely built that way to keep people out. I waded into the ocean up to my knees—holding onto the fence—while Bear swam ahead and around the chain link, and then we were in the compound. Because the compound was secure, I cut Bear off leash and let him go search. He began to go all around this boat that had a tarp in it. He then jumped in the boat. The guy was hiding under the tarp.

"This guy was full on goal-oriented, full on muscle. He was going to do whatever he could not to go to jail. He grabbed Bear and was punching Bear in the face the whole time Bear was on him. Bear stayed on the bite with him even though he was getting kicked, getting headlocked and punched. I was using pepper spray. The guy got Bear off him and jumped out of the boat and began to run, but Bear went right after him and was able to bring him down by biting onto his leg. Again, a barrage of punches from the suspect rained down on Bear. I was right there with Bear delivering strikes, trying my best to subdue this guy so that we could handcuff him.

"Bear and I didn't quit. Finally other officers arrived. They didn't know how we got in, swimming around the fence. In the end they climbed the eight-foot chain-link fence, and with their assistance we were able to place the suspect under arrest."

"Wow, that is intense!"

"Yeah. I knew Bear was okay after that.

"About a year after that he had a bulged disc in his lower back and he had to go for surgery. We were off for three months. After those three months Bear was his old self again. We continued to compete at all the national trials. We won the national champion in 2007. We were the runner-up team in 2008. In 2009 he retired. There were lots of trials and tribulations with him, but Bear was a great dog."

"What was your kids' and your wife's relationship with Bear?"

"Bear was a cuddler. Any time he saw anybody he'd throw himself onto you and be like, 'Scratch me, scratch me!' Because my dogs live in kennels, it wasn't like he was a pet. He went everywhere with me, but to me first and foremost he's a police dog."

"Is that typical, or do some dogs live in the house?"

"We don't have a steadfast rule in our unit that says the dogs must live in their kennel, but if officers ask our opinion, we say that is the preferred method. Being in their kennel, it's their way they can relax.

"When Bear retired, his back end started to go, his feet started to drag. We brought him inside and made a bed for him in the basement. Right next to him was a blow-up bed, where my wife (if I was on nightshift) and I took turns sleeping next to him. When the time had come that enough was enough, we knew. He was urinating, defecating, his dignity was all but gone, that's not who he was. We decided that it was time to put him down. Because he was now incontinent, he was sleeping in the garage. For the last few weeks I began sleeping with him in the garage on the floor."

It seems to be an unwritten requirement of the job of police dog handler, that willingness to sleep on the floor next to your dog when he needs you.

"Bear's second to last day, I loaded him into the police SUV behind the driver's seat. I opened the door in the middle so he could hear the police radio and see me. We drove around my neighborhood, around Coquitlam and Port Moody, pretending like we were on patrol, hunting as a team once again.

"The next morning I took him up to Buntzen Lake with the family. He loved the water. I let him chase the stick. My kids were there and my wife was there; they said their good-byes. After that I drove over to Bill's house, another handler in our unit who was very close to Bear, so that he could also say good-bye. I asked Bill to put a bite sleeve on. I slung Bear in a sling under his lower abdomen and then I gave him his command to bite. I ran with him, slinging him for a bite, a last big bite with the sleeve. I let Bear carry his prize back to the truck. Then Bear and I, we headed back toward the city.

"We were passing by Main and Terminal McDonalds. It dawned on me that Bear had never eaten anything like that before. I said, okay, I'm gonna get a Big Mac and large fries for me and for Bear. The night before I also bought him four rib-eye steaks for his last meal.

"One place Bear always loved was the grass fields that overlooked the oceans and mountains at the old Justice Institute. I didn't want anyone with us, just me and him. It was my time alone with him. I brushed him one last time.

"He ate his rib-eye steak dinner, and then I said, 'Hey boy, I got another treat for you!' I gave him the Big Mac. He looked at it and smelled it, like 'What the heck is this?' He'd already eaten four rib eyes, then he gobbled this up, too.

"We stayed there for about three hours, and then I took him to the vet. By that time I'm a bag of crap, sobbing and crying. I carried him in there and the doctor came in. I was with Bear, talking to him, in his ear, while he was eating a little cookie, and then it was his time to go. It was a day-long celebration of our life together."

Tears spring to my eyes. I don't want to think of when our sweet Dandy dog has to go. But when she does, I'll do right by her. I'll make sure that the family and I give her a day-long celebration of life, of all her favorite places and foods and things to do, and then I'll let her go easy, whispering in her ear. Just like Sergeant Wong did for Bear.

"With our police unit, you work one dog, then you leave. You can stay to be a trainer if there's an opening, but if there's not, most guys leave and go for promotion to be a sergeant. I know with the RCMP, you can be a dog handler for life, as long as you pass the physical fitness every year. With us, you get one opportunity. After Bear, I continued to raise dogs with the unit and I continued teaching on our annual advanced course. I always kept in touch. I knew I'd want to come back as a supervisor. I raised three dogs (Echo, Tusk, and Scout), two of which are currently in our unit. When the other sergeant finally decided to retire, I competed and was selected. I returned in Jan 2014."

"You said you didn't come from a police family. What was your family's reaction when you became a cop?"

"I'm first generation, so for my mom and dad I'm sure policing was looked down upon. Coming from China, policing was for the uneducated. I know for a fact they wanted me to be a doctor, a pharmacist, or an engineer. That was never going to happen, but they would always try. My dad was the more vocal of the two. I remember in grade ten, me and my friend Grant—who is now an inspector with the Victoria Police Department—wanted to do ride-alongs with our school liaison officer from the Saanich police for two weeks. I remember thinking, 'Uh-oh, we'll have to get that parental release form signed.' I forged my dad's signature to do that two-week ride-along, and kept it a secret. I remember this officer taking us to the gun range. He passed us his gun and gave us a basic lesson. This must have been 1983, when I was fifteen. He said, 'Whatever you do, do *not* shoot yourselves, or I will be in a world of shit.'

"We said, 'Okay, sir!'"

This officer later went on to become the chief of police, Chief Constable Mike Chadwick, now retired. Wong's son has also joined the Vancouver Police Department. "You know, it's like father, like son. He knew he always wanted to be a police officer. He got in when he was twenty-one; he's now twenty-three."

"Do you see each other sometimes at work?"

"Oh yeah, lots of times, he'll come to my calls, we'll go for coffee together."

"Do you worry more about him because he's your son?"

"It bothers my wife more so than me. I know he's got a good head on his shoulders. I know the type of people that he is surrounded by. The thing about municipal policing—and again I'm not slagging any other police force—but the experience in the uniform patrol division is long and professional; it's safe and tactically sound. How we do things here is probably a lot different, because we have a constant high level of experience, and a high volume of calls. We have officers from specialty units like K9 and ERT who will always return to patrol division."

"What has it been like, being an Asian cop?"

"I've never had the race card pulled on me because of my background. The main people we obviously deal with are who you see in everyday life here: East Indians, Asians, people of Persian descent."

"So what do you think of these racist incidents being broadcast on social media?"

"We will never understand that level of racism that we see in parts of the U.S. There is no bias here. The conspiracy theorists out there may think so, but it's not true.

"My mom worked as a dishwasher for thirty-five years at the Empress Hotel. My dad was a line cook. Their furniture stayed the same, the house was the same. What was important was their kids were going to be better than they were. My brother went on to become an engineer. My sister got a masters in biochemistry. She wanted to do a doctorate, but at that point my parents said, 'Enough. You're a woman, it's time to start a family.' All they did was work hard to make sure their kids were better prepared and better educated. I'm sure there was racism. I can't even imagine what my dad would have suffered as a young man in this country. But when I see families take no responsibility, not doing the right thing raising a family, suddenly it's policing's fault?"

We're cruising Vancouver's notorious Downtown Eastside. The streets are full of people, even though it's late. There are well-dressed hipsters heading in and out of clubs and restaurants. There are also drug-ravaged men and women who shuffle down sidewalks, converging in clusters on the corners.

"What do you do when your life is in danger?" I ask.

"In dangerous situations, it's about survival. The human spirit, the will to live and to overcome adversity, kicks in. We all have it in us. It's just a matter if we'll be pushed to that point. Survivors can live through it, fight their way through. When I was with Bear in that boat compound? Bear had arrested over a hundred seventy-five guys in his career. There were only two instances, and that was one of them, where we were losing. Two times we needed help. I was worried. It was just me, this guy, and my dog. He was staying in for the fight, but in a fight you don't want it to continue like that. It comes down to life and death and who's going to survive. I honestly believed we were going to potentially lose without help. Some people will just do whatever they can not to go to jail. He was a known criminal, with warrants for his arrest. He knew he would be spending time in custody should he be taken in to custody. It was that fine balance, not to the point where I could shoot him yet. I did not want to escalate to that point. After a while, even the toughest dogs if they are wailed on continually, they will give up. I'm pepper-spraying the individual, striking him with my fists, but he's not complying. In this compound, surrounded by chain link, with no parking nearby, backup didn't see how we waded in. They had to run down to the boat compound, scale the eight-foot fence, and then come and assist us. When they came, they all grabbed a limb and applied different strikes to him until he finally submitted. Then the guy gets walked out. They called an ambulance for his dog bites. He went to jail. Now I look back and go, 'That was crazy!' and then I move on."

It's the same refrain I've heard from other officers: Never give up, even when you are losing. Never give up. Is this what courage comes down to, in the end? Just to keep on fighting as long as you have breath in your body?

"Where was Bear from?" I ask.

"He came from Saskatoon, but his blood line was from Germany. We already had two other dogs in our unit from that blood line. All throughout Edmonton police, they had that same blood line as well."

"How about Hunter?"

"Hunter I selected at Adlerhorst International Kennels. The owner is Dave Reaver, a former law enforcement member in California who is very experienced and well known in the policing world. Adlerhorst trains and sell dogs to all police departments. They have a very good reputation for bringing in strong dogs for the police and military. I tested about ten dogs over the course of two days that had arrived from Europe. Hunter excelled in every category that we looked for. Hunter was from Slovakia. All his commands are Czech, so I just kept them in Czech. Hunter flew back on the plane with me."

"What do you look for when you look at a dog?"

"First thing I look for: Is he trying to bite me? That's probably a bad thing. Does he just want to play? Is he acting kinda hinky or skittish? I look at teeth, are they broken, are they ground down because he likes to chew chain link? I look at body structure, are all his toes there? I look at play drive. What's his intensity like? Does he rip out to the field and he's a fiend looking for his ball? If he's very intense looking for the ball, that's a good quality.

"For police work, we've taken the ball away and added a human. If a dog is keen on looking for his ball, that's prey drive. There's also hunt drive. We'll show him his ball or tug, but prior to releasing him we'll spin the dog in circles, then cut him loose. We're judging the same thing, What's his intensity level, is he methodical, does he abandon the search quickly? In Hunter's case, he's gridding it, making a search pattern, working in a hunt pattern, you could see his tail going around and around.

"I put pressure on them in the bite. I put him in a harness, take him away from other dogs, other stimulus. I'll tie a line to a post, then leave the dog alone. He's getting to settle down. We're watching the dog's observations. Is he starting to yawn? The yawning is a sign of stress; it's something to take notice of. Is he relaxed? Is he showing signs of anxiety?

"I will then start to stalk the dog, advancing toward him with no equipment. I'm looking at his body language. Is he curious? Is he getting nervous? Does he want to bring the fight to me? As I get closer, the dog's true character will begin to emerge. I challenge him, go, 'Hey!' What does he do? Does he growl, does he start to back off, does he retreat? If he starts to retreat we have a big problem. After that, I'll get equipment on. An exposed bite sleeve to start, with an agitation stick or a crop, usually about three feet, used to stimulate the dog. Is he punching out, trying to get me? Does he close his eyes as the crop is raised, or does he show true character? Does he want to bite me out of fear or dominance? Then I will let him come in for a bite. Is it crushing or is it frontal? We look for crushing, not frontal, because with that comes compliance and the ability to hold, making it safer for the dog and the suspect. I'm assessing the quality of grip. I'm now putting pressure on him when I raise my arm and stick as I'm about to strike him. Is the grip now softer? I will now strike the dog with the crop.

"There's speed coming down, but at the last second, I pull away, like this," he says, snapping the back of his hand on my arm, "so it doesn't hurt." (It *hurts*.)

"I want to see whether the dog will wrap his front legs around me and drive his body into me. They are saying, 'I am dominating you.' They'll stay in the fight and they are going to win.

"I will then go into full bite suit. Each country does something a little bit different, French Ring Sport, or KNPV." (Similar to Schutzhund and French Ring, KNPV or Royal Dutch Police Dog Sport, trains dogs for service and protection work, and perhaps for a future career as police dogs.)

"In Schutzhund, for example, they don't do chest bites, leg bites, back bites. Just because a dog bites deep and hard on the sleeve does not mean he will do the same on the suit. If the dog is biting deep and hard on the second, third time, I know he's a very strong-minded dog. I'll see if they are comfortable biting the core. A dog that will fight in the core and is comfortable in it is a very strong dog. Some dogs will bite and start to pull you. That's called the counter. That can sometimes be interpreted as stress, especially if his grip is weak, and he's doing whatever he can not to fight you up close and personal. I want to see whether or not he's comfortable biting my chest, my tricep, also my legs. I will then start to slowly wrap him with my legs like I'm going to suffocate and choke him. The dogs that starts to release, that's not something that we look for.

"We will then move to environment. We'll take the dogs for a walk, over obstacles, up stairs, including see-through stairs, linoleum floors, tile floors, seeing if they'll bite in dark places, on slippery floors." All this time I'm taking notes, imagining how Sergeant Wong chose Hunter, how he had worked this dog to make him shine.

Sergeant Ray Wong has been through it all as a cop. He experienced the worst, watching Bear electrocuted and dying before his eyes, and the best, as he and his fellow officers brought Bear back from the grave. Above all, Sergeant Wong is a man guided by love: love of what he does, love of his family, his dogs and his country.

Not every dog owner is blessed with a bond so tight that a dog becomes family, but for every K9 handler I met, this is the truth they live. You do whatever it takes for your dog. Somehow, you do K9 CPR. You buy four steaks to make his last days on earth extra special. You break cover to protect your dog, and other police officers have to hold you back from risking your own life to save his. When your dog is knifed to death in front of you, he visits you in dreams. This is the bond that endures beyond the grave. The love of dogs defines every officer in every Dog Lover Unit, no matter what they face on the road, no matter where they are from. Whether their dogs are purebreds or rescues, whether they themselves came from police families or just followed a dream they held since they were kids, every single K9 team is defined by a loyalty that transcends language, and a bond of the heart between human and dog that makes them each better than they ever could be alone.

# Epilogue

"All over the world, you will find police forces and approaches to policing that are very different. But K9 cops? They are basically the same everywhere."

—Commandant Sylvain Heritier,
Paris, Brigade Cynophile

"The police, they pickle the world, preserve it the way it is. They are guard dogs keeping us afraid and obedient."

—Sunil Yapa, *Your Heart Is a Muscle the Size of a Fist*

"Policing is a loss of innocence."

—Vancouver Police Department Sergeant Valerie Spicer

"It seems to me that criminals' rights are respected more than your right not to be victimized."

—Royal Canadian Mounted Police
Dog Handler Constable Darrell Moores

The original spark for *The Dog Lover Unit* came from my wife, Isabelle. Even though our relationship was in trouble at that point, we were still (mostly) on polite terms. One evening, Isabelle casually tossed out the idea that would lead to this book. She came home from work (she is a police doctor for the RCMP) and told me about an amazing chase and capture of a dangerous criminal by one of the police dog teams. I said, "That's incredible! Someone should write a book about that." That someone was never going to be me. I couldn't hang out with cops. I couldn't shoot a gun, jump fences, or tackle a bad guy and cuff him. Not only was I a stressed-out mom of three young kids, I was also a dissident leftie feminist poet. Wrong person, wrong political orientation, wrong genre. I only wanted to *read* the darn book. Secretly. But soon after, Isabelle mentioned that the RCMP had organized a police dog funeral for a dog killed in the line of duty. Isabelle told me about it: the dog's flag-draped coffin, the tear-wrenching speeches. Once again, my heart skipped a beat. "You know, *you* could write that book," Isabelle said.

"I don't think so," I said. But a voice within whispered, *I think so.*

The odds were against me. My career had stalled, we were in debt, and the sessional teaching I did barely covered the cost of the sitters I had to hire, train, and hope would show up reliably to watch our kids. I had no reserve left for this dangerous challenge, which must be why that inner voice told me to go for it. I fought it every step of the way. But that voice within is my true self. That voice knew that the only way through hard times was to commit to even harder challenges.

The relationship between humans and animals has always been a central part of my identity. The first dog I ever loved, Jackson, belonged to my father. I was only a toddler, but my earliest memories include Jackson—leaning against his furry bulk, sitting and looking into his brown eyes. Jackson was a big black German shepherd mix with golden eyebrows—gentle with me and hell on wheels with every other living thing. When I was three, Jackson was shot and killed for chasing deer. I kept waiting for him to come running home from across the fields, but he was gone.

Over the years, I rescued boxes of abandoned kittens, brought home stray cats, toads, and snakes (and, memorably, a rabid bat), rode cows until I got my first pony, and was never without the company of a dog if I could help it.

I was raised to love animals. My mother always loved dogs and horses, and every other kind of creature. She taught me how to be in the company of animals. She also raised me to steer clear of people in positions of authority. My mother spoke with real fear of the FBI agents who regularly infiltrated their student organizations when she was at Stanford, provoking mayhem and disruption. My parents were so disgusted with the U.S. government during the Vietnam War that they fled the U.S., ending up on the small island in Canada where I was raised. I learned that cops, especially American cops, were tools of the state, and the state had no compunctions about crushing its own citizens.

In 1999, my brother, Jefferson, was teargassed in Seattle at the World Trade Organization protests. His best friend, writer Eli Hastings, along with hundreds of others, was teargassed, jailed, and held without access to a lawyer. Many others had rubber bullets fired at them. (A federal jury later found the city of Seattle liable for arresting protestors without probable cause, in violation of their constitutional rights.) The attacks on these protestors made me sick. My brother was assaulted by police simply for peaceably protesting against unfettered global capitalism and for social and economic justice, a right every citizen in every democratic nation holds. I had proof that those in authority could abuse their powers.

But on a deeper level, I already had all the proof I needed. When I was sexually assaulted at eleven years old, the thought of going to the police seemed as improbable as developing the power to teleport myself out of there. We were at a mining camp at the end of the world, in the Aleutian Islands in Alaska, where my father was prospecting for gold. I couldn't even open my mouth to speak to my father about what was happening, let alone call up strangers in uniform to ask for help. Suppose I had told, and been believed.

Perhaps my tormenter would have been beaten up. Perhaps he would have quietly disappeared down a mineshaft, the black water closing over his head. There might have been an "accident." Everyone had a gun there. Even now, I recoil at the possibility of unleashing such violence on anyone. Even him.

The choice I had was silence or violence. Silence had its price and I paid that price. But speech has its price, too, and silence seemed the better bargain. I moved on, but I never forgot.

I had tried once before to press charges. When I finally told, I learned that there had been other girls like me. I was twenty-one years old, living in Montreal. Soon after I told my father, my abuser contacted him looking for a job out of state. My father called the police. That was when I learned about the abuser's criminal record, though I never saw it. My father's call led to this man's rearrest for violating the terms of his parole by leaving the state of Alaska. So that was something. But I wanted more. I contacted another officer and told my story. It was difficult to get the words out. I was told that the statute of limitations had run out for me just the month before. I had no chance at justice. I understand that the law is the law, though I think statutes of limitations should be struck down for sexual assault. But what would have made all the difference when I was on the phone with this policeman was a single moment of human empathy. Even just hearing from that officer, "Thank you for calling," or "This must be difficult for you," would have helped. A good dog, sensing pain, would have moved closer and tried to assist. A good cop should, too. But this cop was direct to the point of rudeness, asking me to go into detail about what had happened to my body and then telling me I would get no help from the law. At that point, I gave up, pushed it out of my mind, and tried to move on.

It was in Innisfail, tracking with the police dog teams, that I had the impulse to hunt down my abuser, to find out the rest of the story. I can pinpoint the time with precision: I was listening to Constable Robert Shanks talk about a case of child rape in the remote north, where, despite overwhelming evidence and a guilty plea, the victim was once again living with the perpetrator. I gripped the door handle, hot with rage, as Shanks spoke of his own frustration at having to live with this deeply compromised judicial system.

*Justice*, I thought. *I want justice.* It surprised me, the force of my anger after all these years. I would find the perpetrator. I'd hunt him down like a dog on a track, ruthless and determined. I thought he would be very hard to find, and I wasn't quite sure what I'd do with him when I did find him, but I put that aside. I wanted to track him down; that was all I knew.

And so, as I was riding with K9 teams across North America, I began my own track for the criminal who had abused me decades before. I took courage from the dogs themselves, and from their handlers. These teams were relentless in pursuit. Obstacles in their way became problems to solve, not doors that slammed shut.

In the end, it was as easy to find him as picking up the phone. I called the Homer Police Department in Alaska. The woman who spoke to me was brusque.

"That long ago? We don't have anything. We have a ten-year retention of records, and there were no digital records at that time."

"Don't you have anywhere I might try to search?"

"Do you know his name?"

"His name?" I repeated, stupidly.

"Do you know the name of the assailant?"

I gave her his name.

"Check Vinelink Alaska, that's the offense registry for the Alaska

Department of Corrections," she said. "I'm pulling it up right now. Here he is. Community supervision. That means he's on parole."

"You mean you already found him?"

"Yes."

As I said good-bye and thanked her, I found him online as well. It was astonishingly easy. I scanned his criminal record. Convicted of sexual abuse of a minor in the first degree, count 1, count 10, and sexual abuse of a minor in the second degree, counts 6, 9. For each count, he served eight years; for counts 9 and 6 he served eight years time and eight years suspended. I look up what the counts are for, but then I fold that knowledge away and shut it in a drawer. I can't keep it in mind; my mind doesn't want it.

But there he is. Simple to find. Age sixty-nine, white male, reason for supervision: *Abscond*. In 2003 he had been charged with another offense, violated parole, and was now being monitored. I printed out a copy and held it in shaking hands. "At no time," I read, was he to have under his control "a concealed weapon, a firearm, or a switchblade or gravity knife."

And then I went to pick up my kids at school. It was my day to take my youngest child swimming. We hung around at the playground while he ate his apple and cheese string.

"Mom," he said, totally randomly, as he walked around the perimeter of the sand box. "If you eat eggs, vitamins, ice, and leeks, will you become evil?"

"No," I said, startled. I was slow on the connection, the little acrostic poem he'd made: EVIL. "People become evil when they decide to do bad things."

"I knew that," he said, and then we went to float in deep water. I swam laps while he took his lesson, and I tried to forget myself in the immersion, in the chatter of a six-year-old, in my present blessings.

So I had found my abuser. Now what was I going to do with him? For so long I had wanted to find the man who had once hurt me. I wanted to force him to look me in the eyes, and see my humanity. But once I found him, I was surprised by my indifference. He was an old man. He could teach me nothing about how to live. He had nothing for me, nothing to offer me. He was null and void. He was nobody.

He wouldn't see my humanity any more than he'd seen that of the other victims, and there were at least several of us. How many were there? Where were they now?

Finding him made me interested in his victims, in the girls who had been so much more courageous than I was, the girls brave enough to make that call to the police, to file charges. I had said nothing at the time, nothing to authorities until it was too late. Now I saw that five years after he'd abused me, there were new charges laid against him. Could I have stopped him, prevented the next assaults if I'd had a way to press charges?

I tracked down my abuser's former boss, and had a couple of painful conversations with him. He told me how sorry he was for ever hiring him—as if he could have known—and I told him to put that out of his mind. He also told me about what happened to my abuser's family. His wife had died of cancer soon after he'd been locked up, leaving their very young children orphans, with no close family. That stopped me. I felt a dull pain in my side.

I remembered them, those little children visiting the mining camp with their mother, maybe three and five years old, the way their father pulled them on his lap. Those children were righteous victims, too. How could I keep looking for their father, without adding to their incalculable loss? What good would that do in this broken world?

I know what a price victims pay to go through the criminal justice system. But at least some of the other children he assaulted had pressed charges, and found a measure of justice. How had they become so brave? Who had helped them? I wanted to meet them, to ask them in person, to learn their stories.

I wasn't the girl who had stopped him. I can't change that truth, but maybe I could write about why so few victims were able to trust the police, about the immeasurable distance between an abused child and justice. Maybe I could advocate for change on this side of the past. Because I know now that some of the police dog teams out there are hunting down guys exactly like him. They do it single-mindedly, tirelessly, and relentlessly. I've been on a stakeout for a child abuser, and watched the takedown. That helped. But being arrested is just the first step. It's so easy to get away with evil.

When I realized I was no longer interested in the perpetrator, but in the other victims, I interviewed RCMP Victim Services Coordinator Cynthia Helgason. She wanted me to know what victims are still up against when they press charges. "The chance that you'd go through the whole system without coming up against some difficulty is almost zero."

I thought about Helgason's job. "How do you find the courage to sit with people who have been traumatized, who have just survived the worst events of their lives?"

"I have trouble thinking of it as courage," says Helgason. "What I do makes an immediate, concrete difference in people's lives. I think it would be very hard to do something else, although there are days I dream of it."

"Which days?" I ask.

"Often we are in bleak situations where we cannot actually help. We can't make it better. We can't take action. We just need to be with them in their moment of pain."

Cynthia Helgason says something else that stays with me. "Police officers are action-oriented people. Don't ever let anyone tell you they are not helpers. More than anything, police have superhero complexes. They want to save the world. Whatever happens down the road, the vast majority sign up because they want to help."

What would it be like to have police officers so familiar, so worthy of trust, that even child victims would know who to call and would feel safe doing so? What if every neighborhood and every kid at school had a team of police officers whom they knew by name, who were a little bit more like social workers and a little bit less like soldiers? What if their obligation was not to the state, but to the people?

As a society, despite so many shattering examples of injustice, I believe we are moving in the right direction. It is inspiring to see specialized K9s being trained to support victims by organizations such as PADS, the Pacific Assistance Dogs Society. Tara Doherty, the PADS Communication Manager, speaks with pride of the accredited facility dogs her organization has raised and trained, dogs capable of supporting and comforting victims in court, or helping disabled individuals function out in the world. These dogs include Merlot, a black lab who now works with the Regina Police Department, and yellow lab K9 Caber, the first accredited trauma dog working in Canada.

I would like all victim services departments to have K9s available for therapeutic support. Sometimes even the most well-intentioned support from humans is more than a traumatized person can bear. Sometimes even words meant to comfort can come across as judgmental. But K9 support doesn't require the right words. It is the calm and solid presence of one being lending strength to another.

I went to the dogs seeking courage. I found what I sought. I wanted to change my life. I wanted to grow braver and love more wholeheartedly. I wanted to learn all I could about how police dogs live and work. I followed that obsession through four different countries. And, as I did all this, something surprising happened: my views of police officers shifted, sometimes radically, as I spent time in their company. I needed to learn this. I needed to see that there were indeed men and women in uniform who were worthy of respect, that there were cops I could trust with my life.

As I was experiencing this transformation, another shift was also taking place: the cracks in the relations between certain members of the community and certain police departments became an abyss. There was a number, a shocking and growing number, of police killings of young black men caught on video. Activists across the U.S. protested this brutality. One narrative took hold in the U.S., and drifted to Canada: that not just individual cops, but entire police forces, were racist and corrupt. The narrative bled along with the body count: cops, all cops everywhere, are racist and corrupt.

Seattle K9 Sergeant Steve White had some insightful comments about public mistrust of cops generally.

"Most people don't have antecedents about cops. The lens they see us through is a borrowed lens," he tells me, over pie and coffee at a diner outside Seattle. I have trouble reading maps and a ridiculous resistance to using GPS; consequentially, I have gotten terribly lost getting here. I cried in my car in despair of ever finding the place we were supposed to meet, and kept Steve White waiting. Now I concentrate on my pie, and on pretending to look like a professional. I am sure Steve sees through my façade, but he's too much of a gentleman to comment.

"You mean what we see of cops is filtered through the media, through what we read?"

"Generally, yes. Everybody's antecedents are different. Most of them, when they come to police, are borrowed. Almost nobody comes out of an interaction with the police, thinking, 'That was *really* called for.' The thought is, 'I wonder if he does two more, if he gets a toaster.' It is not in human nature to respond well." We have a wide-ranging and interesting conversation about everything from propaganda to police protocol, and Steve tells me about the cops who mentored him when he was a latchkey kid. I regret not having had time to stop in and see his dog training facility, but my family is waiting for me, and it's a long drive home.

It is true that humans resist being controlled by others, and that is where we need to find opportunities to make the public buy into policing, to have input into the kind of policing they want as a community.

I want the incompetent and racist cops out; they are dangerous for all of us. I also want police officers trained by experts in diffusing tense or potentially lethal situations. I want police departments to be well funded and well supported. There are bad people out there, doing terrible things, and I want good cops available to protect the rest of us from them. I want police departments to be ethical and compassionate and brave, and both representative of and deeply invested in the communities they serve. I want the U.S. to move to greater gun control, so citizens can live more like those in London do—without the fear and paranoia of being members of the world's most heavily armed culture. And I want North American police forces to learn from countries like France and the UK, which have radically refocused policing to make themselves accountable to the public. But this accountability goes both ways: citizens of these countries have also made themselves accountable to police by being unarmed, and thus less dangerous to serve. Most of all, I want police officers patrolling our streets to be like the men and women I've gotten to know.

It is hard to ride with cops and not taste despair. But K9 cops have an advantage. Misunderstood and distrusted by the very public they put their lives on the line to protect, they turn to their dogs and trust them like they trust no other. With their dogs, and sometimes only with their dogs, they allow themselves tenderness.

K9 police officers have told me about drug-addicted mothers

who've pimped out their thirteen-year-old daughters. They've told me about witnessing child rape, about the toll of serial killer cases that they've investigated, about being deliberately stabbed by a syringe just used by an HIV-positive individual resisting arrest. They've seen children killed by those who should protect them and women stalked like deer. They've walked through puddles of blood in dark hallways. They've pumped the hearts of lifeless bodies knowing there is little hope, but praying for a miracle. They've been spit on for the uniform. These officers work so hard to be the wall between criminals and the rest of society. But unlike walls, they are not made of stone.

One of the most frequent reasons for police dog calls is domestic violence. It was disturbing, to say the least, to hear cops talk about trying to rescue women from men they live with who want to kill them. I heard things I wish I had not, about broken noses, ribs, jawbones, about men who shot at the cops who came to intervene and protect. An average of three women are killed every day in the U.S. by their partners, most of them shot to death. Family members and law enforcement are also at grave risk due to domestic violence.

We have these impulses, as poet Denise Levertov notes: the violent and the creative. In her essay "Paradox and Equilibrium" Levertov writes, "We humans cannot absorb the bitter truths of our own history, the revelation of our destructive potential, except through the mediation of art."

But the mediation of art, of poetry, does not protect me these days. I learn of the attacks in France, and I scan the news for names of the police officers I know. I see the images of black men pulled over for broken taillights and then shot to death, and it tears me up. Who are these people so full of hate and suspicion of the other that the first impulse is violence?

All my work as a poet involves speaking for those who are denied a voice, speaking out against injustice and oppression. So I find myself in the position of speaking out against both police brutality and against hatred of the police.

Novelist Chimamanda Ngozi Adichie has spoken powerfully about the danger of a single story. There is one story about cops in my leftie circle: they are brutal, power-hungry, racist thugs. There's another story, I'm sure, among right-wing law-and-order types, about how cops are self-sacrificing heroes who are always on the right side. I fear that people in the arts community, who might have supported my work and the spirit behind it, will not support this work. People on the right politically will likely not support me, either personally or ideologically. And yet, here I am.

There are many stories about the police, about victims and violence and the state. I am not a journalist or a statistician. Nevertheless, I have grappled with facts and with statistics published in studies across the U.S. and Canada, the United Kingdom and France, in the process of writing this book. They don't paint a clear picture. Are African American men more likely to be shot by police?

Not so, according to economist Roland Fryer, who says that Blacks and Hispanics, while more likely to experience nonlethal force, are less likely to be shot than whites.[1] Other data has made it clear that Blacks and Hispanics have far more encounters with police. Each encounter carries statistical risk, and more encounters dramatically increase the likelihood of a violent end result. But, as economist Sendhil Mullainathan makes clear, the racial bias that permeates the U.S. cannot be pinned on individual police officers; it is a bias that runs through all U.S. institutions, and is both more entrenched and more challenging to fight. Police officers, Mullainathan writes,

*are at least in part guided by suspect descriptions. And the descriptions provided by victims already show a large racial gap: Nearly 30 percent of reported offenders were black. So if the police simply stopped suspects at a rate matching these descriptions, African-Americans would be encountering police at a rate close to both the arrest and the killing rates.*

*Second, the choice of where to police is mostly not up to individual officers. And police officers tend to be most active in poor neighborhoods, and African-Americans disproportionately live in poverty.*

*In fact, the deeper you look, the more it appears that the race problem revealed by the statistics reflects a larger problem: the structure of our society, our laws and policies.*[2]

■

Statistics matter. Accurate facts matter. They are not my realm of expertise, though. I am a writer, a poet. I observe at the level of the individual.

And individuals matter. One person killed under questionable circumstances by the police means the death not only of that individual, but also the death, for his friends and family, of any faith or trust they have had in the system.

The system, in certain parts of North America, appears broken. In Chicago, police shootings of African American men, including teenagers like Laquan McDonald, have reached a point where the mayor's own task force lambasts the Chicago Police Department: "C.P.D.'s own data gives validity to the widely held belief the police have no regard for the sanctity of life when it comes to people of color."[3] In a city plagued by homicides and gunfire, the police department has both individual and systemic problems with training, transparency, and accountability.[4] Chicago is by no means alone in having such issues.

But what is to be done about crime prevention? As David Yassky, dean of Pace University School of Law, writes, there is a myth that most of the people swelling the U.S. prison population are in there for drug dealing. Yassky notes that only about one-fifth of those entering prison since the 1990s are there because of drug offenses. "When we talk about 'mass incarceration,' we are mostly talking about people convicted of relatively low-level crimes of violence or theft—a stolen iPhone, a street-corner fight, a few-hundred-dollar burglary from a clothing store."[5] While Dean Yassky believes such crimes need an "enforcement response," he urges reform of the American correctional system, focusing on mental health services, and putting rehabilitation at the center.

I would ask what kind of enforcement response is appropriate for stealing an iPhone. To me, it is certainly not a criminal record, not the trauma of being locked up. I would consider community service, as well as counseling, an appropriate response.

Police departments would do less harm if they were explicitly aligned with protecting the citizens they serve, as well as the state. That would prevent such conflicts of interest as seen in the states of Texas and Arizona. As Arizona's Institute for Justice notes,

> *In Arizona, law enforcement personnel have a strong incentive to seize as much property as they can because they keep up to 90 percent of the funds raised through civil forfeitures. Allowing police and prosecutor to wield both the purse and the sword threatens the fair and impartial administration of justice, endangers private property rights, and can place police officers in unnecessary jeopardy. Forfeiture proceeds are used for a variety of expenditures, ranging from equipment to travel to salaries, benefits and overtime. Over the time period examined in this paper, law enforcement increased its forfeiture revenue almost 400 percent—from $11.8 million in 2000 to $50.1 million in 2011.*

*These large and increasing sums give reason to worry that forfeiture has become, or is becoming, a way for law enforcement agencies to self-fund outside the normal budgetary process.*[6]

Accurate statistics must guide policy, and no state can be legitimate with unjust criminal and penal laws. It is an imperfect process, one that will take time, as each of these countries grapples with how to treat its people and how to deal with crime. But accurate statistics don't replace compassionate policing.

Beyond the statistics, there are individuals. There are those whose lives are lost to violence, whether a young mother killed by a violent ex-boyfriend, a young police officer killed by a rampaging suspect, or a young black man killed by an officer who pulls him over for a broken headlight.

But the whole idea of taking sides is equally troubling. The beauty doesn't cancel out the abuse. Good cops and good training in one unit don't erase police brutality in another. And telling the true good stories doesn't negate the truth of the stories of suffering and injustice.

We need each other: I know this as surely as I know that I'm breathing. And we need to do better at taking care of each other. The first step is seeing each other accurately, listening to one another's stories, and admitting our interdependence. People need good police; the police need good people. And victims know in their bones something that the radical left has a hard time admitting: there are evil people out there, people deeply invested in hurting innocent people, and it will take great efforts to stop them.

As a victim, it is hard to accept the truth: that another human being has decided to do you harm Until that truth becomes a part of you, however, you are split off from what actually happened. Now you have joined the club no one wants to join. The fact that it happens all the time makes it no easier to bear. These invisible stories of crime victims deserve their own book, and I would like to be the one to write it. I hate injustice; it sickens me, and I want to fight it with my pen, to expose it to the light of day, as I have since I published my first book of poetry.

The police have told me again and again of their frustration at catching criminals, only to have those people walk away unpunished. Prosecutors refuse to take cases that they can't win, and victims are left knowing that those who violated them got away with it. In Canada, for example, according to the Department of Justice: "Only 9% of the cases coming into the court system are resolved by way of a trial. Of the 91% percent of cases that do not go to trial, 41% do not result in a conviction; they are withdrawn by the Crown or resolved without a conviction in some other way."[7]

Police officers I talked to spoke about learning not to follow the cases of the criminals they arrest. Even when they catch someone in the act, it is evident that guilt does not necessarily lead to a conviction. How many times did I hear "we have a legal system, not a justice system"? Even those criminals the prosecutors take through the court system who are in the 59 percent resulting in conviction may not receive a sentence commensurate with the harm they caused. For cops who put themselves in harm's way to protect the public only to see the perpetrators and the guilty walk away unpunished, this is a difficult truth to bear.

In her article for *The New York Times Magazine*, Parul Sehgal writes about how survivors of sexual assault are encouraged not to consider themselves victims.

*The logic of "compulsory survivorship" neatly anticipates the conditions so many victims of violence face: the disbelief or indifference, the paucity of social support—to say nothing of the fact that, as Jon Krakauer notes in his book on campus rape, "Missoula," if an individual is raped in America, more than 90% of the time the rapist will get away with it. It makes sense that an ethos of pluck and hardiness has taken hold. There is simply no alternative.*[8]

Didn't I go to the dogs wanting to reject the victim identity? Yes. I wanted to be around survivors who had seen it all, and who would make me tough just by being in their presence. I wanted to find resilience—and I have. But it doesn't look like I thought it would. I've found the strength of self-compassion and vulnerability. I'm a victim, a righteous victim. There are so many others. Of course most of us survive. But I carry scars.

Perhaps it would be better for victims to feel they had been hit by lightning, or stricken by some other natural disaster. As much harm as the weather can do, we don't take it personally. We are not chosen; we didn't call down the floods or fire, and we don't expect justice from a tsunami. That is one true lesson I learned from tracking down the record of the man who assaulted me. It wasn't personal, once I saw the file and registered the facts about the other kids. Him? He was just lightning, and I was just a tree in his path that caught fire.

The weight of human injustice is sometimes so oppressive that despair can set in. I have seen what criminals will do to victims. We smell the blood of weakness, and it just as often disgusts us as arouses our compassion. I have, to my shame, experienced this phenomenon within myself. Who wants to be on that team? That's the losing team. To be a victim is to have come face-to-face with the truth that perhaps we all come up against sooner or later: life happens to us. Our fate is only sometimes in our hands. You can say you are a survivor until you run out of breath, and, while it may give you the dignity to keep fighting, sometimes it might be more honest to say you are a righteous victim instead, because it allows you the dignity of making space for your suffering. And in allowing yourself this tenderness, perhaps you will find tenderness to be moved by the suffering of others.

The fear in reclaiming the term victim is that we will allow ourselves to be stuck in time, like insects in amber, never growing past the worst moments of our lives. But the forced narrative of the survivor does us no favors. Attempts to appear tougher than we actually are can impede healing.

For me, all those ride-alongs were transformative. I had time to witness the cops and their dogs deal with criminals, and it healed something in me. I believe it to be true, what I heard from different police officers, that a very small percentage of people commit the vast majority of crimes. They can leave a huge number of victims in their wake. You can call them evil if you want, or sociopaths or terrorists. They might just as well be rising levees, or rabid wolves. All I know is that if left unimpeded, they will take innocent people down with them until they can't do it anymore.

Hearing the stories from those who have made it their life's work to stand between victims and criminals was a shift in perspective I am so grateful for. Cops hear and see into the lives of so many people. If they see people at their worst, if they are inclined to cynicism, they also see both the results of bad fortune and bad choices. It was freeing, to know both how little control we have over what happens to us, and also, paradoxically, how much. Somehow, the cops I got to know held both those truths close to their chests.

The hardest cop in the world can be killed in a matter of seconds by any deranged assailant with a gun, any ex-boyfriend who wants to kill the woman who left him and is mad about being thwarted. No matter how much they put it out of their minds, every cop knows this. Toughness doesn't mean invincibility. And dogs, even the toughest dogs like Cade and Chrisa, know what it is to be powerless and to be victims. They are at the mercy of the humans who care for them, and also at the mercy of the humans they encounter on the street, as working animals. Despite this, most dogs somehow never lose their capacity for wild joy, or their capacity for loving deeply.

Riding with the dogs allowed me to free myself, and my family, from the trap I was in. In the middle of a hard situation, I took on something harder, but something very different from the quotidian. And saying yes to that one hard thing allowed me to take the other steps I needed to: to confront my past, to be vulnerable without giving in to shame, to ask for help for our child and our relationship, and to be open to listening to others without pretending I had any of the answers anymore. Not having the answers made space for the love. And in that respect, there is no better role model than a good dog. A good dog has no guile. He is sad when he is sad—dejectedly so, when the situation merits it. A good dog is unafraid of hard work or the unknown. He lives in the moment. A good dog is able to move past adversity and take joy in the present reality. His heart retains the capacity to love, though he does not forget those who abused or mistreated him. And he is always, always up for the next adventure. I had lost my joy to fear, my sense of adventure to routine, my capacity to be openhearted to the demands of family life. Going to the dogs gave it back to me. Just being in their company, and in the company of their handlers, provided the transformation I needed, that first step on a new path. It was so simple, really, but so profound. When I had this sense of wonder and curiosity back, when I had my *self* back, my family thrived.

When I was a girl, we had one family we were very close to, who lived in the house just below ours. These were the girls I rode ponies with, the girls I played T-ball with. Their father, Peter, walked us all to the bus stop every morning and waited with us by the road until the school bus came.

Coming home one day, Peter saw a dog sitting by the side of the road, a handsome dark sable German shepherd. The dog sat quietly with a worried expression on his face. He sat there for three days and nights after being abandoned. He didn't move from the spot, even though it was a road where cars whipped past at forty miles an hour. On the third day, he followed Peter home. Because he was a large, threatening Shepherd who charged and barked at the mailman, Peter drove him to the pound and left him there. But that night the girls cried so much and made such sincere promises that they would take care of him that the following morning they all rushed back to get him and bring him home. Poocho had found his family.

I don't know why Peter gave him the undignified name Poocho, for this was a dog that embodied dignity. But Poocho he was, and for the rest of his life he was Peter's dog—loyal, attuned, and deeply attached to the man who had taken him in. Poocho walked us to the bus stop with Peter every day, and watched over all of us kids with grave affection: me, my little brother Jefferson, Rohina and Mimosa and the youngest, Katy May.

In another way, Peter gave him the perfect name: Pooch, an affectionate word for dog, a word of unknown origin. Poocho couldn't tell us about his former owners, or why they had abandoned him by the roadside. He could only do what he did, which was to wait loyally and obediently for his owners to return, wait like the very best dog in the world. When that didn't happen, Poocho became Peter's dog, and our playmate. But what strikes me now is how he never lost his capacity to love, and to connect, despite what had happened to him.

Most dogs are greathearted like that. Most dogs, I think, have more ability to love than humans do. We humans get in our own way. I saw that when I was just a toddler, with my father's German shepherd, Jackson, the one who used to let me sit on his back, put paper bags on his head, pretend he was my pony.

We kids usually rode in the back of the old 1953 Chevy truck, so rusted through in places we could see the road running along underneath. We were always happiest with Poocho in the back with us, though Poocho most loved riding shotgun next to Peter. We kids stole sugar cubes from the coffee self-serve at the grocery store and bounced unbuckled over the gravel road, one hand on Poocho's steady warm back, crunching sugar. He would grin into the wind, taking in the scent of deer and dust and the next adventure.

We parents think a lot about good role models for our kids: coaches, teachers, aunts, and uncles. But looking back, some of my most powerful and important role models were dogs and horses. They modeled curious exploration of the environment, and running for the pure joy of running. They modeled interspecies loyalty and quiet companionship. (And also—let us be frank—the delight of jumping in the lake for impromptu swims, occasional overeating, and lolling in the sun.)

Going to the dogs gave me a space to step out of my life, but they also gave me a way back to loving the wonderful person I was with. People are so stupidly complicated in the way they love. Dogs love without conditions. They don't say, "I'll love you if you talk to me more about your feelings and remember to call the accountant and buy the nonfat Greek yogurt, not the two percent." They don't say, "I'll love you if." They just love you. Scent is not the only area where dogs have far superior ability to humans. Their heart ability is also superior. Human hearts are not as resilient as canine hearts. When people get hurt as children, or even just roughed up by the years, we shut down, sometimes permanently. Dogs shut down, too, but it's almost never permanent. They always have that spark within them, that willingness. Find a sad dog, abandoned somewhere, and odds are good that, given a genuine invitation to bond, she will jump at the chance. Sometimes we humans have to get very close to a dog to learn from them how to live and love openheartedly again. I know I did. In fact, I needed to get close to a lot of dogs.

During our breakup, I had to give up changing Isabelle, and find my way back to seeing who she actually was, beyond the crazy schedules, the work, the kids and their needs, the fact that she hated vegetables and I wanted to move to a plant-based diet. She had to give up changing me, too. We broke up, and then we asked the question we had lost sight of: Who are you? I don't know anymore; who are you?

I wouldn't have gone to the international writing program at Iowa if I hadn't first started riding with K9 teams. Every handler on the force spends 180 days away from home, pursuing their dream with everything they've got. Yes, most of them were men, but women went to Innisfail too, mothers included. Couldn't I take half that time for a writing residency, my first, even though I was a mother?

I came to the point of believing in myself, the point where I said yes, and Isabelle saw the yes that shifted everything and met it with one of her own. We worked out the rest of it. She had to take a leave of absence from her intense work as a police doctor, and become a full-time mom for those months. But I said yes to my dream of writing, and all the discipline it would require. We were able to see, both of us, how to get the help our child needed. When I was out of the picture, the picture became much clearer, and with that clarity came the chance to ask for professional support. One yes led to another: I said yes to her proposal of marriage soon after I came back.

We stepped back, took measure, and found each other again. It's not a story I've seen written much: the end of a marriage and the beginning of another, but with the same person.

It is humbling to confess how much lack of sleep and the inability to talk helped heal our relationship. But when I came home from the dogs incoherent with fatigue, wrung out but happy, and sat with my family on the couch, watching TV, there was really nothing that needed saying. The first few weeks we sat on different couches, then we sat together, then we held hands. The love was still there, dormant, like a bulb in winter. When we got out of the way, the ground thawed and the green shoots broke through. Love opened like a peony.

After nearly twenty years together, we eloped in a beautiful ceremony by the sea, with just us, our two best friends, the dog, Dandy, and the kids. We read each other vows, and the children said vows too, though the dog chose not to speak. The whole day, in January in Vancouver, was magic—filled with bright cold light and so much laughter. *So this is marriage*, I thought. How can it be so startling after twenty years to enter the great mystery of it all?

■

Dandy, our own sweet dog, brings my child closer to us again. Even though we don't touch, we can snuggle through the dog, each of us on one end of her little fluffy body. We can laugh at her, at the way she sprawls on her back, softly snoring, legs splayed in utter repose, at the way she scratches our hands to get us to scratch her head.

■

Since the pit bull incident, Dandy has made it clear that she will take a running leap at any dog, no matter how big, and sacrifice herself for us. I know it's not healthy. I know she smells my anxiety and reacts to it. But it's also incredibly touching, to be in the presence of such love. She is a part of us. Each member of the family responds to her animal to animal, connecting beyond language, beyond species.

In order to help my child, I had to stop and change course entirely. In this, too, I learned from the K9 teams. Sometimes a dog tracks a scent to a dead end, or the scent disappears. The suspect could have been picked up in a car, or the scent could have been washed away or otherwise disturbed. It's hard to let go the illusion of having all the answers. But only with that acceptance can a team change course to a direction that might prove to be the right path.

Dandy may be small, but she loves adventure. Her happy place coincides with my own: on a boat, in dazzling light, paddling out to sea in a kayak. She stands on my knees, nose in the wind, quivering with joy.

The rescue dogs I spend time with are three female dogs, Djimathie, Nicky, and Isis. They are all working in Paris, all rescued from difficult situations. Two of them were days away from being put to death before the Dog Lover Unit decided to adopt them, rescue them, and retrain them as police dogs. All three of these girls have been given one more chance, and they have seized it. They smile while they are at work.

In the end, that is what I most needed to learn: that some of us, the lucky ones, are given another chance, and it is up to us to seize it. I went to the dogs looking for a way out. Riding with the cops I heard of human evil that broke my heart, and I saw human goodness that healed it. But most of all, I saw courage in the face of trauma, a courage that was magnified because it passed from cop to dog and back again: the courage of K9 and human united, working as a team. If they were on a track, and it was a matter of saving a life, they never gave up.

Whoever you are, no matter how lost, never give up.

# Note to Readers

This is a true story, though some names and details have been changed. Although the events in *The Dog Lover Unit* happened over four years, they did not occur in the chronological order in which they are told. I have moved both major and minor events around, compressed conversations and events for dramatic effect, and followed only the timeline of what the story demanded: the themes of justice, violence, and the animal-human bond.

I have done my best to recall and describe my experience of events accurately; all errors of recollection are my own. When I began the ride-alongs, I carried a recording device, which quickly proved useless much of the time, as we were outside running around. What worked best for me was to bring my computer along in the cruiser or truck, and to type things in real time when I could, and type the rest just after the shift. Of course I had to remember and sometimes reconstruct conversations and details, and of course I don't have perfect recall. I have also on various occasions contacted the officers or persons involved and asked them to explain or clarify something that didn't make sense and otherwise to confirm the accuracy of my recollections. For readability, I have often included their explanation as part of the conversation.

These are the experiences of a civilian and a poet, not a police officer. Despite my best efforts, as recounted in the book, I have learned that I am an unreliable witness at high speeds, or when I am afraid. This may, I am well aware, drive the cops I rode with crazy; for this I apologize. You are trained to be witnesses in a court of law: I am on the scent of the truth in a story as seen through my eyes, and as I choose to tell it, with all my imperfections as a poet and storyteller. Even if I have gotten some few facts wrong, I hope I have gotten the great truths right: the truths I learned about courage and canines and cops.

Also, because the various police dog units were so welcoming to me, and made time to connect with me, keep me safe while letting me see what they do, and answering my many, many questions, I would like to give back. Five percent of my postadvance profits from the sale of this book will go to the National Police Dog Foundation: https://nationalpolicedogfoundation.org/faqs/, and Pacific Assistance Dogs Society (PADS): http://pads.ca/

# Acknowledgments

I am grateful to the BC Arts Council and the Canada Council for the Arts, who gave me the gift of time to write this book. Their support made all the difference, as it has for so many Canadian writers and artists.

This book is dependent on the brave and dedicated men and women who shared their stories with me. I cannot thank them enough for letting me into their lives and sharing so openly. Not all of them made it into the final book; every officer I talked to deserved his or her own book. They all took a risk talking to me, trusting me with their experiences, and their traumas; I take that honor very seriously, and hope that this book will provide a bridge, opening the door for greater understanding and dialogue between police officers and the citizens they are entrusted to protect and keep safe.

Love and immeasurable gratitude to my wife, Isabelle Fieschi, who believed in this book, and in my ability to write it, even when I did not, and who managed things at home so I could be out on the road. Thank you, my love. I'm so glad that following the dogs helped bring us back to each other.

My agent, Hilary McMahon, believed in the dogs from the beginning, and saw this book through to the end. Peter Joseph and

Cameron Jones have been the best editorial team I could have wished for—sympathetic, incisive, and responsive. To have worked with two professionals at the top of their game is an incredible gift.

Many people cheered me on, read and edited my proposal, and helped me move the project forward. Some helped me a little and some helped me a lot, but it all made a difference, and I'm so grateful that the right assistance came when it was most needed. I will pay it forward! Carol Shaben steered me to Westwood and offered excellent advice on the proposal. Lori Shenher and Maggie de Vries lent support from early days, as did Adrian Harewood, Andrew Westoll, Alison Pick, Judy McFarlane, Michael Gruber, Elise Gruber, Valerie Truelove, Elee Kraljii Gardiner, Christine Gross-Loh, Cori Howard, and Karim Alrawi. Kara Stanley believed even when I couldn't see how I was going to get there. Brock and Lisa Crawford of Action Photography allowed me to use their excellent photos of Cade.

Thank you to dear neighbors and friends Edward and Stella Tang, Nancy Meagher, Christabel Shaler, and Janet Clark who lent me their quiet houses as oases of quiet whenever they were away traveling. Jim Prier and Shelley Mason, parents and grandparents extraordinaire, picked up the kids from school when I was on the road, read drafts and offered encouragement and clear, useful editorial advice. My mother, Mary Rose, read the book with care and attention, and gave me source materials about how dogs think that were very informative. Bob Rose and Jefferson Rose played devil's advocate about human nature and policing, and challenged me while still supporting me. M. L. Lyke supported me every step of the way, reading drafts with her acute journalistic ability, homing in on what needed work. My aunt Susan and uncle Tim Gonzales drove me to jail and picked me up again, and Aunt Sue and I shared an unforgettable night involving dogs and helicopters. In London, Superintendent Robyn Williams gave me a tour of Scotland Yard, talked to me about how police forces in London function, and generously shared her experiences as an activist and early member of the National Black Police Association, who felt policing was the best way to accomplish her social and activist goals. Catherine Fieschi gave me precious time to work while taking her niece out on the town, all on a broken ankle. Celia Moore loaned me her beautiful flat in London. In Paris, Michèle Fieschi and Jérôme Fouan took care of everything so I was free to write, and helped me with French questions.

# Notes

## Chapter 1

1. Patricia T. O'Conner and Stewart Kellerman, "What Kind of Abbreviation is K-9?," *Grammarphobia*, January 7, 2013, http://www.grammarphobia.com/blog/2013/01/k-9.html.

## Chapter 2

1. Constable Darrell Moores is right that individuals with a criminal record are screened out by the RCMP, and I was not able to find evidence of police officers being hired who had prior records (though those with juvenile records are considered on a case-by-case basis). While this screening is carried out in Canada, in the U.S. it is another matter. According to *The New York Times* on September 11, 2016, there have been a number of police officers fired by one department because of criminal convictions, who then are unknowingly hired by another department in another state.

2. Carson Gerber, "Dog Training Facility Replaces Police Dog Killed in Paris Terror Attacks," *Kokomo Tribune*, December 18, 2015, http://www.kokomotribune.com/news/dog-training-facility-replaces-police-dog-killed-in-paris-terror/article_0a70a554-a4ff-11e5-a9e2-9f5101d26a1e.html.

3. University of Iowa, when I checked, was rated in the top ten of U.S. party schools, but mostly, in 2016, seemed to be around #5 or #6: "2017 Top Party Schools in America," *Niche*, https://colleges.niche.com/rankings/top-party-schools/.
   "Playboy's Top Party Schools," *Playboy*, September 15, 2014, http://www.playboy.com/articles/playboys-top-party-schools.
   These rankings are based, in part, by density of bars within one mile of campus, and alcohol and drug violations reported each year by the schools.

4. "New Iowa City K-9 Team Tracks Down Suspected Armed Robbers," *WGEM.com*, December 31, 2012, http://www.wgem.com/story/20475668/2012/12/31/new-iowa-city-k-9-team-tracks-down-suspected-armed-robbers.

5. In July, a UNICEF report found that twenty-eight people under nineteen were killed by police every day in Brazil, double the number when the country passed a law to protect minors in 1990. This death rate is higher than in war zones, according to the agency. "UN Body Accuses Brazil's Military Police of Killing Kids to 'Clean Streets' for Olympics, World Cup," *teleSUR*, October 13, 2015, http://www.telesurtv.net/english/news/UN-Brazils-Police-Kill-Kids-to-Clean-Streets-for Olympics-2015 1013-0044.html.

## Chapter 3

1. Are K9 teams actually more likely to be shot than general duty patrol officers, as I was told by both Deputy Moses and Sheriff Davis, as well as most of the police dog handlers of the RCMP? A number of K9 officers take this as fact. But when I tried to find statistics for either the U.S. or Canada, it was surprisingly difficult. The RCMP keeps records of all police fatalities, but does not separate them into categories based on police specialty. In the U.S., Seattle Police Sergeant Steve White, Canine Unit supervisor, said in his experience over many years of conducting officer safety seminars, the number of K9 officers who say they've been involved in shootings are two to four times as high as general duty officers. But Sergeant White says it's more complicated than that. While he has observed in his own work that K9 officers are more likely to be involved in dealing with suspects who have shown their willingness to resist or flee, and simultaneously are less likely to give up pursuit of these suspects than the average officer, he also believes that some K9 officers may skew statistics because they were involved in shootings outside of their K9 duty assignment. In Canada, Senior Trainer Tom Smith had also heard how much more dangerous K9 policing is than general duty. He stressed that there were no statistics, but shared his observation with me. "I kind of don't agree with that in some ways," he told me. "In thirty-five years I've been in we've had three police dog handlers killed. It's not because they were dog handlers so much; it's because they were policemen. I think dog handlers respond to more dangerous calls, but so does ERT (the Emergency Response Team). I think constables who are working in remote places where there's no backup for hours, they're on their own, they're at risk." It would be useful for both the public and the police officers to know the risks, in order to best guide policy.

## Chapter 4

1. "Sonoma County Main Adult Detention Facility," *Yelp*, accessed April 4, 2016, https://www.yelp.ca/biz/sonoma-county-main-adult-dentention-facility-santa -rosa.
2. "Justin Bourque Statement to RCMP Shows No Remorse for Killings," *CBC News*, October 27, 2014, http://www.cbc.ca/news/canada/new-brunswick/justin -bourque-statement-to-rcmp-shows-no-remorse-for-killings-1.2814230.
3. Michael MacDonald, "Justin Bourque Apologizes Saying His Rationale for Killing Mounties in Moncton Was the Talk of Some Arrogant Pissant," *National Post*, October 28, 2014, http://news.nationalpost.com/news/canada/justin-bourque

-apologizes-saying-his-rationale-for-killing-mounties-in-moncton-was-the-talk-of
-some-arrogant-pissant.

4. "Position Statement on Pit Bulls," *ASPCA.org*, accessed December 2016, http://
www.aspca.org/about-us/aspca-policy-and-position-statements/position-statement
-pit-bulls.

5. "On the Blue Water: A Gulf Stream Letter," Hemingway, Ernest, *Esquire*, April 1936.

## Chapter 6

1. Bob Paulson, "Statement of Apology to Women in the RCMP and Announcement of
Settlement," Royal Canadian Mounted Police website, October 6, 2016, http://
www.rcmp-grc.gc.ca/en/news/2016/5/statement-apology-women-the-rcmp-and
-announcement-settlement.

2. Katherine Spillar, "How More Female Police Officers Would Help Stop Police
Brutality," *Washington Post*, July 2, 2015, https://www.washingtonpost.com
/posteverything/wp/2015/07/02/how-more-female-police-officers-would-help
-stop-police-brutality/?utm_term=.4cdd0c1306a8.

3. "Table 74: Full-Time Law Enforcement Employees by Population Group Percent
Male and Female," FBI Uniform Crime Reporting website, 2013, https://ucr.fbi
.gov/crime-in-the-u.s/2013/crime-in-the-u.s.-2013/tables/table-74.

4. "RCMP Sets an 'Ambitious' New Goal: Recruit as Many Women as Men," Canadian Association of Police Governance website, October 27, 2014, http://capg.ca
/rcmp-sets-an-ambitious-new-goal-recruit-as-many-women-as-men/.
I learned a great deal from reading the PhD dissertation by retired RCMP Sergeant
Orville Nickel. Nickel was a use-of-force expert, who taught a number of courses to
officers about appropriate use of force. His gender-based research about when force
is applied is fascinating reading. He writes: "If policewomen are successful in de-
escalating confrontational circumstances without the application of physical force,
what does that say about the need for using physical force for purposes of gaining
control in most if not all situations? Are there equally effective means of gaining situational control other than by physical force?" His study offers compelling affirma-
tive answers to this question. Orville Nickel, "Critical Factors in Police Use-of-Force
Decisions," (PhD dissertation, Walden University, 2015), http://scholarworks.waldenu
.edu/cgi/viewcontent.cgi?article=2269&context=dissertations.

5. Peter Tyson, "Dogs' Dazzling Sense of Smell," *PBS.com*, October 4, 2012, http://
www.pbs.org/wgbh/nova/nature/dogs-sense-of-smell.html.

6. Jane Onyanga-Omara, "Gun Violence Rare in U.K. compared to U.S.," *USA Today*,
June 16, 2016, http://www.usatoday.com/story/news/world/2016/06/16/gun-violence
-united-kingdom-united-states/85994716/.

7. Sue Sutton and Gene Sutton, "Springers in Law Enforcement," English Springer
Spaniel Field Trial Association website, accessed November 2016, http://www.essfta
.org/english-springers/versatility/springers-in-law-enforcement/.

8. "Pit Bull Kills Therapy Dog in Vancouver," *CBC News*, November 3, 2016, http://www.cbc
.ca/news/canada/british-columbia/pit-bull-kills-therapy-dog-in-vancouver-1.2821946.

9. "National Statistics: Police Workforce, England and Wales," UK Government website, March 31, 2015, https://www.gov.uk/government/publications/police -workforce-england-and-wales-31-march-2015/police-workforce-england-and -wales-31-march-2015.

10. Griff Witte, "What Can US Trigger-Happy Cops Learn from Britain's Gunless Police?," *The Independent*, June 12, 2015, http://www.independent.co.uk/news/world /americas/what-can-us-trigger-happy-cops-learn-from-britains-gunless-police -10316119.html.

11. Ben Kesling and Cameron McWhirter, "Percentage of African-Americans in U.S. Police Departments Remains Flat Since 2007," *Wall Street Journal*, May 14, 2015, http://www.wsj.com/articles/percentage-of-african-americans-in-u-s-police -departments-remains-flat-since-2007-1431628990.

12. "Hispanic Americans by the Numbers," *Infoplease*, accessed 2016, http://www .infoplease.com/spot/hhmcensus1.html.

13. See note 11 above.

### Chapter 7

1. Alexander Stille, "Can the French Talk about Race?," News Desk, *The New Yorker*, July 11, 2014, http://www.newyorker.com/news/news-desk/can-the-french-talk -about-race.

2. "Moins de Policiers Tués, Mais Toujours Autant de Blessés en 2015," *Le Monde*, October 18, 2016, http://www.lemonde.fr/les-decodeurs/article/2016/10/18/moins -de-policiers-tues-mais-toujours-autant-de-blesses-en-2015_5015889_4355770 .html.

3. "Thousands Rally in Paris to Protest Crime Targeting Chinese," *Reuters.com*, September 4, 2016, http://www.reuters.com/article/us-france-crime-chinese -idUSKCN11A0TY.

4. Carla Power, "Why There's Tension Between France and Its Muslim Population," *Time*, January 8, 2015, http://time.com/3659241/paris-terror-attack-muslim-islam/.

5. Anne Vidalie, "La Diversification Ethnique de la Police S'opère Par le Bas," *L'Express*, February 16, 2015, http://www.lexpress.fr/actualite/societe/la-diversification-ethnique -de-la-police-s-opere-par-le-bas_1650383.html.

6. L. Martin, "Polices Municipale et Nationale, Gendarmerie : Quelle Place Pour les Femmes?," *Emploipublic*, February 3, 2015, http://infos.emploipublic.fr/metiers /les-secteurs-qui-recrutent/les-metiers-de-la-securite/polices-municipale-et -nationale-gendarmerie-quelle-place-pour-les-femmes/apm-4409/.

### Epilogue

1. "Quantifying Black Lives Matter: Are Black Americans More Likely to be Shot or Roughed Up by Police?," *The Economist*, July 16, 2016, http://www.economist.com /news/united-states/21702219-are-black-americans-more-likely-be-shot-or -roughed-up-police-quantifying-black-lives.

2.  Sendhil Mullainathan, "Police Killings of Blacks: Here is What the Data Say," The Upshot, *New York Times*, October 16, 2015, http://www.nytimes.com/2015/10/18 /upshot/police-killings-of-blacks-what-the-data-says.html?_r=0.

3.  Monica Davey and Mitch Smith, "Chicago Police Dept. Plagued by Systemic Racism, Task Force Finds," *New York Times*, April 13, 2016, https://www.nytimes.com/2016 /04/14/us/chicago-police-dept-plagued-by-systemic-racism-task-force-finds.html? _r=0

4.  ibid.

5.  David Yassky, "Unlocking the Truth about the Clinton Crime Bill," The Opinion Pages, *New York Times*, April 9, 2016, http://www.nytimes.com/2016/04/10/opinion /campaign-stops/unlocking-the-truth-about-the-clinton-crime-bill.html.

6.  Tim Keller, Diana Simpson, and Dick M. Carpenter II, "Arizona's Profit Incentive for Civil Forfeiture," Institute for Justice website, December 2012, http://ij.org/report /arizonas-profit-incentive-in-civil-forfeiture/.

7.  "The Final Report on Early Case Consideration of the Steering Committee on Justice Efficiencies and Access to the Justice System," Department of Justice, Government of Canada website, last modified January 7, 2015, http://www.justice.gc.ca /eng/rp-pr/csj-sjc/esc-cde/ecc-epd/p1.html.

8.  Parul Sehgal, "The Forced Heroism of the 'Survivor,'" First Words, *The New York Times Magazine*, May 3, 2016, http://www.nytimes.com/2016/05/08/magazine/the -forced-heroism-of-the-survivor.html?_r=0.